# Demystifying Hinduism
# A Beginner's Guide

*Understand the basics of Hinduism. Sanatana Dharma simplified for the Modern World, the Hindu Identity, Spiritual Wisdom, Philosophy, the symbolism of Rituals, Scientific Truths, Mythology, and Ethical Practices.*

**Understanding Hinduism Series – Book 1**

# Sahasranam  Kalpathy

## Disclaimer

All the facts in the books and the statistics given are taken from authentic sources. The suggestions and opinions expressed in the book are the authors own and do not in any way intend to hurt the feelings of anyone or any other religion. Some of the interpretations of the scriptures and texts given in the book may be seem slightly different from the conventional descriptions as it is known that such exegesis can vary depending on the commenting author.

# TABLE OF CONTENTS

# ACKNOWLEDGEMENTS

I wish to pay my respects to Late Swami Chinmayananda, Swami Udit Chaitanya and Swami Chidananda Puri for bringing Hinduism and its concepts close to the masses. I was also one who benefitted from their *satsangs*.

My parents and my elderly relatives like uncles and aunts (numerous to be named) have helped me in the spiritual journey in my life. I have to acknowledge their help and guidance with gratitude.

The Swamijis in the Ramakrishna Mission in Kozhikode, Kerala, India have helped me immensely by providing many books on various aspects of Hinduism and spirituality. I humbly bow before all the Swamijis with gratitude.

My family has stood by me during my days of authoring this book and supported me in all manner possible. I will be failing in my duty if I do not acknowledge that.

I must place on record my sincere thanks to Mr. Som Bathla, my mentor in this author journey and all the affectionate members of the Author-Helping-Author (AHA) community who have always given me constructive suggestions at various stages of my writing and publishing.

My thanks are due to 'Revandesigns' for the beautiful cover designed for this book.

*With profound gratitude and reverence, this book is dedicated to the enlightened sages and seers whose timeless wisdom has guided generations through the multifaceted tapestry of Hindu philosophy, unravelling the mysteries of Hinduism and inspiring seekers across time and space. Their teachings continue to kindle the flame of spirituality in the hearts of seekers*

# A Humble Request to the Reader

Thank you for buying and reading this book. May I request your indulgence for one more favour.

I hope you enjoyed reading this book and derived benefit from the assorted topics discussed.

**Kindly give your sincere and valuable review of this book in the Amazon site.** Your rating and candid review will be a great inspiration and encouragement to me.

I would also request you to check my other books – ***Tell Me a Story, Grandpa*** and ***Grandpa Tell Me More Stories*** which are a compilation of short stories with morals, written with children in mind.

Also, the book of '***In Search of a Bridegroom***' is an interesting Autobiographical Fiction which will be of great interest to the reader.

Two books on the Health Problems faced by the Elderly are available under the names, "***How to face the Health Challenges While getting Old***" and "***Old Age Health – Challenges and Solutions***" These deal with the Health Challenges in old age, their Early Recognition, Prevention and Treatment.

My last book named "***Understanding the Electrocardiogram***" is a book written for the benefit of the Medical fraternity. It is a book for doctors, residents and nurses.

You can contact me at my email address ramani2911@gmail.com

https://www.linkedin.com/in/sahasranam-dr-k-v-3231a13a/ (Linked In)

https://medium.com/@ramani2911/membership (Medium.com)

https://www.amazon.com/author/sahasranamkalpathy

(Amazon Author Central)

Thank you for your Co-operation.

# Here is a FREE Gift for you

## Discover The Secrets To A Healthy Heart

### Download Your FREE eBook Today!

Did you know that heart disease is the leading cause of health problems worldwide? Don't wait until it's too late — take charge of your heart health today with my **FREE** eBook, "**Diseases of the Heart**."

FOUR major heart conditions you need to know about are explained.

*Coronary Artery Disease*: Learn all about it before it's too late. *Heart Failure*: Understand the symptoms and steps for managing this serious condition. *High Blood Pressure*: Discover how to keep your numbers in check and protect your heart. *Atrial Fibrillation*: Find out what causes this common yet dangerous irregular heartbeat.

Click the **LINK** below to download your copy.

Get Your **FREE** eBook Now! **CLICK ON THE LINK BELOW:**

**https://sahasranam.ck.page/708a4d8aa7**

**Or SCAN the QR code below.**

# BOOKS BY THE AUTHOR

## NON-FICTION

**How to Face the Challenges while Growing Old**
Problems of Elderly Book 1

**Old Age Health Challenges and Solutions**
Problems of Elderly Book 2

**Understanding the Electrocardiogram**
Medical Book on ECG

**Demystifying Hinduism**           Understanding
Hinduism Book 1

**The Avadhoota**
Understanding Hinduism Book 2

**Daily Musings**           Understanding
Hinduism Book 3

**How to Master Essential Life Skills**      Skill sets for
Success Book 1

**How to Achieve Professional Excellence**    Skill sets for
Success Book 2

## FICTION

**Tell Me a Story, Grandpa**       Short Stories for Children
Book 1

**Grandpa, Tell me More Stories**    Short Stories for
Children Book 2

**In Search of a  Bridegroom**   An Autobiographical
Fiction

**The Truth Lies Out There**    A Family Drama of Suspense

**Code Black**           A Hospital based Thriller

**PREFACE**

Hinduism has been a baffling and enigmatic religion for the Western world. However, for an average Hindu who may have only a limited knowledge of the *Vedas* or *Upanishads*, it is a way of life that he has been accustomed to from childhood – a faith that his parents and spiritual teachers have inculcated in him from the time he was born. For a Hindu, Hinduism is simple and uncomplicated. He believes in one God or a few Gods and is intensely devoted to them. He lives his whole life devoted to that God, not necessarily knowing the great philosophical truths that  are expounded in the ancient Hindu scriptures. Because for him, Hinduism is an unwavering faith in the God who will give him *Moksha* (<u>salvation</u>) at the end of his life.

In the bargain, the average Hindu learns various virtues and moral rectitude, which he faithfully follows lest he defy the God whom he deeply reveres. This he learns from his parents and other elders in the family, who instill the basic knowledge of Hinduism in him right from the time he is born. Even the lullabies his mother sings to him extol the greatness of the Gods.  The average Hindu feels that an in depth knowledge of the *Vedas, Upanishads* and other scriptures is not essential for him to practice the

9

faith. Simple devotion and capitulation before his favorite God is enough for him.

But Hinduism is much more recondite than what it appears to be superficially. It is not easy for a person to learn all about it in one's lifetime. The seeker who is a beginner often flounders in the sea of scriptures, philosophies, and rituals in Hinduism that he does not know in which direction he should turn.

This book was written with the intention to clear some misunderstandings about Hinduism and to help the beginner understand the basic concepts in Hinduism. Hence the name, *'Demystifying Hinduism'*. It is more like a primer on Hinduism. Let me at the outset declare that I do not know all about Hinduism. I am still a humble student of Hinduism. What I know would amount to a mere thimble-full compared to the vast ocean of knowledge that is Hinduism. What little I know and have learnt is by tuning in to the speeches, <u>discourses</u> (*Satsang*) and works of great scholars and Swamijis and spending a lifetime reading their works and the scriptures. My parents and many of my elderly relatives, who are no more, have contributed to my great journey. In addition, my resources were a large number of online articles, discourses, speeches, and printed books. I have shared these resources at the end of this book.

I have been immensely benefitted by the *satsangs* of Poojya Gurudev Late Swami Chinmayananda, Swami Udit Chaitanya, and Swami Chidananda Puri who have greatly influenced my thoughts and helped to mold my vision and perspectives. Knowledge regarding Hinduism, from any quarter was welcome to me. I have freely drawn inspiration from their speeches, reflections, blogs, and writings. Late Swami Chinmayananda needs special mention as he was instrumental in guiding me during the formative years of my life – the teens, when every individual is in search of the meaning in one's life. His exposition of *Karma Yoga* from the *Bhagavad Gita* had touched my heart as a teenager and has stood me in good stead all my life.

In order to simplify the concepts and philosophies, I have written the book in a **Question** and **Answer** format as has been done in most of our scriptures including the eminent *Bhagavad Gita*. The whole book is in the form of a conversation between a grandfather and his three American-born grandchildren who visit him in his village in India from the United States during their summer holidays. The children, eager to understand Hinduism, request their grandfather to answer their questions about the religion and in the bargain get answers to most of their doubts about the *Sanatana Dharma*.

The whole book is written in simple English and provides effortless reading for the beginner. The simple language, interspersed with examples enables the neophyte and children to comprehend the deep philosophical precepts easily.

A **Glossary** has <u>not</u> been included deliberately at the end of the book, but the meanings of Sanskrit words are given in the text itself wherever they have been used. *Sanskrit words are in italics and their meanings are given nearby <u>underlined</u> for ease of understanding.* This makes it easier for the reader and  avoids the laborious process of turning to the glossary every time a new word is encountered in the text. A detailed list of **Resources,** both in English and Malayalam has been added at the end to benefit the reader who may seek more information and an in-depth study of the Hindu way of life.

This is a book both for the youth and children of the modern age. The book mainly targets the flummoxed youth of today who are interested to know their roots but do not know whom to ask or turn to. Often the American-born Hindu youth of today do not have a working knowledge of Hinduism. This book proposes to bridge this gap in their knowledge regarding the Hindu way of life. Many a parent today is busy with the fast-paced modern life that they do not find time to address the doubts that arise in the minds of the youngsters regarding religion in general and Hinduism in particular. The book has been written with a view to help such youngsters get a better understanding of Hinduism and to clear many of the misconceptions and fallacies about the religion in their minds.

Some of the essential facts in Hinduism find repetition in different chapters. This is not due to an oversight but was deliberate in order to emphasize the importance of the fundamental doctrines involved. There have been many commentaries on various Sanskrit texts in Hinduism and there are subtle variations in these interpretations from scholar to scholar. The author wishes to point out that there may be slight such variations in this text also from what the reader might have understood or heard previously from other sources. But this does not in any way vitiate the basic principles and tenets that are discussed. Some of the thoughts expressed in the text regarding Hindus, Temple worship and the modern culture are personal opinions of the author and are not made with any intention to malign or disrespect any person or any other religion.

With these simple words, I humbly submit this book to my dear readers.

Sahasranam Kalpathy.

(Dr. K. V. Sahasranam) **email:** ramani2911@gmail.com

# 1. INTRODUCTION

Hinduism, better called *'Sanatana Dharma'* is the oldest religion in the world. Unlike many other religions which have a single, major religious text , Hinduism is unique in that the number of writings and scriptures available are numerous. Unfortunately, many of these valuable texts have been lost due to the lack of preservation of the recorded texts. Since ancient times, these scriptures and passages were handed down from generation to generation through word of mouth and learnt by rote. Hence the possibility of variable nuances in the interpretations and commentaries always occurred.

It is humanly impossible to delve into the details of Hinduism and learn all that is given in our scriptures in one lifetime. Neither can it be condensed into one small book like this. As the Tamil poetess Avvaiyyar said, *"What is known is a handful ; the unknown is as vast as the universe."* In addition to the various scriptures, texts and lyrics which are available, there are many commentaries which have been written on the scriptures by various seers and scholars. There are always subtle variations in the interpretations of the scriptures as these were originally written in Sanskrit which is the language of the *Vedas* spoken by the sages of ancient India or *Bharat*. In Hinduism, Sanskrit is considered the language of the Gods.

Translations of almost all the Hindu scriptures are now available in most of the Indian languages as well as in English and other European languages. One such text is the *Bhagavad Gita* which has commentaries and translations in most of the major languages of the world.

Many of the Hindu scriptures, especially the *Gita*, have influenced and dominated the thoughts of great philosophers, scientists, statesmen and scholars of the world.

Swami Vivekananda described the Gita as *"a bouquet composed of the beautiful flowers of spiritual truths collected from the Upanishads"*.

Aldous Huxley in his writings said, *"The Bhagavad Gita is perhaps  the most systematic spiritual statement of the Perennial Philosophy"*.

Mahatma Gandhi said, *"When disappointment stares me in the face and all alone, I see not one ray of light, I go back to the Bhagavad Gita"*. Thus was the influence of the Bhagavad Gita in the lives of these great souls.

Hinduism never negates philosophies of other religions. India with its rich cultural heritage of Hinduism has always welcomed other religions with open arms in its midst and provided a fertile base for all religions to thrive and grow in India. The basic tenet of Hinduism is tolerance. One common prayer in Hindu scriptures from the *Yajur Veda – Taittiriya Upanishad* runs thus:

ॐ सह नाववतु ।
सह नौ भुनक्तु ।
सह वीर्यं करवावहै ।
तेजस्वि नावधीतमस्तु मा विद्विषावहै ।

*Om Saha Naa Vavatu |*
*Saha Nou Bhunaktu |*
*Saha Veeryam Karavaavahai |*
*Tejasvi Naav-Adhiitam-Astu Maa Vidvishaavahai |*

It means, *"May He protect us all together; may He nourish us all together; May we work conjointly with great energy, May our study be vigorous and effective; May we not mutually dispute (or may we not hate anyone)"*.

Another prayer runs thus:

असतो मा सद्गमय ।
तमसो मा ज्योतिर्गमय ।
मृत्योर्मा अमृतं गमय ।

*Om Asato Maa Sad-Gamaya |*
*Tamaso Maa Jyotir-Gamaya |*
*Mrtyor-Maa Amritam Gamaya |*

It means- *"Lead me from the Unreal to the Real; Keep me not in the Phenomenal World of Unreality but lead me towards the Reality (of Eternal Self)"*, - *"Lead me from Darkness to the Light; Keep*

**16**

*me not in (the Ignorant State of) Darkness but lead
me  towards the Light of Spiritual Knowledge",
-"Lead me from Mortality to Immortality. Keep
me not in the World of Mortality but lead
me  towards the World of Immortality (of Self-
Realization)"*.

Unity in diversity is the hall mark of Hinduism. While the Hindus worship numerous Gods, still Hinduism accepts that the Absolute Truth or Universal Consciousness – the *Brahman,* is One and the only indivisible Supreme. This fascinating plurality while accepting the one and only Brahman as the Supreme Consciousness is the unique characteristic of Hinduism. All the various 'God Forms' are regarded as the manifestations of that one *Brahman.* The goal of every Hindu is ultimately  to realize the *Brahman* and become merged with it to be released from the eternal cycle of births and deaths, which is called '*Samsara*'.

This book is written in a conversational style of **Questions & Answers** that discusses the basis of religion and Hinduism. The simple division of *Scriptures* in Hinduism is discussed and how a Hindu *Worships* his Gods is discussed in the fourth chapter. The concepts behind *Idol worship* and *Temple worship* are rationalized, and a brief synopsis of the *Hindu festivals* is given in the seventh chapter. The importance of *Meditation* in Hinduism and its role in the realization of the *Brahman* are discussed in the eighth chapter.

*Yoga* and its various divisions are discussed followed by a discussion on *Dharma* which is the crux of Hinduism. *Dharma* is one word in Sanskrit that defies definition in English. It can be interpreted to mean many concepts which change contextually. _Karma and Reincarnation_ are much debated topics and are elaborated in some detail. Hinduism is rife with mythology as any other religion. The importance of _Mythology_ in Hinduism and the various mythological texts are chronicled in the twelfth chapter.

The concept of _Avatars_ or the incarnations of the Divine are next considered and the division of human fields of work into the four socioeconomic groups is elaborated under the _Varna Ashrama_. A brief look into _Diet and Vegetarianism_ is considered in the fifteenth chapter and the role of _Arts in Hinduism_ as seen in the ancient texts and scriptures is examined in the sixteenth chapter.

Science and belief may be at loggerheads in many religions and religious beliefs may run counter to scientific truths. But in Hinduism many of the ancient scriptures belie this fact and indicate that science and religion are but two sides of the same coin. Many of the seers and sages of ancient India have been scientists as well and their contributions are brought out in the discussions. _Science and Hinduism_ is discussed in the seventeenth chapter.

The _Concept of Time_ in Hinduism has been appreciated by many scholars from the rest of the world and these have been referred to in the eighteenth chapter. The magnitude of time expressed in ages (*Yugas*) and the minutest division of time have been explained.

Death is an all-time mystery. It creates both awe and perplexity in the minds of man. Death and reincarnation have been  controversial topics in most religions. Hindus, for one believe that the soul is eternal, and reincarnation is the basis on which man is born in this world to expiate one's *Karma*. *Death and Reincarnation* has been discussed in the nineteenth chapter.

Of the numerous sages and seers in Hinduism, *Adi Sankaracharya and Swami Vivekananda* are the two stalwarts who strode the Indian subcontinent. They have received a brief mention in this book for the youngsters to be inspired by them. Adi Sankaracharya was instrumental in popularising the Advaita philosophy and consolidating the practice of Hinduism throughout India attempting to put an end to the misinterpretations of the scriptures and superstitions of the period. Swami Vivekananda on the other hand, was responsible for giving a modern touch to Hinduism and making it a feasible and practicable religion in the modern world. He popularized  Hinduism in the West by his famous speech in the World's Parliament of Religions in the United States in the year 1893. Swami Vivekananda targeted the youth of the country when he promoted Hinduism. His birthday 12th January is celebrated as the National Youth Day in India. His popular quote and advice to the youth of India was:

उत्तिष्ठत जाग्रत प्राप्य वरान्निबोधत।

*Uttiṣṭhata jāgrata prāpya varānnibodhata |*

It means, *"Arise, Awake and stop not till the goal is reached."*

The book concludes with a <u>*Miscellaneous*</u> assortment of questions that often beleaguer the minds of the novice attempting to  understand Hinduism. An attempt has been made to answer most of such questions. But the author is fully aware that this is an incomplete list and there are many more lingering questions that crop up in the minds of the reader  begging  an answer.

The list of <u>*Resources*</u> at the end of the book are references that have been used to prepare the manuscript. The author is greatly indebted to many of the Swamijis and scholars whose speeches and *satsangs* have been useful in formulating the questions and answers that are discussed in this book. But for their guidance, this book would be incomplete. The speeches and *satsangs* have been so numerous that they cannot be quoted or attributed here in detail.

# 2. RELIGION & HINDUISM

**"What is Religion, Grandpa? How did religion originate? Why do we need religion at all?" Aditya the grandson who was in middle school in the United States set the ball rolling with his first question.**

Grandpa smiled and began explaining. Children, you must first understand the etymology of the word. The word *'religion'* is derived from the Latin word *'Religare'* meaning 'to bind.' Briefly, I will explain how Hinduism began as a religion.

Ancient man was in awe of nature – the earthquakes, the floods, the torrential rains, the lightning and thunder, the land slides, and avalanches, all instilled in him a fear of the unknown. He realized that there was an invisible **Power** above him which was controlling all these fearsome forces of Nature and began seeing it with awe and reverence. This engendered in him devotion and fear towards these unseen and unknown 'forces' or 'power'.

It was this *"Fear of the Unknown,'* that inculcated in him a reverence which metamorphosed itself into devotion and worship. He realized that there is an unknown force that controls everything in Nature. That unseen power,  he named as "<u>God</u>" or *"Ishvara"*.

That was not all. Man saw his companions dying and leaving back a body which disintegrated and decayed to mingle with the elements of the earth. Something left this body on death – the spark of life. Where did it go? He recognized that the body is composed of the five elements – *Earth, Fire, Water, Air* and *Ether* (space). The body returned to its original source- the five elements, when it was burnt or buried. These <u>five elements</u> were called the *Pancha Bhutas*. But where did that verve or vitality which was in the human body before death, go when man died? What was it that was keeping the human body *'conscious'* when he was alive? Where did it disappear when he died? These questions were one of the reasons for man's quest for the unknown force or power which controlled all these, and  he came to refer to it as '<u>the soul</u>' ,  *'Atman'*, *'Jiva'* or  *'Jeevatma'*.

He inferred that if the body returns to the *Pancha Bhutas* (<u>five elements</u>)  from where it came, then that power or *"Chaitanyam"* (<u>Spirit</u> ; <u>Energy</u>) in the body, should also be returning to the same source from where *it* came. His ruminations culminated in the conclusion that there was an unseen power – a *'Universal Power'* or *'Universal Consciousness'* to which the spirit or the *Atman* returned. He called it the *Brahman.*

Man, thus recognized a superior force or Consciousness which he began to respect, revere and worship. This was the essential origin of the Hindu religion. Of course, initially, this began as worship of the forces of Nature, like the Sun, the Moon, the Rivers, the Mountains etc. In different countries and climes, man's thought and mindset differed, and the religions born of these were also hence different. As man evolved, the religious beliefs also became refined and concretized.

**"Can you tell us about how the *Santana Dharma* originated? What are your thoughts about it?" Jaya, the sprightly intelligent girl who was to move to middle school the year after posed the question.**

Man recognized that he has a mind, but the mind of each one differed from that of the other. Even in the same family, different siblings had different mindsets and different characters. This set him enquiring about the mind. Thus, on one side, he was enquiring about the outside world (Nature) around him. But another group of men began to enquire about the mind by looking inward into their minds.

Thus, man's enquiry <u>with</u> the mind led to unraveling *'Material or Scientific Knowledge'* about nature and the world around him. He began to delve into his own mind through *contemplation* and *meditation*. This enquiry <u>about</u> the mind led to *'Spiritual Knowledge.'* The deep contemplations and reflections led him deeper into his mind and he experienced certain revelations which he perceived as coming from that 'Universal Consciousness' or

'Power,' which he called 'Ishvara', 'Chaitanyam', or 'Brahman' (God). He realized that this was an Unseen force, a Formless power, and an All-Pervasive Entity. His contemplations led to the realization that all living beings are a fragment of this 'Power' or 'Entity'. That was what gave him life and that he was also a part of this *Power*. Hence, he concluded that the *Atman* and *Brahman* were the same.

His reflections further led him to find out that the *Atman* (soul) which is part of that All-Pervasive power had to return inevitably to its origin – the *Brahman* when it left the body. The physical body in turn returned to the five elements when it was interred or cremated. Furthermore, his meditations revealed that the ultimate goal of man was to realize this truth that he was part of the *Brahman* and his goal in life was to return to *Brahman*. Till then he had to come back into this world multiple times. This gave him an idea about *reincarnations*. The few who realized these truths through meditation and reflection came to be known as *Rishis* (sages).

**"But why did man lay down rules and laws for every religion to follow? Is it so in Hinduism also?" Vijaya, the youngest granddaughter who had a wise head on young shoulders had this skeptical question.**

As man progressed, religion too evolved and a series of do's and don'ts emerged to keep society under control. Man could not live alone. So, he started living in communities as he learnt that he could not forage for food and face the rigors of nature alone and needed companionship and help. This community living demanded the creation of a set of principles, guidelines and values to keep people in the community in check. This necessitated the formulation of commandments, tenets, mandates, and rules which had to be followed by every member in the community. Thus, religious discipline had to be pursued by everyone in the community. This was how organized religion began. Religion promoted emotional support to humanity through its values and morals. It kept the whole community cohesive and bolstered unity in the society. This is a common factor for all religions.

Hinduism also set forth laws and rules to be followed by everyone. But the rules of the game are a bit different in Hinduism. Nobody punishes a Hindu if he goes against these laws or tenets. God does not punish man, according to Hindus, but they punish themselves. We will see more about it when we discuss *Karma*.

Does your class teacher not lay down rules in the class for you to follow and be disciplined? If the teacher did not impose some rules in the class, students would become unruly and boisterous, wouldn't they? It was exactly the same reason that the sages or *Rishis* of yore imposed or laid down rules and principles for mankind.

**"So, does Religion mean the rules and laws that have been laid down or the mythology that we hear?" Aditya was back with a sharp query.**

Sure, your question is well founded. Understand that every religion has three aspects. They are:

1.    Theology & Philosophy.
2.    Mythology.
3.    Rituals.

**1. Theology** is the study of Divine things or religious truths as expounded by the masters, sages, or prophets. It deals with Nature, God, and all religious beliefs. **Philosophy** is the study of the fundamental nature of knowledge, reality, and existence. It deals with the rational investigations of the truths and principles of being, knowledge, values, meaning of life and conduct.

**2. Mythology** is a collection of legends or myths about Gods, demigods, or heroes. It is an entertaining way to teach the difficult principles of philosophy to the common man in a simple and understandable manner through stories and parables. Understanding a mythological story does not need any education. Even the ignorant could understand these and through these mythological stories they were taught the philosophical principles, morals, and values in an easy manner. Every religion has its own quota of these mythologies.

**3. Rituals** are solemn religious ceremonies where a series of rites are performed according to prescribed protocols as a part of worship. Rituals are common to all religions. It can vary from simple rituals to very complicated and elaborate rituals performed by a single individual at home or multiple individuals jointly as in temple festivals and *Poojas.* Rituals are part of the Hindu religion as also of other religions like Christianity, Islam, Judaism, or Buddhism.

**"Grandpa, can you tell us why we are called Hindus? What is the meaning of the word 'Hinduism'? Who coined this term?" Jaya wanted to know.**

Conservative estimates put the origin of Hinduism to about 5000 years ago. But some of the scriptures denote that it was present much before that, even as early as 9000 BCE. Hence, Hinduism is decidedly the oldest religion in the world predating all the other religions. Some historians and evolutionary psychologists peg the origin of Hinduism between 2300 – 1500 BCE. But since Hinduism did not have one single individual as its founder, its origin cannot be precisely dated. It is said to have had its roots in the Indus valley along the banks of the river *Sindhu* (Indus river). This river is one of the longest in the world nearly 2000 miles long. It arises in the Himalayas near mount *Kailas* and *Manasa Sarovar*, in Western Tibet and flows through parts of Tibet, India and Pakistan. The Persians stumbled upon the inhabitants to the south of this river when they invaded the region. The Persians pronounced the word **'S'** as **'H'**, hence the river was *'Hindu'* for them. The people who lived south of this river in the Indian subcontinent were called *'Hindus'* by the Persians. The Arabs called the region *'Al-Hind'* and later by the 13th century, it was called *'Hindustan'* – the land of the Hindus. The suffix *'ism'* (doctrine ; practice) was added to the word Hindu to coin the word *Hinduism.*

**"Is Hinduism a popular religion? How many people in the world are Hindus? Are there Hindus elsewhere in the world besides India?" Vijaya, the little one, always came up with an interesting question.**

Grandpa continued. Today, Hinduism is world's third largest religion next to Christianity and Islam. Approximately 1.2 - 1.35 billion people follow Hinduism world over. Ninety-four percent of the Hindus live in India. Interestingly, as I told you earlier,  the word *'Hindu'* was given to us by the Persians; it is an exonym. The term Hindu is more a *geographical term* than a religious one. The real name (endonym) of our religion is "*Sanatana Dharma*" or "*Vaidika Dharma*" (<u>religion of the Vedas</u>).   For practical purposes of our discussion, we will continue to call it *'Hinduism'* for the time being.

In addition to India, Hinduism is also the faith most followed in Nepal, Mauritius, and Bali (Indonesia). Hindus are present in most parts of the world as they have migrated from India. Ancient records prove that in olden days, Hinduism was popular in many countries of Asia. Even today relics are identified in these countries which testify to this fact. One important aspect of Hinduism is that there is no single prophet or founder for Hinduism. It was founded or originated from the revelations of multitudes of <u>sages</u> of yore called the "*Rishis*", who through contemplation and meditation realized the eternal truths which form the foundation of Hinduism. They passed these revelations on to their disciples who popularized them. Thus, Hinduism is built upon the epiphanies of a large group of *Rishis*, many of whom are anonymous.

Dr. S. Radhakrishnan who was the president of India was once asked as to who a Hindu is. His answer was, *"By negating all the religions, that is, one who is not a Muslim, not a Christian and so on, whoever is left is a Hindu"*. Just like the United States which is a country that honors diversity, Hinduism is also a pluralistic religion believing in diversity.

Sree Ravishankar has said, *"Diversity is the DNA of Hinduism"*. Diversity is seen even among the Hindus. The North Indian Hindu is different from the Hindu in South India. It differs from region to region as far as dress, rituals, and traditions are concerned. But still, all are classed as Hindus.

The main texts of the Hindus are the *Vedas,* and these are the bedrock on which the whole edifice of Hinduism stands. We will deal with these in more detail later.

**"Do Hindus have a religious leader like the Pope in Rome for the Christians?" Aditya, who was the senior of the three wanted to know.**

Grandpa smiled. Hindus do not have a religious head like the Pope. Hinduism was not founded by a single Prophet or Messiah. A single sage or Rishi cannot be credited as the founding father or patron saint of Hinduism. There are many sages who are mentioned in our scriptures who have contributed to the growth of Hinduism like Sage Vyasa,

Yajnavalkya, Patanjali, Valmiki, Kaanad etc. The list is so long that it is impossible to remember all the names offhand. But there are also many more unnamed sages whose revelations were included in Hinduism.

But we have *Gurus* (<u>religious teachers</u>) who are also leaders or religious heads like the Sankaracharyas in the various *Madoms*. Adi Sankaracharya unified the various concepts in Hinduism and put forth the *Advaita* philosophy and popularized it during the 7th century CE by traveling on foot throughout the length and breadth of India. He established four monasteries or *Ashrams* in four corners of India. They are in *Sringeri* (Karnataka), *Badrinath* (Himalayas), *Dwaraka* (Gujarat) and *Puri* (Orissa). The priests there are called 'Sankaracharyas' and they are the religious *Gurus* who teach and help to popularize and promote Hinduism. But they are not the sole religious leaders of *Sanatana Dharma*. We will discuss later about Adi Sankaracharya in our dialogues.

**"Does Hinduism convert people from other religions to its faith?" Jaya had a mischievous question.**

Grandpa burst into laughter. There is no proselytization in Hinduism, and no one is coerced into conversion. There is freedom of religion in Hinduism. No one is compelled to follow the tenets and principles laid down in the scriptures. There are plenty of Hindus who are proclaimed atheists, like the Communists. Hinduism does not force anyone to follow its tenets or principles. It is a sort of voluntary choice of the person. A person can follow the Hindu way of life without going through any rituals like baptism to become a Christian or reciting the Shahadah to become a Muslim.

# 3. SCRIPTURES IN HINDUISM

"Grandpa, what are the scriptures in Hinduism. You mentioned about the Vedas. What are they? Are they the only available scriptures for Hindus?" Aditya was always the first to initiate the discussion.

Grandpa began. The *Vedas* are the oldest available literature and texts on Hinduism. The word 'Veda' is derived from the root *"Vid"* which means 'Knowledge' or 'to know'. Hence the Vedas are packed with knowledge of the great truths in Hinduism.

"Can you elaborate on these a little more, grandpa?" Aditya added.

The ancient knowledge of the *Rishis* was divisible into six categories. They are:

| | | |
|---|---|---|
| 1. *Shruthi* | | 4. *Ithihasa* |
| 2. *Smrithi* | | 5. *Aagama* |
| 3. *Purana* | | 6. *Siddhanta.* |

**Shruthi** means is "that which is heard". They are the *Vedas*. They were revealed to or 'heard' by the ancient rishis during meditation. They are the aggregate of all the revelations to the various *Rishis* and not to one person alone. These were transmitted from generation to generation by word of mouth till the recorded word became a reality. The language of the *Shruthis* is Sanskrit. The *Shruthis* are considered Divine revelations and are hence are considered Eternal Truths which an unchangeable.

**Smrithi** means "that which is remembered". These were the various experiences of sages which were chronicled. Various sages have composed these *Smrithis* and there are 18 *smrithis* named after the various sages. It includes a diverse group of texts that were written down. These writings were, of course, inspired by the Vedas. Examples of *Smrithis* are *Bhagavad Gita, Ramayana, Mahabharata, Manu Smrithi* etc. All the remembered and written texts come under this group. The *Smrithis* dictate rules that govern society. What was relevant a thousand years ago may not be relevant today. Hence, *Smrithis* can be altered or amended according to the times, whereas the *Shrutis* are eternal unchangeable truths. For example, many of the precepts given in the *Manu Smrithi* are irrelevant today and they have been changed accordingly.

The **Puranas** are ancient literature which were written centuries ago. They comprise the legends of Gods, their history, their powers, their achievements, and parables connected with them. These stories contain the philosophies and doctrines advocated in the *Vedas* in a subtle form for the common folk to understand. Anything conveyed through stories gets assimilated easily by the average person.

There are 18 Major *Puranas* (*Maha puranas*) and 18 minor ones called *Upa Puranas*.  I will just name them. Most of them are named after the Gods in Hindu Mythology. The major ones are:

Vishnu Purana

Bhavishya Purana

Bhagavatha Purana

Vamana Purana

Skanda Purana

Kurma Purana

Varaha Purana

Markandeya Purana

Narada Purana

Brahmanda Purana

Garuda Purana

Siva Purana

Vayu Purana

Ganesha Purana

Varaha Purana

Devi Bhagavatham

Matsya Purana

Padma Puranam.

Many more are there which are classified as *Upa Puranas*. You do not have to remember all these names. I have mentioned them just to make you aware of the vastness of spiritual literature available in Hinduism. The *Puranas* were written and compiled by the great *Rishi  Veda Vyasa* or *Krishna Dvaipayana*.

The **Ithihasa** (<u>ancient history</u>) literally means '*indeed it was*'. The two main *Ithihasas* are the *Ramayana* and the *Mahabharata*. They are the most important epic poems of the Hindus. The *Ramayana* tells the story of Sri Rama and his wife Sita and the *Mahabharata* that of the Kauravas and Pandavas and the great war fought between them. We will discuss this in more detail at a later time.

The **Aagamas** (<u>tradition</u>) extensively deal with theology and epistemology. The *Aagamas* indicate practices which have been handed down the ages as tradition. It includes architectural principles of temple construction, details of rituals, how to perform *Pooja* with idols, and the art of sculpture (*Shilpa Shastra*- <u>Science of Architecture</u>).

The **Siddhantas** (<u>tenet</u> ; <u>doctrine</u>) are principles in different branches of science and philosophy like Astronomy, Astrology, Cosmology. There is *Sushruta Samhita* which is a treatise on the principles of Medicine and Surgery, *Aryabhattiyam* which deals with the principles of astrophysics, *Arthasasthra* by Chanakya which deals with economics and administration, *Charaka Samhita* by Sage *Charaka* dealing with *Ayurveda* – the traditional Indian System of Medicine, *Rasendra Mangalam* by Nagarjuna dealing with the science of Alchemy and many more. I am naming them only to make you aware of the extent and vastness of scientific and philosophical knowledge which has been discovered and recorded by our sages.

**"Wow, grandpa, you have swamped us with names and the details which are mind-boggling. To imagine that these were all committed to memory by our ancestors! It is inconceivable!" Vijaya, in her little voice squealed with surprise.**

No, my children, you don't have to commit all this to memory. This is just to make you understand the importance and grandeur of our ancient heritage. When you have finished these discussions and are older, you can read about these texts and gain more knowledge about our ancient heritage.

**"Grandpa, can you throw more light on the *Vedas* in a bit more detail. You said that they are the foundation of *Sanatana Dharma*." Jaya was inquisitive.**

Grandpa continued. As we said earlier, the *Vedas* are the scriptures filled with knowledge and were handed down the ages from the *Guru* (teacher) to the *Sishya* (disciple) by word of mouth. The language was ancient Sanskrit. It was only around 500 CE that the *Vedas* began to be written down and recorded.

There are four *Vedas* the *Rig Veda, Yajur Veda, Sama Veda* and the *Atharva Veda* (also called *Atharvana Veda*).

Each Veda in turn has four sub-divisions called the *Samhitas, Aranyakas, Brahmanas* and the *Upanishads*.

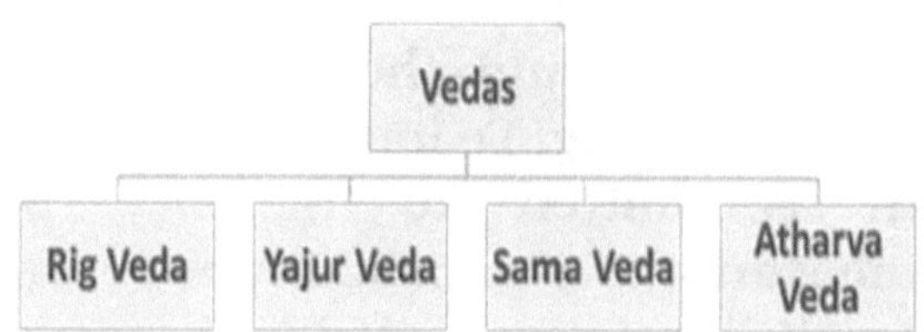

The **Samhitas** (<u>collection</u>) are compilations of lyrical poems in praise of God, Nature and the various aspects of nature worshipped in Hinduism. Expostulating the glory of Nature, they invoked the Gods. These *mantras* (<u>chants</u>) were for invoking the benediction of Gods like *Indra* (God of Heaven), *Agni* (<u>Fire</u>) and *Varuna* (<u>Water</u>) for prosperity, success, and welfare of the community.

The **Aranyakas** (<u>forest texts</u>) were compiled by those who retired to the forest to meditate after completing their life as a householder. The *Aranyakas* discuss rituals and sacrifices that are performed to venerate and appease the Gods.

The **Brahmanas** (<u>explanation of the sacred knowledge</u>) also deal with the rituals and their performance. They are *prose* commentaries on the mantras and rituals used in worshipping the Gods.

The **Upanishads** (<u>sitting near ; beside</u>) are mainly <u>philosophical texts</u>. They were learnt by sitting beside the *Guru*. The *Upanishads* indicate a transition from the ritualistic religion to the meditative and contemplative religion where the concept of the *Brahman* and the Truth beyond rituals and ordinary worship are discussed. These *Upanishads* were appended to the *Vedas* later and hence are called the 'Vedanta' (<u>end of the Vedas</u>). Commonly, they are in the form of a dialogue or question-answer format between the *Guru* and the *Shishya*. They propound esoteric knowledge regarding the Absolute Truth or Universal Consciousness or *Brahman*.

There are about 108 *Upanishads* of which 12 are important. There were many more *Upanishads*, some of which have been lost to posterity. The important ones are:

| | |
|---|---|
| Brihadaranyaka U. | Taittiriya U |
| Svetasvatara U | Isavasya U |
| Keno U | Chandogya U |
| Mandukya U | Aitareya U |
| Katha U | Mundaka U |
| Prasna U | Kaushitaki U |

In addition to these, each *Veda* has six <u>ancillary supportive texts</u> called the *Vedangas* (<u>limbs of the Vedas</u>). I will briefly touch upon them in the interest of time and to avoid confusing you. There are six Vedangas namely, *Siksha, Vyakarana, Chhandas, Niruktha, Jyothisha* and *Kalpa*. Let us look at each of these in brief.

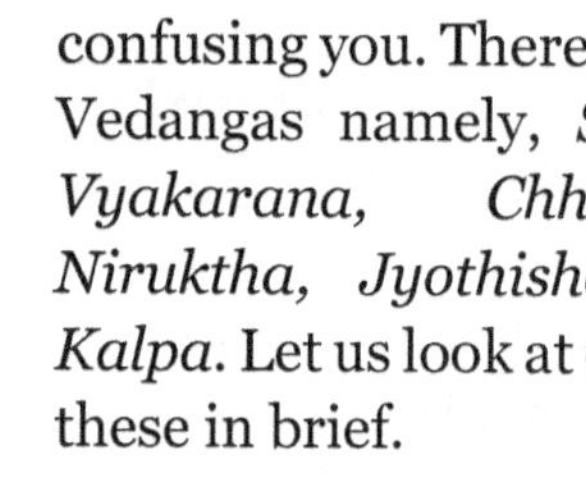


*Siksha* is the branch dealing with <u>Phonetics</u>, letters of the Sanskrit alphabet and the combinations of words during recitation of mantras.

*Vyakarana* is the study of Sanskrit grammar, construction of sentences, syntax, and the use of words in sentences.

*Chhandas* includes the study of Prosody, the study of poetic meters and versification. This is essential in the construction of the *mantras* (chants) to rhythm. When there is a rhythm to the chanting, memorization of the lyrics becomes easy.

*Niruktha* deals with Etymology, the origin, and the meaning of words according to the context in which they are used.

*Jyothisha* deals with Astronomy and Astrology. It focuses on time keeping and identification of auspicious times for rituals and festivals.

*Kalpa* includes the standardized procedures for various rituals like marriage, obsequies, and birth, performed during the life of an individual.

In addition to the *Vedangas*, there are four *Upavedas* which also deal with secular aspects of Hinduism. They do not deal with spirituality. The four *Upavedas* are:

1. ***Ayurveda*** (Knowledge about Life) which is the study of Medicine and Life Sciences. It deals with wellness in life - wellness of the body, mind, and soul. Various texts in Ayurveda are available. Ayurveda is still practiced extensively in many parts of India and there are universities rendering courses in

Ayurveda, especially in the state of Kerala in South India.

2. ***Arthasasthra*** which is the study of <u>Business administration and Economics</u>. It also deals with Man, Material and Money management, political science, sociology, trade & commerce, engineering etc. There are many texts available in this too.

3. ***Gandharva Veda*** which deals with <u>Arts, Music, and Dance</u>. The *Gandharvas* are celestial beings in mythology who are artists and musicians. Sixty-four types of arts are described including poetry, sculpture, theatre, painting, carpentry, needlework and many more.

4. ***Dhanur Veda*** is the science of <u>Warfare</u>, <u>Martial Arts</u> and <u>Archery</u>.

In addition, the scriptures contain a wealth of knowledge on various aspects of science like Mathematics, Biology, Physics, Chemistry ad Geometry and Astronomy. We will discuss this on another occasion later in our dialogues.

# 4. WORSHIP IN HINDUISM

**"Grandpa, which are the ways in which a Hindu worships the Gods?" was a relevant question from Vijaya.**

Grandpa began. There are many ways in which a Hindu worships God. First of all, we should understand that in Hinduism each one can have an *Ishta Devata* (<u>favorite</u> <u>God</u>) and worship that God. Or one can worship more than one God at a time.

The types of worship are divided into two.

***Nitya*** (<u>daily</u>) worship which means the type of worship one does daily. The *Sandyavandanam*, the daily poojas, and *Nama Japam* (<u>chanting</u>) are examples of *Nitya* worship. The other types of daily worship are *Mantra* chanting, Meditation, and *Bhajans*. Visit to the temple is also part of  daily worship.

***Naimittika*** (<u>special    occasion</u>) worship means worship done on special occasions like on a person's birthday, *Ganesha Pooja* done when taking up residence in a new home, or *Devi Pooja* done for overall prosperity in the home or *Poojas* done on specific auspicious days of the year like Rama Navami, Durgashtami, Sri Krishna Jayanthi etc.

**"What is Sandhyavandanam, Grandpa?" Aditya was curious.**

This is the worship done thrice daily by those who wear the *Upaveetham* or *Poonal* (<u>sacred thread</u>). (*Sandhya* means '<u>twilight</u>'). It is performed in the morning before the sun rises, at noon when the sun is above our heads and evening before the sun sets. It has many components. The *'Gayatri Japam'* is the repetition of the Gayatri Mantra 32, 64 or 108 times daily. This is a mantra to the All-pervading *Brahman* to enlighten our intellects. As the sun is a manifest form of that *Brahman*, the offerings are directed to the sun. There are many steps in the performance of *Sandyavandanam*. Along with chanting of excerpts from the *Vedas*, the person also performs the *Pranayama* (<u>breathing exercise</u>) and *Tharpanam* (<u>offering of water</u>) to the Gods, planets, and the <u>ancestors</u> (*Pithrus*).

*Sandyavandanam* is performed by the Brahmanas, Kshatriyas and Vaishyas who wear the sacred thread or the *Upanayanam.*

**"What is the *Gayatri* mantra? What is its meaning?" Aditya wanted to know, "My *Upanayanam* ceremony is planned for this year".**

Yes, every Hindu must know what the *Gayatri* mantra is. *Gayatri* mantra is the most sacred mantra of the Hindus. It is one of the oldest *Vedic* mantras in Hinduism. Sage *Vishwamitra* is said to have composed the *Gayatri* mantra. It is directed towards the Sun (*Savitur*) God considered as the manifestation of the Brahman and the protector of all beings. It runs thus.

ॐ भूर्भुवॢ स्सुवः तत्सं वितुवरेण्युं<br>भर्गों ढ़ेवस्यं धीमहि  धियोॢ यो नः प्रचोॢदयात् ॥

Om Bhoor-Bhuvah Suvaha<br>Tat-Savitur-Varennyam<br>Bhargo Devasya Dheemahi<br>Dhiyo Yo Nah Prachodayaat ||

The meaning of the mantra is "*We meditate on the glory of that Being who has produced this universe; may She enlighten our minds.*" (Swami Vivekananda)

"*We meditate on the effulgent glory of the divine Light; may She inspire our understanding.*" (*S. Radhakrishnan*)

"*We meditate on the adorable glory of the radiant sun; may She inspire our intelligence.*"

Many English translations are available for the *Gayatri* mantra, but all ultimately mean the same thing requesting that All pervasive *Brahman* to enlighten our intellect.

**"What is _Upanayanam_ ceremony?"** Vijaya's was curious.

_**Upanayanam**_ is a ceremony that is performed for boys usually between the ages of 7 and 13. The _Yagnopaveetham_ or _Poonal_ or _Janeu_ as it is called is the 'Sacred Thread' that is worn by the three _Varnas_ (division ; caste) - _Brahmanas_, _Kshatriyas_ and the _Vaishyas_. It marks the entry of the boy into the 'Brahmachari' or student stage of life. The ceremony marks the initiation of the boy to the scriptures, and he is required to perform _Sandyavandanam_ three times a day after the ceremony. He becomes qualified to perform the rituals and study the _Vedas_. We will discuss the _Varnas_ at a later date.

After the _Upanayanam_ ceremony, the boy is said to be 'reborn'. That is why he is called _**"Dvija"**_ (twice born). This is his second birth considered as his 'spiritual birth'. During the ceremony, the father who acts as the _Guru_ chants the _Gayatri_ mantra thrice in the right ear of the boy, thus initiating him into the world of the scriptures.

The _Yagnopaveetham_ also called _Janeu_ or _Poonal_), is the sacred thread which is worn across the chest from the left shoulder to below the right arm. It consists of three strands which represent the three natures of man – _Sattva, Rajas,_ and _Tamas._ (This will be discussed later). It is also said to represent the three Goddesses, _Gayatri_ (Mind), _Saraswathi_ (Word) and _Savithri_ (Action). The three strands are also represent the _Rig, Yajur,_ and _Sama Vedas._ The single knot on the thread represents the _Brahman._ The sacred thread is supposed to be worn on the chest for the rest of the life of the person. It is renewed every year after an elaborate ritual during the *Avani Avittam* festival (*Raksha Bandhan* day) which falls during August-September months.

**"Don't girls wear the sacred thread? Is there no *Upanayanam* ceremony for girls?" Jaya's concern as a girl was genuine.**

In ancient days the girls also underwent the *Upanayanam* ceremony at a young age. But as they were married early in olden days, this ritual was coupled with  the marriage ceremony. Even today, during the marriage ceremony, a ritual equivalent to the *Upanayanam* ceremony is performed for the bride. She accepts her husband as a *Guru*. The woman does not wear the sacred thread. But wearing her upper garment (<u>*sari*</u>) across the left shoulder is symbolic of the *Yagnopaveetham* for the woman.

**"Can we get back to the methods of worship, Grandpa?" Aditya steered me back to the main topic, "How and why do we perform *Pooja* to God?"**

There is a ninefold path in the worship of God which is described by Prahlada in the *Srimad Bhagavatham*. I will now, just name the nine-fold path of worship of God. We will discuss this in more detail when we discuss the topic on *Yoga*. This comes under the discussion of *Bhakti Yoga*. But just to name them, – *Shravanam* (<u>listening</u>), *Kirtanam* (<u>singing</u>), *Smaranam* (<u>contemplating</u>), *Padasevanam* (<u>service</u>

at His feet), *Archanam* (pooja), *Vandanam* (prostrating at His feet) , *Dasyam* (devotion), *Sakhyam* (friendship) and *Atmanivedanam* (self-surrender).

We will discuss this another day. I will now tell you briefly why and how we do *Pooja* as a part of worship.

In one of our previous discussions, I mentioned about the concept of *Ishta Devata*. Each one can have a favourite God, *Siva, Vishnu, Ganesha, Lakshmi. Saraswathi, Durga* or any other God or Goddess. *Pooja* is performed to the God or Goddess whom we worship. It is a way of offering our homage to the deity. Interestingly, *Pooja* as a method of worship was not described in the Rig Veda which is the oldest scripture in Hinduism. *Pooja* was also not part of the worship in the *Satya (Tretha) Yuga*. *Poojas* are performed daily in the household, during special ceremonies like the *Upanayanam*, marriage, birth of a child, birthdays of an individual, on auspicious occasions like Deepavali (*Lakshmi Pooja*), Navratri (*Durga Pooja*) etc. It is regularly performed three times a day in temples by the chief priest of the temple.

*Pooja* need not necessarily be to the deities or their idols. Poojas are also offered to rivers, mountains, trees, animals like the cow, *Go-pooja* (Go = cow), elephant, *Gaja-pooja* (Gaja = elephant) or cobra, *Naga-pooja* (Naga = snake) and so on. It is well known that in the *Srimad Bhagavatham, Sri Krishna* encourages his village folk to worship the mountain *Govardhanam* as it is a protector of their village and provided a grazing ground for their cattle.

There are many steps in the conduct of a *Pooja*. It is called the *Shodasa Upachara* (*Shodasa* = 16; *Upachara* = service: courtesy) or the 16 steps in the conduct of the Pooja. The deity is first invoked, offered a seat, and so on. It is akin to honouring a guest who has visited your home. The deity is offered clothes, sandal wood paste, followed by offering flowers (*Archana*), praised with mantras, offered food (*Nivedyam*) prostrated before and then finally bid farewell. The devotee seeks the blessings of the deity during the *Pooja*.

**Pooja Room in a Home**

The *Nivedyam* (oblation ; food) offered to the deity is then distributed among the devotees as *Prasadam*. However, many of the *Pooja* rituals today have become more of a monotonous routine stereotyped procedure and seem to lack the genuine fervour and earnestness on the part of the doer.

**"Grandpa, what are the other methods by which we worship God?", Vijaya wanted to know.**

The *Homam* or *Havan,* as it is called in North India, is another method of worship. This is a ritual performed by a priest for the blessings of the deity for the whole community (as done in temples) or for a household (when performed at home). The *Agni* (sacred fire) is invoked in the fire-sacrifice and offerings like ghee, grains, cooked rice are offered into the fire to the recitation of mantras. The pit for the sacred fire (called '*Homa Kunda*') is made of clay or with bricks arranged in a square or other geometrical patterns. There are also elaborate *Homams* which are called

**VILAKKU IN POOJA**

'*Yagnas*' done at the community level in temples with a large gathering of devotees. *Yagnas* are performed for the welfare of the community or for other blessings like adequate rains, good harvest, good health of all community members etc.

In Hinduism *Agni* (sacred fire) is considered the purest of the five elements as it purifies everything without itself getting tainted. (unlike water or air which get tainted when impurities mix with them). Hence *Agni* or a *Homam* is an integral part of all the *Poojas* and Hindu ceremonies like marriage, *Upanayanam* or death rites. At home the sacred fire,

*Agni* is symbolized by the <u>oil lamp</u> or *Vilakku* which is lit in the *Pooja* room.

**"What is *Namajapam*?  What is the role of chanting in worship?**

*Namajapam* or *Namasankeertanam* is where the devotee chants the *mantra* or *mantras* worshipping the *Ishta Devata*. Chanting of mantras is called *Japam*. It can be performed by repeating the name of the God like *"Om Namah Shivaya"*, *"Om Namo Narayanaya"*, *"Om Namo Bhagavathe Vasudevaya"* and so on. There are other chants also which are recited during the *Namasankeertanam*.

It can also be chanting the multiple names of the God in a rhythmic metered verse. The thousand names of *Bhagavan Vishnu* as in *Vishnu Sahasranamam* and that of the *Divine Mother* (*Shakthi*) in

*Lalitha Sahasranamam* are some of the mantras chanted daily by many Hindus.  Many devout Hindus repeat the *Gayatri mantra* 108 times daily or 1008 times on special occasions. There are many more such mantras and chants which are intoned daily by the Hindus at home, in temples and in community gatherings.

There are many <u>couplets</u> in Sanskrit called *Slokas* (singular = *slokam*). They are in praise of many of the deities. Thus, there are *slokas* for *Vishnu, Siva, Ganesha, Lakshmi, Saraswathi, Durga, Hanuman* and so on. These are simple and easy to commit to memory and are often chanted by children in the morning and at dusk when the *Vilakku* (<u>oil lamp</u>) is lit in the *Pooja* room. These simple verses are taught to children even from the tender age of two or three when they quickly memorize them and learn to recite them by heart.

A simple mantra which is said to give liberation in these modern times is the *Maha mantra.* (<u>Great Mantra</u>):

हरे राम हरे राम राम राम हरे हरे

हरे कृष्ण हरे कृष्ण कृष्ण कृष्ण हरे हरे

*Hare Rama, Hare Rama,  Rama Rama Hare Hare,*

*Hare Krishna, Hare Krishna, Krishna Krishna Hare Hare.*

Chanting *mantras* mentally while meditating leads to calmness of the mind and peace. It reduces stress and improves the power of concentration of the mind. Children are encouraged by the elders to chant the slokas daily morning and evening (*Sandya Japam*) so as to enhance their academic performance. Also, the chanting of mantras in a home creates positive vibrations which give a positive feeling to whoever enters the home. Have you not noticed that when you enter some homes, you get a very pleasant and positive feeling. This happens whatever the religion the family follows. Any home where there is regular prayer and chanting, be it a Christian or a Muslim or any other religion, gives this positive feeling. I am sure most of you would have felt these vibrations.

**"Should we not pray to God for material gains when we worship Him at home or in the temple?" Aditya asked this naughty question with a twinkle in his eye. "I could pray for an A+ in all my examinations".**

Grandpa smiled. Hinduism is not a religion which encourages you to beg or entreat God for material gains. God is Omniscient. He knows what your wants and needs are and will reward you accordingly. Remember, *you will get what your deserve, not what you covet.* That is the *Law of Karma.* We will discuss this another day.

We will always get what we deserve, and we have to learn to accept with grace whatever we get. In our previous discussions we have said that we should do our duty sincerely leaving the reward and results to God. Whether it be success in your examinations or success in your life, you will be rewarded for your efforts. But do not solicit God with your requests.

One prays for enlightenment and liberation and not for the earthly benefits when one goes to the temple. If you surrender yourself completely to Him, you will get all that you deserve. He perfectly well knows what you need.

*Vandanam* is the other method of worship. It can be loosely translated into 'prostration at the feet of God' in English. But remember that it does not mean 'beseech' or 'beg'. Prayer should be for prayer's sake only. Sing or chant God's praise to your heart's content without putting in any requests or demands. The English poet Tennyson aptly said, *"More things are wrought by prayer than this world dreams of...."* Prayer can work wonders for the mind and the soul, and the power of unconditional prayer is often felt by the devotee. The miracles wrought by prayers have been described in many anecdotal instances. Sincere prayer touches your soul and melts your heart.

**"What is the offering that we should give God during worship?" Vijaya asked.**

Ah! That is a very good question. You tell me what God does *not* have. You cannot 'give' anything to God because, everything in the Universe is His. But then why do you give the offering to God. It is like you giving a beautiful set of color pencils to your friend for her birthday. It is not because your friend cannot afford a pencil set. You give it out of your love and affection for her. Isn't it so?   Similarly, your offering to God is to express your love and devotion to Him. In fact, in the Bhagavad Gita, Bhagavan Sri Krishna has said:

पत्रं पुष्पं फलं तोयं यो मे भक्त्या प्रयच्छति ।
तदहं भक्त्युपहृतमश्नामि प्रयतात्मनः ॥ ९-२६॥

Patram puṣpam phalam toyam yo me bhaktyā prayacchati
Tadaham bhaktyupahṛtamaśnāmi prayatātmanaḥ

It means, *"If one offers to Me with devotion a leaf, a flower,  fruit, or even water, I delightfully partake of that offering by My devotee with love  in pure consciousness".*

So, you can see that God will accept anything given with sincere devotion. It is not the cost or the value of the offering that is important, but the devotion with which it is offered that is important to God.

**"What is *Bhajan*?" Jaya had a simple question .**

*Bhajans* are songs with a religious theme often in praise of a deity. '*Bhajanam*' in Sanskrit means 'reverence'. These lyrics are set to beautiful *ragas* (tunes) and sung in groups in  community halls or temples. *Bhajans* are also sung individually at home in front of the deity in the *Pooja* room. There are many *bhajans* in praise of all the deities in Hinduism. The rhythmic cadence of the *bhajans* give an emotionally charged feeling to the mind and soul. Listening to *bhajans* is also enlivening.

*Bhajans* when sung in groups, generates a sense of belonging and camaraderie in the group. The emotionally and spiritually charged ambience and the elation and bliss that one feels during the *bhajan* must be experienced to be believed. The devotee feels oneness with the Supreme *Brahman* during the ecstatic moments while singing the *bhajans*. *Bhajans* also have a therapeutic value. They are a good antidote for depression, stress, and anxiety. They help improve the power of concentration and focus of the individual.

After a session of *bhajan*, the devotees feel a sense of being spiritually charged and elevated.

Most of the *bhajans* are in praise of the deity or are based on the Hindu epics like *Ramayana, Mahabharatha* and the *Srimad Bhagavatham*. The rhythmic melodies have a mesmerising effect on the mind and soul. Every Hindu child is taught a few simple *bhajans* by their parents or spiritual teachers and these songs are ingrained in their minds from childhood.

**"What is '*Satsang*'? Why are we asked to attend the *satsangs*?", asked Aditya.**

Let us first look at the word meaning. '*Sat*' means 'truth' and '*Sangha*' means 'friendship', 'company' or 'association'. It literally means to be associated with people who are devoted to God or with pure and truthful people. In other words, *Satsang* means being in the company of good people. It also refers to a community or group of people who are engaged in spiritual discussions and debates. Group chanting or *bhajans* are also called *Satsangs*. It also denotes listening to spiritual discourses from *Gurus* or scholars who have studied the scriptures and give us the specific details and philosophy in a simple assimilable manner.

Man's innate nature is to absorb evil as easily as a sponge mops up water. Just like water flows downward, our thoughts, if left unchecked, tend to gravitate towards negative tendencies and evil deeds. Our aim should be to steer clear of the negative tendencies and evils and aim towards self-improvement and enlightenment. Adi Sankaracharya in his composition *"Bhaja Govindam"* says,

सत्संगत्वे निस्संगत्वं, निस्संगत्वे निर्मोहत्वं।<br>निर्मोहत्वे निश्चलतत्त्वं, निश्चलतत्त्वे जीवन्मुक्तिः

Satsangatve nissangatvam nissangatve nirmohatvam,<br>nirmohatve niscalatattvam niscalatattve jivanmukti

It means, *"Through the company of the wise or the good, there arises non-attachment; from non-attachment comes freedom from delusion; where there is freedom from delusion, there is abidance in self-knowledge, which leads to freedom while alive".*

The aim of *Satsang* is to achieve spiritual upliftment and this is done by keeping the company of good and *Sattvic* people. We live in a world with temptations all around us and it is very easy to slide into corrupt and immoral ways by falling into bad company. Hence the importance of being in a good company.

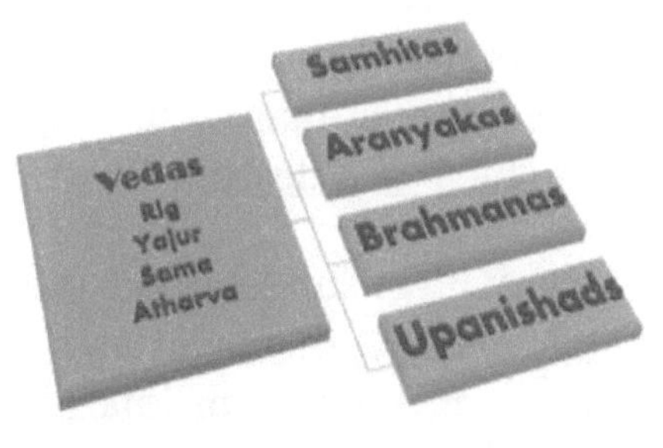


A *Satsang* is often led by a *Guru* or a teacher, or a scholar well versed in the scriptures of Hinduism. It starts with a prayer or a series of slokas followed by a discourse by the *Guru* on some topic and is concluded with a *bhajan* or a *Kirtanam* (<u>song</u>). There may be *Satsangs* going on in a series for several days like the *"Srimad Bhagavatha Sapthaham"*. Here the whole scripture

55

(*Srimad Bhagavatham*) is read and explained by the *Guru* in detail over a period of seven days. (*Sapthaham* = <u>seven days</u>) in a simple manner for the average person to understand.

## "What is the meaning of Tantric worship, grandpa?" Aditya asked.

*Tantra* literally means '<u>weave</u>'. The word '*tantu*' in Sanskrit means '<u>thread</u>' or '<u>filament</u>' and indicates the Naadis or energy channels in the body.

Tantra is the practice to harness these Naadis into a unified whole and transform the person into a sublime human being. All the energy channels of the body are thus bonded together by the *Tantra* practices. *Tantra* uses mystic sounds or syllables, mystic diagrams or *Yantra* (<u>instrument</u>; <u>drawing</u>) and objects in their rituals. Metal sheets embossed with a picture of the *Yantra* is used in the *tantric* rituals. Ultimately, the aim of *Tantra* also is to free the human soul from the bondage of *Samsara* – <u>birth and death</u>.

*Tantra* has been a misunderstood practice. People believe that it deals with magic and occult practices. This is not true. It is only a spiritual practice which helps evoke the hidden inner power of the human consciousness to reveal the inner divinity within us.

The *Mantra* tradition where the chanting of mantras during rituals is often combined with *Tantra* tradition and a combination is used by most of the practitioners of rituals in worship. *Tantric* practices use *Mudras* (hand gestures). These gestures by hand are used in the worship of Gods to seek their blessings. Many of the *Tantric* practices have not been committed in writing and they are traditionally taught in person from *Guru* to *Shishya*.

Often it is *Bhagavan Siva, Bhagavan Vishnu,* and *Goddess Durga* (*Shakthi*) who are worshipped through *Tantric* rituals. In the state of Kerala in India it is the *tantric* rituals which are followed in most of the temples. The priests are brahmins called 'Namboodiris' whose worship is more *tantric* than *mantric*. They are experts in *Tantric* worship. *Tantric* rituals are aimed at dispelling the negative energy from the body and ushering in positive energy into the body and mind.

# 5. IDOL WORSHIP

**"Why do Hindus worship idols? My friends make fun of me saying that we Hindus have too many Gods with weird faces and forms. How do I respond to them?" Jaya had a genuine concern.**

Grandpa smiled. Children, First of all, you should understand the main concept of **"God"** in Hinduism. When you were tiny tots your mother pointed out various idols and pictures and told you the names of various Gods and stories about them. Isn't it so?

[The children nod their heads in agreement].

In the ancient *Vedas*, God was not described in any form. Many of the things in Nature were worshiped as Gods – the mountain, the river, the sun, fire, and even plants and trees were all worshipped. Man worshipped the *'Power'* in Nature which he thought, protected him. The *Vedas* and *Upanishads* describe the 'All Powerful', 'All Pervasive' God as the

"*Brahman*". The *Brahman* is formless, eternal - without a beginning or end and is present everywhere. Everything in the Universe is a part of that *Brahman*. So are you and so am I. [Grandpa, pauses for effect]. Remember, *idol worship is not idle worship*. It has a deep meaning.

**"Then why should we worship the idols if you say that God or *Brahman* is Formless and All Pervasive?**

Good question, children. Now listen. Can you concentrate and think of an object called '**Quintoplemoth**'? [Grandpa pauses for an answer]

[The children look at each other and raise their eyebrows] "**Grandpa, you are making fun of us. How can there be a thing with that strange name which nobody has seen, heard, or described?**"

Exactly, *what the mind does not know, the eyes do not see*. Similarly, it is not possible to imagine or contemplate something which has no form. Now, close your eyes and try to imagine "sweetness".

[The children shake their heads in unison, meaning "**No**"].

But if I say '*Candy*' or '*Laddu*' you will immediately see the form in your mind's eye, will you not? (*Laddu* = an Indian sweet made from flour and sugar).

[The children smile and nod vigorously].

Sweetness cannot be imagined, but only perceived. Similarly, it is very difficult to think of and imagine something abstract. So, you give it a form. This is called '***Personification***' in English. And that is what an idol does in Hinduism. <u>The idol is not God.</u> It is only a symbol or manifestation of that Absolute Power or Universal Consciousness that we recognize as God. God does not reside in the idol, but we see and feel God's presence by looking at and worshiping the idol. The idol is made of wood, metal, stone, clay or marble and it is a finite substance. You can break it, destroy it, or burn it. But that does not 'destroy' God! That is why the Hindu is able to dispose the idols into the sea or river after the *Pooja* as is done after *Ganesh Chathurthy* without any remorse. He understands that 'God' is beyond idols and symbols. That is the reason why, when the Mughals destroyed many of our temples and idols, nothing happened to Hinduism. It still continued as strong as ever.

I will give you one more example. All three of you have learnt algebra. When you have to find an unknown factor, how do you start working.

The children chorused, "**We name that unknown number or factor as "X" and start working through the equations and derive the answer in the end." Aditya pops up with the answer.**

"Well, after you have calculated and got your answer to your problem, what do you do with the **X**"?

**"We no longer need the X as we have got the answer already. We discard it."** the children replied.

It is the same with the idols in Hinduism. The beginner who cannot contemplate upon the unknown and formless God or *Brahman* resorts to worshipping the *Brahman* through the idols. Later when he reaches the higher planes of spirituality through meditation and contemplation, he no longer needs the idols and rituals to know and experience God. He does not practice any rituals and does not worship or pray to any idols. He is able to perceive and experience God without the help of any external aids like idols or symbols.

That is the basis on which idols are worshipped. You must understand that a vast majority of Hindus worship the idols as they have not reached the spiritual maturity to realize God without the help of idols which are only props in our spiritual journey.

I will give you one more example. All three of you take part in sports. There is a high jump event in sports where you try to jump to great heights without any aid. But what do you do when you have to jump to a height of 7 feet?

**"We use a pole for vaulting – we call it <u>Pole-Vault</u>" replies Aditya.**

What do you do when you pole vault? You run forward with the pole, use the pole to raise yourself to a great height, more than you can normally jump and when you reach the top, *you let go of the pole*, don't you?

[The children nod vigorously in unison].

Idol worship is like pole-vault. You use the idol to reach great heights in spirituality and when you reach that stage, you let go off the idol and meditate on the formless. The idol is your pole and the height is the spiritual heights that you strive to reach. Do you get it? But in fact, only a few are able to reach those great spiritual heights.

**"So do you mean that idol worship is for the beginner, and you don't need it when you are well advanced in your spiritual journey?" queries Jaya.**

Exactly, you are spot-on. Idol worship which should be really called 'Deity Worship' is seen in all religions even if they deny it. The Muslim turns towards the *Kaaba* in Mecca when he prays and stones the 'devil' which is symbolized by a pillar, the Christian uses the cross as a symbol of worship and bows before the idol of Jesus and Mary in church. Every religion has an idol or a symbol which it uses for worship.

The idols are mere gizmos which help you realize God. Hinduism asserts that God is present in everyone. Every being in the Universe, living or dead is *Brahman*. You are, I am, that tree, and that bird on the tree is all *Brahman*.

What we call *'Soul'* or *'Atman'* in the human body is *Brahman*. It is the *'Life'* or *'Jeevatma'* in a human body. Imagine a human body without the *Atman*. What will happen?

**"It will be a dead body" pipes up Aditya.**

Yes, *Atman* or soul is the presence of God or *Brahman* in each one of us. Our five senses are Sight, Hearing, Smell, Taste and Touch. These are called the *Jnana Indriyas* (*senses*). We experience the world around us through the five sense organs which are the Eyes, Ears, Nose, Tongue, and Skin respectively. But remember that there is a *Power* behind the eye that makes us see. The eye is the fleshy anatomical part of the body. A power behind the nose makes us smell, a power behind the ear makes us hear, isn't it so? But for the anatomical eye to perceive an object in the world outside, it needs a power or an inner Energy which empowers it.  The fleshy eye is also part of a dead body, but can it see anything, can the nose smell, can the tongue taste? No, it cannot. This is because the inner spirit or *Power* that empowers the eye to see, the nose to smell, or the tongue to taste is gone.  That is the *Atman.*

**"It is very confusing Grandpa; can you make it simpler for me to understand? Why can't we see God?" Vijaya, being the youngest, found it difficult to follow.**

[Grandpa closes his eyes for a minute and then opens it with a smile]. "What do you see in the ceiling", he asks.

"The ceiling fan".

"What do you see on the table there?"

"The Table lamp"

"What is there in the wall above the window?"

"The Air conditioner".

Okay, now what are these different items? They are all equipment with different functions, do you agree? The fan generates movement of air and helps to keep the room cool. The air-conditioner cools the air in the room in hot weather. The table lamp gives us light in the dark. All three of them have different functions, don't they?

[The children nod their heads].

"What energy or power runs all these appliances?"

"Electricity", they answer.

Have you seen electricity? Have you tasted it? What is its shape? How big or small is it? Now can you close your eyes and visualize electricity?

[The children chuckle, looking at each other.]

Electricity is power or energy which has no form but is needed to run all these equipment, do you agree? Once you remove the electricity from the equipment, it is just a metallic frame with a combination of wires and machinery. It cannot function. Now think of *Brahman* as this electricity. It is formless, it is all pervasive and it cannot be seen. It is everywhere. Are there different types of electricity like Indian electricity, American electricity, or Russian electricity? No, isn't it? But you can feel its presence when you touch a live wire. Similarly, *God has to be experienced but not 'seen'*. You can see the fan in the ceiling, you can see the lamp on the table, and the air-conditioner, but they do not represent electricity. They are only the means through which electricity expresses itself as light, cool air or heat depending on which equipment you use. Thus, light, heat or cold are expressions of electricity which itself in invisible and formless. So is *Brahman.*

So, coming back to our discussion of idol worship, let me repeat that idols are not God, they are only personifications or symbols of Gods that we worship. We worship God through the medium of the idols. The idols can be made of anything like stone, clay, metal, or paper, like the picture on the wall. It only symbolizes that *Power* which we call God.

"Have you not seen the priest make a small conical shape with wet turmeric powder, put a tilak of *Kumkum* on it and perform pooja symbolizing it as *Bhagavan Ganesha*?", Grandpa asked.

[The children vigorously nod their heads in agreement.]

**"But there are still people who do not believe in God or in this so-called 'symbolism'." Aditya seemed skeptical.**

I agree. They are the atheists who do not believe in God. Does not matter. But I do not agree that they don't accept 'symbolism'. They definitely believe in symbolism. If I give one of these non-believers a piece of cloth and ask him to burn it will he do it?

"Sure, why not?" was the prompt answer.

Now, if that piece of cloth is the flag of his country, or his political party?  Still, it is a piece of cloth. Will he burn it? No, he wouldn't. Isn't it so? Why? It is because the cloth (flag) now represents Patriotism or Nationalism for him. Doesn't it?

If I give these guys a piece of blank paper and ask them to burn it will they, do it?

"Easily" was the answer from the children.

Now if that piece of paper has the picture of Benjamin Franklin with $100 written on one corner?

[The children begin to chuckle]. **"You have made your point Grandpa", chimes in Vijaya.**

Let me give you a definition of *Brahman* as given in the *Keno Upanishad.*  *"What one cannot think with the mind, but by which the mind is made to think, what speech cannot enlighten but what enlightens speech, what cannot be seen by the eye but by which the eyes are able to see – That is Brahman".* I think that this is the best definition of *Brahman* that I have encountered.

*Bhagavan Sri Krishna* himself says in the *Bhagavad Gita, "for human beings with a materialistic perspective, understanding and worshiping Brahman in an Unmanifested form is extremely difficult. If you are unable to focus your mind steadily on Me, then long to attain Me by practice of any other spiritual discipline, such as a ritual, or deity worship that suits you." (Bhagavad Gita. 12.09)*

Hence, we should resort to idols in the initial stages of worship. This one verse is enough to justify idol worship.

So, I hope you are convinced about the need for idol worship. Idols are needed only in your early stages of development of religious faith and devotion. Once you realize God and his greatness, idols may no longer be necessary for you. When you were in your kindergarten, you had to count using your fingers. Do you do it now? It is the beginner and those in the early stages of spirituality who have to stick to idols and rituals. It may no longer be needed when one has reached the higher realms of spirituality like the student who has moved up the ladder of academic scholarship.

**"But still, Grandpa, some of my friends make fun of me saying that our Gods have all sorts of weird forms and shapes and flaunt different objects in their hands. What is the meaning of all this? I sometimes feels embarrassed." Aditya wanted an answer.**

I understand your dilemma. It may be difficult for you to explain these concepts to your friends, unless you understand the symbolism behind the idols which we worship. I will illustrate this with some examples.

Which is the most common idol you come across daily that you want discussed first ?

**"*Bhagavan Ganesha*" chorused all three together.**

Yes, now let us see what the idol of *Bhagavan Ganesha* symbolizes. The God has the head of an elephant a stout body with a large pot belly and is seen to ride on the back of a mouse! To the observer it may all sound absolutely ridiculous. But the symbolism behind this is profound.

**Bhagavan Ganesha**

The large head of the elephant symbolizes *knowledge*. The large ears indicate that we should keep our ears open and listen to God's praise and acquire knowledge by listening to our teachers and *Gurus*. The trunk is a part of the head which can lift the heaviest of weights like a log of wood or pick a tiny needle from the floor. This indicates that our mind should be able to learn gross ideas and also minute and subtle ideas. The small eyes indicate the power of contemplation. The small mouth indicates that we should speak less but listen and learn more. The mouse on which *Bhagavan Ganesha* rides symbolizes *Logic*. Logic cuts across knowledge like the mouse which gnaws at the net (bonds in life). The mouse is also a restless creature constantly on the run. This indicates the restlessness of the mind, and the *Bhagavan Ganesha* rides on the back of logic and controls the restlessness of the mind.

The <u>axe</u> in one hand of the *Bhagavan* denotes detachment from the world. The axe epitomizes severing the emotional ties or materialistic bonds. The *Ankus* (<u>bullhook</u>) in the other hand denotes the need for self-discipline. The bullhook is an instrument used by the mahout to control the elephant and keep it calm and restrained when it becomes aggressive. The bullhook in Bhagavan Ganesha's hand denotes the need to keep our emotions and  passions under control. The <u>sweet</u> (*Modakam*) in His hand symbolizes the reward one gets for a wise and balanced life. The fourth hand is raised in blessing to the devotee.

Many Gods are seen with various weapons. These do not indicate that the weapons are to destroy the enemy or evil individuals. They are meant to destroy the *negative tendencies* in the human mind. Often the negative tendencies are epitomized as *Asuras* or *Rakshasas. Bhagavan Ganesha's* one foot rests on the ground whereas the other foot is raised. This indicates involvement in worldly matters as well as in higher spiritual matters.

**"Wow!  What an explanation! Now I can counter any argument from my friends"** **Aditya smiles with pleasure. "Tell me Grandpa, why do we always worship *Bhagavan Ganesha* before starting any Pooja or new venture like during the housewarming?"**

There are a couple of *Puranic* legends behind why *Bhagavan Ganesha* is offered *Pooja* before starting any new venture. Once, Parvathy, *Bhagavan*

*Siva's* wife was resting in her chambers. To guard the entry, she created a boy and advised him not to allow anyone to enter. When *Bhagavan Siva* came to visit his wife, the boy refused entry to *Siva*. Enraged, *Siva* cut off the boy's head. *Parvathy* was so enraged that she threatened to destroy the whole world with her intense anger. Upon this *Bhagavan Siva* replaced the head of the lifeless boy with that of an elephant and revived him. *Siva* and *Parvathy* then blessed *Ganesha* saying that henceforth all Poojas and good ventures would start with the invocation of *Ganesha* for its smooth conduct without any obstacles.

Another legend says that once sage *Narada* reached the abode of *Bhagavan Siva* and *Parvathy* with a divine fruit from the heavens. *Narada* was bent upon creating some mischief in the family. He requested *Siva* to give the fruit to his favorite son. *Bhagavan Siva* was at a loss as to whom to give it to – his elder son *Ganesha* or younger son *Subramanian*. *Bhagavan Siva* decided that he would give the fruit to the one who circumambulated the earth thrice in the shortest time possible. Hearing this *Subramanian* took off on the peacock which was his vehicle. *Ganesha* fell into deep thought as he could not do so with his bulky body and his ride which was a mouse. Finally, he folded his hands and went around his parents *Siva* and *Parvathy* thrice and prostrated before them saying that going around one's parents is equivalent to going around the world. Pleased by *Ganesha's* intelligent answer, *Siva* gave the fruit to *Ganesha* and blessed him saying that he will be offered first pooja before any auspicious ritual. This is mentioned in the *Ganesha Puranam*.

It is believed by Hindus that worshipping *Bhagavan Ganesha* always brings success to any new enterprise or undertaking. Every temple will have one shrine dedicated to *Bhagavan Ganesha*. You will find *Bhagavan Ganesha* adorning many of the offices of devout Hindus as a small idol on the table or shelf, or a framed picture on the wall. You can also find Him in many shrines or oratories built in hospitals where patients and their families offer worship. *Ganesha* is the favorite God of the masses.

**"By the way, Grandpa, who is an *Asura* and who is a *Rakshasa*?"**

The *Asuras* are described as beings which have opposite characteristics to *Devas*, who are called 'Suras'. *Asuras* are described in the *Vedas,* and they possess all the negative characteristics like, violence, dishonesty, cruelty, tyranny etc., unlike the *Devas*.

The *Rakshasas* on the other hand are evil beings or demons who live on earth and are constantly trying to destroy the good humans like the sages. *Rakshasas* live in forests and are said to be cannibals. They are evil personified. There are many allusions to *Rakshasas* in Hindu mythology.

You can see that the idols of many of the deities are depicted as killing or subjugating a *Rakshasa* or an *Asura*. Examples are that of *Mahishasura* being conquered by Devi or *Apasmaraka* being trampled on by *Bhagavan Siva* dancing as *Nataraja*. In reality, the Asuras and Rakshasas symbolize the evil and negative tendencies in man. These are symbolic and indicate that the God helps us to suppress these evil and negative tendencies in us.

**"But then, Grandpa,  tell me about the eight hands of *Goddess Durga*" asked Jaya.**

*Goddess Durga* symbolizes the power behind creation. She is a feminine personification of *Brahman.* Her eight arms symbolize the eight quadrants of the universe. They are also said to represent the *Ashtanga Yogas.* She rides a lion as her vehicle. The lion is an animal symbolic of determination and will. The Goddess riding the lion indicates that she has a mastery over these qualities

The conch in her hand symbolizes the sound "*Om*" or '*Pranavam*' (<u>cosmic sound</u>). The bow and the arrows represent *energy.* The thunderbolt in her hand represents  *firmness.* The devotees must stand firm to face the challenges of life. The lotus in her hand represents *success* and *evolution of spirituality.* The lotus is a flower that arises from mud but stands tall above the mud facing up to the sun. man should also rise above the murky earthly life and turn his thoughts and mind upwards to God. The *Sudarshana Chakra* or discus in her hand indicates that the whole world is at her command. The trident indicates the three qualities

Goddess Durga

of *Sattva, Rajas,* and *Tamas.* The *Abhaya Mudra* (<u>gesture of fearlessness</u>) of her right hand represents freedom from fear for her devotees.

**"Why does Bhagavan Brahma have four heads, grandpa?" asks Vijaya wrinkling her brow.**

A good question, dear. Tell me what function *Bhagavan Brahma* performs in the pantheon of Hindus.

**"Creation?", Jaya hesitatingly replies.**

Yes *Bhagavan Brahma* is concerned with creation. And for creation, what requisites do you need? You need <u>knowledge, wisdom, intelligence</u> etc. Now pay careful attention. I will be going into a little bit of esoteric philosophy here.

How do we acquire knowledge in this world? We imbibe knowledge using our five senses which we have discussed previously. These experiences reach our brain through the five sense organs. You know that the brain has many anatomical parts like the cerebral hemispheres, the cerebellum, medulla, pons etc. Different parts of the brain have different functions related to our five senses. Psychologically, or rather spiritually, however, the brain has <u>four levels of function</u>. They are described in our scriptures. These four together

**Bhagavan Brahma**

are named as the '*Anthakaranam*' (*Antha* = <u>inner</u>; *Karana* = <u>instrument</u>; <u>function</u>) It means the total mind along with the feeling of "I", the thinking capacity, the memory etc. These four divisions of *Anthakaranam* are:

1.   ***Manas*** – This is the *Mind*. It receives the <u>sensory perceptions</u> from the five senses and feels pleasure and pain. It is said that around 60,000 thoughts pass through our mind daily. Mind is where <u>emotions</u> like love, jealousy, anger, and hatred occur.

2.   ***Ahamkaram*** – This the *Ego* or Our egocentric attitude in making decisions. 'Me', 'Mine', 'My' are the attitudes that we have. It is one's sense of self-esteem and self-importance. It varies from person to person. It is the view a person has of himself. It is the "I" in a person. Ego is responsible for one's personality and identity. Ego motivates one to work hard to achieve success and reach greater heights in one's calling. Thus, ego has both positive and negative aspects. Hence it is a necessary and important part of our psyche.

3.   ***Buddhi*** – This is *Intelligence or Memory*. This is the human ability to <u>discriminate and rationalize</u>. It functions through logic and reason and has the ability to acquire knowledge, skills, and the ability to solve problems. It is the next higher level in one's psyche. It finds answers to questions and doubts.

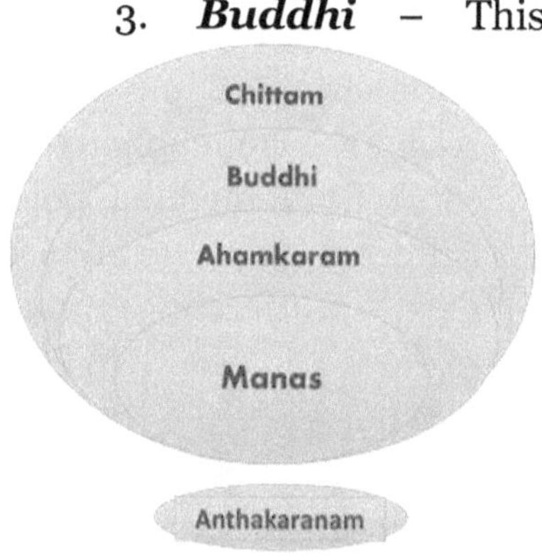

4. ***Chittam*** - This is the *Intellect*. This is the highest level of consciousness and full of positive energy. It is the faculty of <u>reasoning and understanding objectively,</u> especially the ability to figure out abstract matters. It is what makes a person '*clever*' and '*wise*'. It is a collection of memories and is the storehouse of knowledge. It functions to interpret and analyze the knowledge that is received by the mind, processed by the intelligence, flavored by the ego into practical and knowledgeable wisdom.

*Any creative idea needs the active involvement of all these four faculties — the Mind, the Ego, Intelligence, and Intellect.* When they act in unison in a coordinated and sequential manner, we are able to create things and function normally in the world around us. These together form our *Anthakaranam.*

A musician creates a heart-warming melody and composes excellent music. His mind first decides to create a piece of music. His intelligence tells him how to do it, what instrument to use and so on. His intellect gives him knowledge from the storehouse of his memories - from its abundant repertoire, and his ego goads him to create the best composition ever and present it to the world. Thus, you find that the four divisions of his *Anthakaranam* act in conjunction to create the music.

Before an engineer commences to construct a building, he has to conceive the architecture and the plan in his psyche, and it is the sum total of the mind, intelligence, intellect, and ego that help him in his creative work. The same holds good with an author who creates his masterpiece — a book, an artist who paints his best picture ever, a scientist who invents a new machine or a robot, and so on.

*Bhagavan Brahma* is the designated creator of the Universe and everything in it and he does it with the help of this quartet. *And this is symbolized as his four heads — the <u>mind</u>, the <u>ego</u>, the <u>intelligence</u>, and the <u>intellect</u>, called Manas, Ahamkaram, Buddhi, and Chittam in Sanskrit.*

I hope the concept is clear to all of you.  Thus, every deity or image of a deity has many symbolisms attributed to it. We will learn more about this as we move along.

**"What does the symbol 'Swastika' mean. I saw our priest draw this on the floor with a rice flour before the Pooja the other day" Jaya queried.**

Yes, just like we have idols for deities and Gods, we have symbols also in Hinduism.  The *Swastika* is one such holy symbol. It is a hated symbol by the western countries, but it has been a sacred symbol for the Hindus since ages.

Let us look at the meaning of the word first. *Swastika* is a combination of two Sanskrit words *'Su'* which means '<u>auspicious</u>' and *'Asti'* meaning '<u>happen</u>'. It means '<u>*May the auspicious happen*</u>'. This symbol interestingly has been seen in some pottery from

Greece in 800 BCE and in some coins as early as 3000 BCE. It has also been seen in ancient ornaments in Italy, Greece, and Scandinavia in 400- 900 BCE. The *Swastika* is representative of the four *Vedas*, the four *Purushartas*, the four *Varnas*, the four *Ashramas* and the four directions. (We will learn about these names as we go along). It also implies that '<u>let noble thoughts come from all four sides</u>.' The symbol is associated with *Goddess Lakshmi* who confers wealth and success on Her devotees.

Another symbol is the "*Om*" written in Sanskrit. The word *Om* is also called '*Pranavam*'. It symbolises the Supreme Truth, the Universal

OM or AUM - Pranavam

Intelligence or *Brahman*. It denotes the sound of creation and the universe. The word is a combination of the three letters '**A**', '**U**', and '**M**'. They represent the trinity *Brahma*, *Vishnu* and *Siva* and the sound *Om* is said to represent the primordial word or sound which was the beginning of creation. Even Christianity recognises the 'Word' as the beginning of creation with the statement – "*In the beginning was the Word and the Word was with God and the Word was God*". *(Gospel of John)*. Every chant or *mantra* in Hinduism starts with the chanting of *Om* . The very chanting of the word Om creates sacred and powerful positive vibrations in the mind.

Another symbol is the *Yantra* which are geometric diagrams drawn on the floor during rituals. The word meaning is 'machine' or 'contraption' and are associated with specific deities. The *yantras* are also used to adorn the walls and ceilings in temples and places of worship. *Yantras* are also part of the *Tantric* type of worship.

YANTRA

Instead of an idol or an image of God, during a *Pooja* or any ritual, a '*Vilakku*' (oil lamp) is lit symbolizing the deity. *Vilakku* is a Tamil word. In North India it is called '*Diya*'. This is often done during *Pooja* to the *Goddess Devi* or *Durga*. A silver or Brass lamp with five wicks and oil or ghee is lit and placed in the center of a *Yantra* during the *Pooja* symbolizing the Goddess.

VILAKKU IN POOJA

The *Siva Linga* which you see in temples is also a symbolic representation of *Bhagavan Siva*. The *Shaligram* is a stone found in the Gandaki river in Nepal. This is used as a symbolic representation for *Bhagavan Vishnu* in rituals by the Hindus. They are fossils of ammonite shells from the Devonian-Cretaceous period. They are millions of years old.

The lotus symbol, the Trident symbol or *Trisula* are also sacred symbols for Hindus. There are many more such symbols, which I leave to you to find out for yourselves.

**"Wow, what a great number of symbols and deities. You said that the Supreme *Brahman* is one. Grandpa, tell us why we still have so many different Gods in Hinduism with different functions as you would put it. To remove obstacles, we worship Bhagavan Ganesha, Goddess Saraswathi for knowledge, Goddess Lakshmi for success and prosperity, Hanuman for courage and strength and so on. Why so many?" Vijaya wanted an explanation.**

A good question. I will answer this in a different way. We all aim to progress in life. But the progress that we seek may be of different kinds. A student wants success in his exams, a business man wants prosperity in his business, a scholar wants knowledge, a warrior wants victory in war and so on. Agreed that God is one. But his attributes are numerous. So, for the common man to understand, our *Rishis* of yore gave the Gods a duty or function or portfolio each and gave them a form and an identity. You see the idol of *Goddess Saraswathi* with the *Veena* (an Indian stringed musical instrument) and the bundle of scrolls in her hands, *Goddess Lakshmi* is portrayed with a vessel full of gold coins, or *Bhagavan Ganesha* with a couple of weapons which can ward off obstacles in your progress to success. These symbolize the function of the Gods.

Take, for example, our Government. We have a Prime minister and many ministers in the cabinet under him – the finance minister, the home minister, the law minister, the health minister etc. All of them put together constitute the Government. So, when you want a solution to your financial matters, you have to meet the finance minister, the health minister for anything connected with hospitals or medical issues and so on. Similarly, the Gods have portfolios, and many individuals have their *'Ishta Devatas'*, or favorite Gods whom they worship depending on their likes and wonts. For example, the warriors worship *Goddess Shakthi* or *Bhagavan Hanuman*. The businessmen worship *Goddess Lakshmi*. The scholars and the philosophers, *Goddess Saraswati* and so on.

All of the cabinet ministers put together form the *'Government'*. But can you see the government. No, you cannot. Because the *'Government'* is an abstract entity. What we see is the personnel that form the government. But we feel the presence of a government through the Ministers, Administrators, Judiciary, the Army up to the lowest functionary like the housekeeping staff. It is a concept. You cannot *see* the government. You can only see the *functionaries* of the government. But the government is the ultimate authority in matters of the country. You are in awe of the Government. It can impose laws, punish you or take away your freedom. The Government is everywhere. But still, you cannot *see* it. So also, you see the deities in temples, in idols or in pictures and worship them. But you cannot *"see"* *Brahman* who represents the Ultimate Authority like the Government.

**"That is a brilliant example, Grandpa", Jaya commented, "I never thought of the government as a formless entity till now. Now I understand the concept of Brahman and the multitude of deities with their functions.**

**Vijaya had a strange question. "Why is *Goddess Saraswathi Bhagavan Brahma's* consort, *Goddess Lakshmi, Vishnu's* and *Goddess Parvathi* or *Shakthi Bhagavan Siva's* consort? Why do we need female deities."**

Firstly, let us discuss why we have female deities. Everything in the universe has two aspects — the positive and negative. If you take the atom, it has positively charged protons and the negatively charged electrons. Duality is part of the universe. There is good and evil, *Devas* and *Asuras*, violence and non-violence. Thus, the world always needs duality to be complete. If you consider Chinese philosophy, they call it *Ying* and *Yang* — the opposites. Likewise, the opposites are Man and Woman, Night, and Day, Light and Dark, Earth and Sky, Cold and Heat etc. For creation you always need these dualities. The world needs a <u>pair of opposites</u>. These are called *Dvandva*. It is an English word derived from *Sanskrit*.

I will endeavor to give you a logical answer to your question. The *Tri Murthy* (<u>Trinity</u>) or <u>Triumvirate</u> Brahma, Vishnu and Siva have different functions as per the Hindu theology. But we know that they are only manifestation of that one Reality called the *Brahman*. Do you know their respective duties or functions?

"Sure, *Brahma* is the Creator, *Bhagavan Vishnu* is the Preserver and *Bhagavan Siva* is the Destroyer or Annihilator", answered Aditya.

*Bhagavan Brahma* is the Creator. But to create anything what does one mainly need? It is *Knowledge*- you need knowledge to create a computer, an aircraft, or a clone. That is why it is said that *Brahma* is wedded to *Saraswathi,* the **Goddess of Knowledge** who is the "better half" of *Creation.*

Next, we will see about *Bhagavan Vishnu.* He is worshiped as the Preserver and the Protector of the universe. He maintains the life forms in the world. What is created by *Brahma* is maintained by *Vishnu.* But what is the fundamental resource needed in an

organization for maintenance — it is *money* or *finance.* Isn't it? So, *Vishnu* is said to be wedded to *Lakshmi,* the **Goddess of Wealth**. Or in other words, *Wealth* is the better half of *Maintenance.*

Thirdly, continuous Creation and Maintenance will choke the system and the resources in the world, and you need to keep a balance and avoid overcrowding. Further old creations (may it be bridges, buildings, roads, and the like) have to be pulled down to give way to newer creations or constructions. Older technology has to be removed and replaced with new technology in any organization. Always *"old order changeth, yielding place to new"* Imagine a situation in a world where no one died, no animals died, and no trees withered! It would be chaotic. Wouldn't it? *Shiva* is given the task of Destruction. He is the **God of Destruction**, be it in the form of earthquakes, wars, floods, or any natural disasters. He destroys what needs to be destroyed, only to pave the way for *Brahma* to create anew. And for destroying anything you need Power or Energy. Thus, *Shiva* is wedded to *Sakthi* (which in Sanskrit means Power or Strength). *Sakthi* is the **Goddess of Power.** In other words, *Power* is the better half of *Destruction.*

I would describe these as "functional" Gods, a concept which a common man can grasp, understand and worship. So are the multitudes of Gods in Hindu Mythology who are assigned various portfolios of management. But the basic concept of one Supreme Being who is formless would explain the concept of the multitude of Gods in Hindu Mythology looking after the varied functions for mankind.

**"That is a highly logical explanation, Grandpa" commented Aditya. "But tell me why we worship trees, mountains and rivers, animals and hold them sacred in Hinduism?"**

Hinduism holds sacred everything in the Universe. God or *Brahman* or the Supreme Being, whatever you would like to call it as, pervades everything that is present in the Universe —the inanimate objects and the animate objects be it a tree, a plant, an animal, or a reptile.

The five elements which we have already explained at the outset are Earth, Water, Air, Fire and Space (Ether). All objects in these are held sacred. It is also environmental science. From time immemorial, man has recognized that if we nurture Nature, it will reward us with bounties. That is what modern ecology also tells us. Thus, nature's generosity included, adequate rains, sunshine, wind, luxurious crops, copious amounts of fruit and many other largesse. The earth not only yielded crops but rewarded man with precious and useful metals and minerals from its bowels. Thus, man came to revere these objects of nature which were useful to him and made him prosperous. Thus, worship of nature was a sort of 'thanksgiving'.

That is how some trees gained religious sanctity and became worthy of worship like the *Banyan* tree and the *Tulasi* plant. Rivers like *Ganga* and *Cauvery* are held sacred by the Hindus. Mountains like the *Govardhan* (Mathura district of Uttar Pradesh) and the *Arunachal* mountains (Tamil Nadu) are worshipped. Mountains were recognized as essential for rains to occur. There is a parable in the *Srimad Bhagavatham* where Sri Krishna encourages his fellow men to worship the mountain *Govardhan* instead of Indra who is the God of Heaven, since the mountain was more important as it gave them rains and provided a grazing ground for their cattle.

The cow is an animal sacred to the Hindu. Snakes, especially the cobra is worshipped, and it is given milk as offering. The lion, the bull, the peacock, the swan and the tiger have been recognised as vehicles of Gods and Goddesses and their preservation is the duty of every Hindu. Thus, preserving the ecology and conservation of nature was considered to be essential for the survival of man and this assumed the form of nature worship including its elements and its flora and fauna.

# 6. TEMPLE WORSHIP

**"Grandpa, tell us something about temples and temple worship in Hinduism" requested Aditya.**

Temples are the main centers of worship in Hinduism like churches are for Christians and mosques for Muslims. They can be considered as centers for communion with God. Temples are filled with a positive energy that has to be experienced and cannot be described in words. The atmosphere and ambience in temples is highly conducive to worship and inculcates a sense of reverence in the individual.

Let us first see the details about the temple architecture. The Hindu temple is built based on specific architectural designs as given in the *Aagamas.* They are perfect geometrical structures built according to specifications given in the *Shilpa Shastras* (Architectural science) of the *Vedas.* At the center, inside the temple is the *Garbhagriha* (Sanctum Sanctorum), where the deity is kept. The deity is often placed facing east. Its architecture is also according to specific designs and prescribed specifications. There are precisely defined patterns and measurements for the construction of each part of the temple. The *Murti* (idol) to be kept in the temple has to be made according to certain specifications depending on which it has to be sculpted in stone or cast in metal.  The *Poojas* and types of worship to be done in the temple are also defined.

The rest of the temple is built around the *Garbhagriha* in the form of concentric circles or squares. The

temples are often built in perfect geometric shapes of circles, squares, or rectangles. Above the *garbhagriha* is a lofty towering structure often decorated with hundreds of carved statuettes. This is called the *Vimana* or *Shikhara*. It is often dome shaped or pyramid shaped. It may differ in different parts of India. The *Vimanas* in the temples of South India, especially in Tamil Nadu,  are rendered exquisite by the beautiful sculptures in them.

Outer to the *Garbhagriha* is a passage that goes around for the devotees to circumambulate the sanctum. This is called the *Pradakshina* path or *Parikrama* path. There is often a large, adjoining pillared hall called the *Mandapam* which is for congregations and performance of rituals. Additional buildings may also be present. Often there are smaller shrines for additional Gods or Goddesses in most temples. In addition, there is a raised platform all around where devotees can sit and do *japa* or meditate.

Many temples in India do not allow non-Hindus to enter. Similarly, there are strict rules that the devotees should be decently dressed. Wearing hats, caps, shorts, or footwear in temples is not permitted. In some temples in South India, men are required to remove their shirts and enter the temple bare-chested. The scientific reason behind it is that the bare body absorbs the positive vibrations emanating from the *Garbhagriha* and energizes the individual.

*Poojas* are performed in the temples by the chief priest

of the temple and the offerings of food or fruits to God (*Nivedyam*) are distributed to the devotees as *Prasadam*. All temples conduct an <u>annual festival</u> (*Utsavam*) in an elaborate and grand manner. The devotees gather in large numbers and partake in all the festivities.

In many towns and villages during the festival, an idol of the deity is taken in procession around the streets in a decorated *Ratham* (<u>chariot</u>) drawn by devotees. The concept behind this is to carry the idol around the town or village to be seen by those devotees

Ratham

who are laid up with disease and the differently abled devotees who cannot visit the temple due to infirmity or ailments. The concept is that God visits you if you cannot visit his abode, the temple.

**"But why should we go to a temple to worship the omnipresent God if you say that he is all pervasive and present everywhere?" Vijaya had a mischievous glint in her eye while asking this question.**

I will tell you a simple example that I heard from Late Swami Chinmayananda when I was a young boy. One of the naughty youngsters whom he was addressing asked a similar question. The Swamiji's answer was interesting. The Swamiji asked the young boy the composition of milk. He answered saying that milk contains water, proteins, fats, carbohydrates and some minerals and vitamins. The next question by the Swamiji was which parts of the cow's body contained these ingredients. The boy looked surprised and answered, "Why Swamiji, these ingredients are present in every part of the cow's body".

"Then why don't you pull the cow's nose or tail or the horn to get milk? Why do you want to go to a specific organ (the udder) of the cow to get milk from?", and the Swamiji broke out into a guffaw. "My dear friend", he said, "Just like that, to feel and experience the concentrated power and energy of God, you have to go to the temple which is the concentrated source of focused positive energy of the Divine."

The environment and ambience in the temple gives you a psychological feeling of serenity, calmness, and devotion. You feel that your problems will be solved, and a positive energy pervades your *Manas, Buddhi,* and *Chitta*. It is a place of tremendous energy. That is why it has been said that you should go to the temple and sit there for a while. This is to imbibe the positive energy that emanates from the temple.

God is called *Nirguna Brahman* (*Nirguna* = <u>devoid of material qualities</u>). Universal consciousness without an embodied form or image just as our soul in our body. The *Saguna Brahman* (*Saguna* = <u>with attributes or qualities</u>) is the embodied form that you see in an idol or an image. It is only an instrument for you to understand the formless Absolute Reality. Temples are places where you concentrate and focus your mind on the *embodied* form of God because the human mind cannot focus on an abstract concept easily. We have discussed this when we talked about idol worship.

This is especially true of the common folk who are not aware of the deep philosophy and concepts of the *Vedas*. For them, unconditional devotion is the only way to reach God. The devotee coming to a temple surrenders himself or herself completely to God while offering the *Pooja* and partaking in the *Prasadam* which is the offering to God.

**"Grandpa, you said that the offering of fruits, or milk-pudding (*Paayasam*) to God is called *Nivedyam*. But I do not see God eating the fruit or *Paayasam* that is placed in front of Him. Does it mean that God has not accepted my offering to Him?" Vijaya's genuine doubt was bubbling with the innocence of childhood.**

Grandpa smiled. I will ask you a simple question. When you saw the poem *"Twinkle, twinkle little star"* in your nursery rhymes book and memorized it, the poem was retained in your memory was it not?

[The children nod].

Now, since the poem is in your memory, did it disappear from the textbook? No, it didn't. So, the poem is accepted by your mind and stored in your memory but continues to be present in the book for others to read and memorize. So also, whatever you offer to God is accepted by God just by his vision falling on the object and it is returned to you as *Prasadam*. It is like the return gift you get when you give your best friend a birthday gift.

Bhagavan Krishna said in the Bhagavad Gita,

पत्रं पुष्पं फलं तोयं यो मे भक्त्या प्रयच्छति |
तदहं भक्त्युपहृतमश्रामि प्रयतात्मनः || 9:26||

91

*Patraṁ puṣhpaṁ phalaṁ toyaṁ yo me bhaktyā prayachchhati*
*Tadahaṁ bhaktyupahṛitam aśhnāmi prayatātmanaḥ  (9:26)*

It means, "*If one offers to Me with devotion a leaf, a flower, some fruit, or even water, I delightfully partake of that item offered with love by My devotee.*

It is not what you offer to God that is important, but the devotion and surrendering mindset with which you offer anything to God which is paramount. Remember, the whole universe is His and there is nothing that *He* wants from *you*. So do not be under the false impression that by offering costly items like gold, silver, or any other valuables to God, He will be pleased with you. No, it is your mind that God wants. He wants you to surrender to him unconditionally and not simply bestow gifts to Him. After all who are we, ordinary mortals, to give Him gifts and offerings?

**"Is there any other advantage in going to temples to worship God?", Jaya had her doubts.**

Sure, there are many advantages in going to the temple. I will list out a few of them to you, just for completion's sake.

• We have already discussed that the *garbhagriha* where the idol of the deity is kept emanates positive vibrations and the pyramidal shape of the *Vimanam* or *Gopuram* above is said to generate positive energy. The devotee who stands in front of the deity and worships, is charged with this positive energy. The temple thus acts as a spiritual 'charging center' for your mind and soul.

• After visiting a temple and worshiping at the sanctum, the devotee sits for a time in the temple in the *mandapam* and meditates or recites *mantras*. These further calm the mind and helps increase the power of concentration of the mind.

• The ambience in the temple is also conducive to the development of a peaceful feeling in the mind. The ringing of the bells along with the rhythmic chanting of the mantras stimulates the auditory senses. The sight of the lamps lit around the idol stimulates the visual senses, the sweet smell of flowers that adorn the deity, the incense and camphor which is burnt and waved in front of the deity stimulate the olfactory senses. You feel the warmth in your hands when you hold your hand above  the lighted camphor and touch your eyes with your palms. The holy water offered to you with the *Tulasi* leaves and the *Prasadam* which is offered to you also stimulate your gustatory senses. Thus, all your five senses are stimulated when you are in a temple. These stimuli have a positive effect on the corresponding sensory centres in your brain.

• You should be barefoot in the temple and as you do the *parikrama* or *pradakshinam*, you absorb the positive vibrations that are emanating from all sides. The number of *pradakshinams* can vary from three to seven or nine and this is also a good physical exercise for the body. Further walking barefoot on the stony floor offers  acupressure therapy for your feet.

• The priest offers tilak for you to apply on your forehead. It is applied in the center of the forehead between the brows. This point is called the *Ajna chakra* and said to stimulate the brain. Sandal

wood paste or *Kumkum* (<u>vermillion</u>) or *Vibhuti /
Bhasma* (sacred ash)  is given to be applied to the
forehead.

• Removing the footwear and head dress
like a cap or hat is like surrendering one's ego before
God. Even kings and emperors are supposed to
remove their crowns before entering a temple. The
lintel of the door at the entrance to the *garbhagriha* is
often only four or five feet high so that anyone
entering must bow his head to enter.

• The bell in a temple is made of bell metal
(an alloy of lead, copper, cadmium, zinc, and nickel).
The booming tintinnabulation of the temple bells with
their lingering echo in our ears stimulates our brain
and is said to produce a harmony between the two
hemispheres of our brain.

• The temple is also a place where people
congregate and meet each other. The *mandapam* in
the temple is used for *Satsang*. The *Satsang* is usually
a talk or a discussion about religious matters led by a
scholar or a *Guru* or a *Swamiji*. Stories from Hindu
mythology are told to the common folk and the
philosophical truths in the scriptures are discussed.
*Satsang* also depends on the type of audience that is
present. *Satsangs* for children usually revolves
around stories from the *Ramayana*, *Mahabharata*, or
other *Puranas*. This storytelling entertains the
children, but simultaneously instils in them the subtle
values and morals of *Dharma*.

• Temples are also places where food is
provided for the needy. This is called 'Annadhana'.
(*Annam*-<u>food</u>, *Dhana*- <u>donating</u> ; <u>giving in charity</u>).
*Annadhana* is said to be the best type of charity. There
are many temples that perform *Annadhana* on a daily

basis, like the Guruvayur temple in Kerala and the Dharmasthala temple in Karnataka. The reason *Annadhana* is said to be a noble mode of charity is because, however much wealth or material objects you give a person, he may not be satisfied. But when you give food to an individual, he cannot eat beyond a limit when he will say "enough". So *Annadhana* is the only charity that gives satiety to an individual.

•    Unfortunately, now a days the temples have become places where 'applications' are made to God for a fee under the name of *"Vazhipaadu"* (offering with a view to gain something in return). It appears as if God is sitting there to listen to our woes and fulfil our requests. Even though the temple is a place where one should sit silent and meditate on the deity who is in the sanctum sanctorum, many temples are not places of silence. The commotion and bedlam created by the devotees and the loud, blaring music and pandemonium in some of the temples are not conducive to meditation and quietude. Government domination on temples has worsened the situation. Let us not get into a controversy by discussing this further.

**"Grandpa, you mentioned that God does not need anything from us as everything in the Universe is His. Then why are we offering *nivedyam* to Him" Aditya's question was logical.**

Yes, true. We have discussed this already, but it is worth repeating. Everything in the Universe is God's. The universe itself is the manifest form of God. In His benevolence, God has given everything in this world and this universe for us to enjoy. The trees bearing fruit, the rains bringing plenty of food in the form of bounteous crops, the rivers giving us water for our needs, the oxygen in the air sustaining our life – everything is His.  In return we must express our thanks to Him. *Nivedyam* is only an expression of our *gratitude.*  We surrender everything to God and that is the concept behind the *nivedyam.*

**"We have a *Pooja* room in our home. Is it not enough if I worship God in that room?" Jaya was doubtful.**

Good question, dear. Yes, most of the Hindu homes have a *Pooja* room or at least a *Pooja* corner or alcove, especially if you are living in a

**Vilakku**

small apartment. Small idols of deities or their framed pictures are kept in the area. A *Vilakku* (<u>oil or ghee lamp</u>) is always lit during the *Pooja* and flowers are offered. A fruit or a little milk is offered as *nivedyam.* Every morning after the daily ablutions and a bath, the family members worship the deity for a short while by reciting *mantras* or *slokas* in praise of the deities. Each member worships the deity that he or she wishes to worship (*Ishta Devata*).

In the same family, there may be one person who is a staunch devotee of Siva whereas another may be a devotee of *Bhagavan Krishna.* A third may worship *Bhagavan Ganesha* daily whereas the fourth may be a devotee or *Goddess Lakshmi.* This is according to one's own will and inclination.

Every evening also during the *sandhya*, (<u>twilight</u>), when the sun sets, the devout Hindu lights a lamp in the *Pooja* room and worships the deity for a short while. It is the concept of worship and surrender to the deity that is more important. These simple rituals are done in order to inculcate a sense of discipline in the minds of the family members.

We should remember that whichever deity we are worshipping, ultimately it is all one absolute *Brahman* that we are seeking to realize. There is a sloka which is repeated in the *Sandyavandanam* daily. It runs thus...

आकाशात् पतितं तोयं यथा गच्छति सागरम् ।
सर्वदेवनमस्कारः केशवं प्रति गच्छति ॥

*Aakashath Pathitham Thoyam, Yatha Gachathi Sagaram*
*Sarvadeva Namaskaram, Keshavam Prathi Gachathi"*

It means, "*As the water that falls down as rain from the sky finally reaches the Ocean, the worship of any divine aspect ultimately reaches the Supreme Being*"

# 7. HINDU FESTIVALS

**"Grandpa, why do we have festivals in our religion. There are so many of them that sometimes, we are not able to understand their significance. Please elaborate on them" as usual Aditya set the ball rolling.**

Grandpa began. 'Culture and religion are closely interwoven, and together they form a civilization. Every religion and culture has its festivals. The festivals have religious and spiritual significance, but at the same time help to achieve a sense of camaraderie and unity among the individuals in a community and instills the spirit of team work in them. This cooperation is needed for the smooth running of any society. Festivals bring people together for group activities which further strengthens the bonds of friendship and solidarity among the members. Festivals also help the individuals in society to devote some time from their busy materialistic pursuits for spiritual matters. It helps to bring families and individuals together and helps new relationships to be forged. Many marriages also get arranged during these festivities. Festivals are also a great chance for womenfolk of society to get together and exchange ideas and forge newer bonds.

In addition, festivals are times when the whole house and the community is cleaned, decorated, often painted, and given a makeover. This also promotes hygiene and spring-cleaning in homes. It is a time when friends and relatives visit each other, exchange gifts, and share food. Various charitable activities are undertaken during festivals, like giving new clothes to the needy and poor, feeding the needy and providing shelter to the homeless. The festivals are also times when dances, dramas and other art forms are staged and helps people promote their talents. Visit to temples and partaking in group activities like *Poojas*, *Homams* and *Bhajans* form part of the festivals. It helps promote sociological cooperation among members of the community.

The Sanskrit word for festival is '*Utsavam*' (<u>happiness</u>). Many festivals mark the end of a season and the beginning of the next. Some festivals are related to the harvest season when the people enjoy a bounty harvest and celebrate it to please the Gods. It is a sort of 'thanksgiving'. Others are related to the birth anniversary of a God or legendary figure as in *Sri Krishna Jayanthi* or *Sri Rama Navami* (birth of *Sri Krishna* and *Sri Rama* respectively). Others are related to the victory of good over evil (*Navaratri* or *Dusshera* and *Deepavali*). The celebrations are held on a date based on the lunar calendar and not on fixed dates as in the Julian calendar.

A lunar <u>month</u> is called '*Masam*', a lunar <u>fortnight</u> is called a '*Paksham*' and a lunar <u>day</u> is called a '*Thithi*'. The <u>full moon</u> is called the '*Poornima*' and the <u>new moon</u> day is called '*Amavasya*'. Many festivals are celebrated on days calculated based on these parameters.

**"Grandpa, tell us something about the common festivals of Hindus." Jaya was interested in the details.**

Yes, we will start from the month of January. But remember that describing all the festivals may be out of the scope of our discussion as there are many major and minor festivals for the Hindus. But I will elaborate on a few important ones. Also, you must realize that there may be slight differences in the festivals depending on the region and the culture of the groups of Hindus because even among the Hindus there are many sects.

*Makar Sankranti*. (*Makar* = <u>Capricorn</u>; *Sankranti* = <u>transition</u>). This is called '*Pongal*' in South India and '*Lohiri*' or '*Bhogi*' in the north. It usually falls on the 14th or 15th of January. This festival is dedicated to the Sun God It marks the day when the sun having travelled south (which

**Kolam**

is called '*Dakshinayanam*', (*Dakshin* = <u>south</u>; *Ayanam* = <u>journey</u>) during the last six months, begins its journey towards the north which is called *Uttarayanam* (*Uttar* = <u>north</u>). The womenfolk draw beautiful *Kolam* (<u>designs</u>) in front of their homes with rice flour.

The sun transits from the zodiac sign of Sagittarius to Capricorn which is called '*Makara*' in Sanskrit. Various regions celebrate this in different ways. In the south *Pongal* is celebrated by cooking the newly harvested rice with milk or jaggery – called "*Pongal*" and offering it to Gods as *Nivedyam*. Cows are bathed, decorated, and worshipped for *Pongal*.

**Maha Shivaratri.** (*Maha* = great; *Ratri* = night). It means the 'great night of Shiva'. The festival celebrates the wedding of *Bhagavan Shiva* to *Parvathi*. It is also said to be the day when *Bhagavan Shiva* drank the poison called '*Halahala*' which was generated during the churning of the milky ocean. Devotees visit the *Shiva* temples and observe fasting on that day. Many stay awake that night spending their time in *bhajans* and singing praises to *Bhagavan Shiva*. Legends also describe *Shivaratri* as the night when *Bhagavan Shiva* performs his cosmic dance, called '*Shiva Tandavam*'. *Shivaratri* occurs in the month of February/March.

**Thai Poosam.** This is a festival which is mostly celebrated in the South, particularly in Tamil Nadu. (*Thai* = the name of the Tamil month; *Poosam* = the name of the star on that day). It is the day when *Goddess Parvathi* gave the famous spear called '*Vel*' to her son *Bhagavan Muruga* or *Subramanya* to kill the wicked *asura Soorapadman*. It is celebrated in the temples of *Bhagavan Subramanya* or *Murugan* in South India in an elaborate manner. Devotees carry urns filled with milk, honey, and other offerings to the God on their shoulders on specially made wooden arches called '*Kavadi*'. This symbolically represents the burden of *Samsara* which the devotee carries to the feet of God. Many of the *Muruga* temples are situated on hillocks or hills like Palani in Tamil Nadu. The devotees trek up the hill on foot  to offer this to *Bhagavan Subramanya*.

**Holi**.      It is a festival celebrated mainly in North India. It is a festival marked by color and gaiety. People take to the streets and smear color on each other and sing and dance with abandon. Legend describes this festival as commemorating the slaying of the demoness *Holika* by *Prahlada*, and ardent devotee of *Bhagavan Vishnu*. The festival also marks the advent of spring. It also signifies *Sri Krishna's* celebrations with the *Gopis*.  It is observed on the <u>full moon day</u> (*Poornima*) of the *Phalguna* month which occurs in March.

**Sri Rama Navami**.      This      festival celebrates *Sri Rama's* birth. It is also celebrated as the wedding day of *Sri Rama* and *Sita*. Devotees throng to temples dedicated to *Sri Rama*. The celebrations in Ayodhya in Uttar Pradesh in India where *Sri Rama* was born are very elaborate and spiritual. The day is marked by *bhajans* and *Poojas* invoking the blessings of *Sri Rama* and *Sita*. *Annadaanam* (<u>food donation</u>) is offered to all the devotees and the needy on this day.

**Ugadi**.      It is also called *Yugadi* and means 'beginning of the year'. It is celebrated in parts of South India. It falls in the latter part of March or early April. It is the new year day beginning with the *Chaitra* month. People welcome the new year decorating their doorways with mango leaves and drawing beautiful *Kolam* in front of their houses with rice flour. Visit to the temple, wearing new clothes, offering charity to the needy are part of the celebration.

**Mesha Sankranti – Vishu.** This is celebrated on the day the sun transits into the *Mesha* (Aries) sign of the zodiac. On that day offerings are given to the *Pithrus* in the form of water and sesame seeds. The ancestors are remembered on that day. In Kerala this is celebrated as *Vishu*. It is also the festival

**Vishu Kani**

celebrated after a good harvest. Early morning the elders get up before sunrise and lead the younger members of the family to the *Pooja* room where the symbols of a bounty harvest – vegetables, coconut, jack fruit, mango, rice, dhal, gold coins, a mirror, an idol of Bhagavan Krishna etc., are kept in a large platter or basin. The vegetables and flowers are usually of golden yellow color – cucumber, lemon, Laburnum flowers etc. This is called the '*Vishu Kani*'. *Kani* means that which you see first when you awake in the morning. The eldest patriarch in the home gives coins to all the younger members including children. This is called '*Kaineettam*' (<u>gift given for *Vishu*</u>). Following this, the family visits the temple to offer prayers to *Bhagavan Krishna*. In the afternoon there is an elaborate luncheon with many savories and curries. This is called the '*Vishu Sadya*' (*Sadya* = <u>feast</u>). Children welcome the new year by bursting crackers and other fireworks. This is variously called *Bihu* in the north east parts of India.

***Guru Poornima.*** This is the birth anniversary of *Sage Veda Vyasa* and hence, it is also called *Vyasa Poornima*. It is celebrated in the month of *Ashada* (June-July). It is on the <u>full moon day</u> (*Poornima*). This is the day one's spiritual *Gurus* are honored. The disciples honor and offer pooja to their *Guru*. This is the real "Teachers' Day" for Hindus. It is the day when we must honor our teachers. Even in this modern age, such a day to remember and honor our teachers is important to inculcate respect and reverence among students for their teachers in schools and colleges. Unfortunately, these concepts are sadly lacking in today among the modern youth.

***Mahalakshmi Vratham – Varalakshmi Vratham.*** This is performed by married Hindu women to seek the blessing of *Goddess Lakshmi, Bhagavan Vishnu's* consort. *Goddess Lakshmi* is the goddess of prosperity. In South India, especially Tamil Nadu, it is celebrated as *Varalakshmi Vratham*. It occurs on the month of *Shraavana* in the Hindu calendar (July-August). The married women pray for blessing of the goddess for their husbands and for their whole family. *Poojas* are conducted and offerings in the form of savories and *Paayasam* (<u>rice pudding made with milk or jaggery</u>) are offered to the deity as *Nivedyam*.

***Onam***.  Onam is the harvest festival in Kerala. It is observed in the month of *Chingam* as per the Hindu calendar (<u>August-September</u>). It is on the *Thiruvonam* day which is the <u>lunar-star</u> day. Onam is

Pookalam

celebrated for ten days beginning from the *Nakshatra* (<u>lunar-star</u>) called *Athham*. For the ten days, children and womenfolk of the household lay beautiful <u>floral  carpets</u>(*Pookalam*) with multicolored flowers in front of their homes to welcome the *King Mahabali* who visits them during these days. Onam is the official festival of the state of Kerala. The ten-day festival which ends with the day of the *Thiruvonam* star is marked by festivities like dancing, sports, tug-of-war, *Puli kali* (<u>Tiger-dance</u>) and many such events. On the *Thiruvonam* day, an <u>elaborate feast</u> (*Onam Sadya*) is arranged in the family. Often it is organized by the community in community halls in an elaborate manner. Now a days, people from all religions and sects are invited and partake in the Onam festivities.

Onam is believed to be the day when *Bhagavan Maha Vishnu* incarnated as *Vamana*, a young brahmin boy and sought alms from the *King*

*Mahabali*. The king, though being a benevolent king, had become arrogant and wanted to conquer the worlds of the *Devas*. Hence, *Bhagavan Vishnu* incarnated as a young

*Brahmachari* and requested the king for three feet of land measured with his own tiny feet. When the king granted the wish, *Vamana* grew in size to reach up to the heavens and measured the heavens, earth, and the nether worlds with his two feet. As there was no more place to measure, the king Mahabali offered his head where *Vamana* could place his feet. In fact, *Bhagavan Maha Vishnu* blessed the king with his foot on his head and sent him to a nether world called *Suthala* where the king ruled well for the rest of his term in comfort and luxury. Contrary to the popular story being circulated in the state of Kerala by certain misinformed and mischievous elements, the king was not 'banished' to *Paathala* or hell. The *Srimad Bhagavatham* gives this story in detail. You must read it later.

Legend in Kerala says that the king was permitted to visit his subjects in Kerala once a year on *Onam* day to ascertain in person the welfare of his subjects. The present tendency by some perverted elements in the country is to caricature this great and benevolent king in the form of a comic character and malign his image. This corrupts the minds of the children and biases them against the sacred *Puranic* story in the *Srimad Bhagavatham*.

***Raksha Bandhan – Avani Avittam.*** Rakhi Poornima or Raksha Bandhan is a festival celebrated mainly in North India. It falls on the full moon day on the Hindu month of *Shraavana* (July-August). Sisters tie a '*Rakhi*' (amulet) on the right wrist of their brothers. The brothers in turn present their sisters with gifts of money and sweets. The amulet is for the protection of the brother by the Gods.

The menfolk on the other hand vow to protect their sisters at any cost.

This is also the day called *Avani Avittam* (*Upakarma*) by the brahmins in India. It is the day that the brahmins change their <u>sacred threads</u> (*Upaveetham*; *Poonal*) and wear new ones. They recite excerpts from the *Vedas* and *Upanishads* and honor their *Gurus* on the day. It is the day when they perform rituals to honor the sages and *Rishis* who have nurtured the *Sanatana Dharma* and given the *Vedas* and the scriptures to the Hindus. Legend is that this was the day that *Bhagavan Vishnu* incarnated as *Hayagriva* and restored the *Vedas* to *Brahma* from whom two asuras *Madhu* and *Kaitabha* had stolen them. For the Tamil Brahmins, it falls on the month of *Avani* (*Shraavana*) and the *Nakshatra* on that day is *Avittam*.

### Janmashtami – Sri Krishna Jayanthi.

This is the birth anniversary of *Bhagavan Sri Krishna*. *Janmashtami* occurs in the month of *Shraavana* on the *Ashtami day* (<u>eighth day after the full moon)</u> and the *Nakshatra* on that day is *Rohini*. *Bhagavan Krishna* is said to have been born about 5200 years ago at Mathura near Agra in India. The festival is celebrated with great devotion and vigor in all parts of India with *Bhajans*, *Satsangs*, and *Poojas* and plays enacted on the life of *Sri Krishna*. Many charitable activities are undertaken on that day. In South India, especially in Tamil Nadu, footprints of a child are drawn from the main doorway of the house to the *Pooja* room with the belief that *Bhagavan Krishna* would visit their homes on that night. Many sweets are prepared as offering to the God on that day.

*Janmashtami* is a festival that is celebrated extensively in India and world over by Hindus.

**Ganesh Chathurthi – Vinayaka Chathurthi.** This is a festival that is celebrated in many parts of India especially Maharashtra and South India. *Bhagavan Ganesha* is the remover of obstacles. Large idols of *Ganesha* made of clay are worshipped on that day. The festival is to remember the birth of *Bhagavan Ganesha*. *Chathurthi* means the fourth day of the lunar fortnight after the <u>new moon</u> (*Amavasya*). *Ganesha Chathurthi* is celebrated in the Hindu month of *Bhadrapada* (*August-September*). The large clay idols are immersed in the river or sea after the celebrations are over.

**Navaratri.** This means '<u>Nine Nights</u>' (*Nava* = <u>nine</u>; *Ratri* = <u>night</u>). The festival extends for nine days starting from the new moon day in the month of *Ashwin* (<u>September-October</u>). The *Goddess Shakthi* or *Durga* is worshipped in her different forms as *Durga, Lakshmi,* and *Saraswathi.* In different parts of India, *Navaratri* is celebrated in different names. In the north it is called *Durga Pooja* where *Goddess Durga* or *Kali* is worshipped. In Karnataka, it is called *Dussehra*. The festival marks the victory of *Goddess Durga* over the demon *Mahishasura* who assumed the form of a buffalo. *Poojas* are performed at homes and in the temples during this period. Daily *nivedyam* is offered to the deity.

On the ninth day (*Maha Navami*) books are kept in front of the deity, *Goddess Saraswathi* is invoked on that day to bless the devotees with knowledge. Artisans place the appliances and equipment used in their profession in front of the deity and worship them. Books are worshipped on the day as symbols of *Goddess Saraswathi*. This gesture ensures that *Work is worship*. It is also called '*Ayudha Pooja*' (*Ayudha* = <u>weapon</u> ; <u>appliance</u>). The *Kshatriyas* worship their weapons like swords, bow, arrows, and spears on that day. Artisans worship their tools of trade. Businessmen worship their books of accounts. Students place their books in front of the deity and worship the books. Drivers decorate their vehicles like cars, taxis, trucks and vans with flowers and sandal paste.

In South India, this is accompanied by arranging the idols of various Gods and Goddesses on steps made for the purpose. This called '*Kolu*'. The womenfolk in the community visit each other's homes and share the *Prasadam* made as offerings to the deity on the day. The colorful dolls are a sight for sore eyes. Children accompany the elders and render Carnatic music songs in front of the *Kolu*.

The tenth day is celebrated as *Vijaya Dasami*. This is the day when the *Goddess Durga* slayed *Mahishasura,* a demon in the form of a <u>buffalo</u>. It marks the end of *Durga Pooja* festival. In North India it is celebrated as the festival marking the victory of *Sri Rama* over *Ravana* and *Kumbha Karna*. It is celebrated as *Ramlila* where effigies of *Ravana*, his brother, *Kumbha Karna*, and son *Meghanada* which are stuffed with fire crackers are burnt to the tumultuous cheering of the spectators.

In Mysore, Karnataka, *Navaratri* is celebrated as Dussehra. In Kerala and Tamil Nādu,

*Vijaya Dasami* is celebrated as the day children are initiated into the three R's. Toddlers are made to write the initial alphabets with their finger on a plate filled with rice. This is done in a temple or at home itself in the *Pooja* room. This is usually done by an elder member in the family or the temple priest. This is called '*Vidyarambam*' meaning 'beginning of education'. Often this ceremony is conducted before the children are enrolled in school or in the kindergarten classes.

**Deepavali**. *Deepavali* also called '*Diwali*' in North India is a festival which is famous for Hindus all over the world. (*Deepam* = lamp; *Avali* = row). It marks the victory of *Sri Krishna* and his consort *Satyabhama* killing *Narakasura*, a demon king. It isalso said to represent *Sri Rama's* return to Ayodhya after slaying the asura king *Ravana* in Sri Lanka. Rows of lamps are lit in front of the homes symbolic of the reception accorded to *Sri Rama* on his return. It symbolizes the victory of good over evil. It is celebrated on the new moon day in the Hindu month of *Kartika* (October-November).

*Deepavali* is a festival when the families get together. It is also a major cultural festival marked by dances and colorful pyrotechnics. In North India it is celebrated for five days. the third day marks the day of

*Lakshmi pooja* when *Goddess Lakshmi*, the Goddess of prosperity and wealth is worshipped.

In South India *Deepavali* is celebrated mainly in Tamil Nadu by wearing new clothes, taking an oil bath, and bursting crackers. It is believed that on the *Deepavali* day, every water source becomes as pure as the *Ganga*. (Ganges river). Hence having an oil bath on this auspicious day is called 'Ganga Snanam' – 'bathing in Ganga'. Sweat meats are made at home and distributed among friends and neighbours.

***Karthika Deepam.*** This is a festival mainly celebrated in South India especially in Tamil Nadu on the full moon day of the *Kartika* month on *Kartika Nakshatram* day. It is also celebrated by the

Karthika Deepam

Tamil Hindus in Malaysia, Sri Lanka, and other countries. Legend says that the *Bhagavan Muruga* or *Subramanya* also called *Kartikeya* was born on that day from *Bhagavan Siva's* third eye. Six children were born from six sparks from *Bhagavan Siva's* third eye and taken care of by six nymphs called the *Kartikas*. When *Goddess Parvathy* hugged all the six children together, they merged to become one boy who was called *Kartikeya* or *Murugan*. The front yard of the homes are decorated with colorful *Kolam,* and lamps (*Deepam*) are lit on them. Rows of lamps adorn the front of most homes to give a divine atmosphere to the festival. Temples perform special *Poojas* on that day.

So, my children, I have given you a brief account of each of the major festivals that the Hindus celebrate each year. There are many more minor festivals and celebrations, which are beyond the scope of our discussion today. I would suggest that you read about them in more detail if this interests you.

**"That was wonderful Grandpa", commented Vijaya. "Now I understand why my dad bought me new clothes for Deepavali and why he gave me ten dollars when he woke me up early at 5 am on April 14th !"**

**Everyone broke into loud laughter.**

# 8. MEDITATION

**"Grandpa, please tell us all about Meditation today" requested Vijaya.**

Grandpa began, The Universal Consciousness or *Brahman* about which we have discussed, is present in all life forms in the universe – plants, animals, and humans. The expression of this consciousness varies depending on the living being through which it is manifests. Thus, its manifestation in a rabbit, a lion or man will be different even though the 'life' or 'soul' in them is the same. The mind does not evolve in an animal or bird. Whereas in humans, the mind has the four levels called the *Anthakaranam*. That is why humans are considered as the highest in the evolutionary tree.

Electricity is energy that is subtle and all pervasive. But its expression is through various equipment like the light bulb, the heater, the radio, or the television. Depending on the sophistication of the equipment which expresses it, the function of the equipment changes. But electricity remains unchanged. So also, is the Brahman which is present in all of us.

There are two terms that you have to familiarize yourself with before we discuss meditation. One is the word '*Sraddha*'. This means '<u>Unwavering Faith</u>' or '<u>concentration</u>' and the other word is '*Bhakti*' which is '<u>Devotion</u>'. You must have heard these two words previously. *Sraddha* is discipline for the head (intellect) and *Bhakti* is energy for the heart (mind). *Love is the language of the heart and knowledge is the language of the head.* <u>Meditation</u> which is called '*Dhyana*' strives to invoke both *Sraddha* and *Bhakti* in us.

Attaching our mind intensely to God with love is *Bhakti* yoga and attaching our mind to God and selflessly acting in the world outside is *Karma* yoga. Elevating our mind to God through meditation is *Jnana* yoga. We will discuss more about these when we discuss the topic Yoga. Meditation is the main tool in *Jnana* Yoga.

**"Tell us, Grandpa, how can I practice meditation to discipline myself?" Aditya was enthusiastic.**

I will explain how it is done. I will explain the theoretical aspect of learning to meditate first. But remember that meditation has to be taught properly by a *Guru* to the pupil and is not learnt from a text book. We will have a practical session on Meditation later on when I will teach you how to meditate. But meanwhile we will learn the basics of meditation today.

**"Before that, Grandpa, please explain to me what you mean by the word '*Guru*' and who is a '*Sishya*' asked little Vijaya.**

The *Guru* has been defined in the dictionary as '*a personal religious teacher and spiritual guide in Hinduism*'. The word meaning of *Guru* is 'one who removes darkness'. (*Gu* = darkness; *Ru* = one who removes). The darkness in a student is ignorance. The *Guru* enlightens the student with knowledge. In religious parlance, a *Guru* is one who initiates, guides, and correctly maps the route in the journey of a student seeking spiritual knowledge and self-realization.

The *Guru* is well versed in the *Vedas* and all scriptures and imparts this knowledge to his disciples. These disciples or proteges are called '*Sishyas*'. The *Sishya* usually stays with the *Guru* in his ashram and lives like one of the households. The *Guru* imparts spiritual and religious knowledge along with training in practical skills so  as to make his disciple fit for functioning and living in the outside world. The ashram is often a secluded place in the outskirts of the village or in the jungle. This is called the '*Gurukulam*' (home of the Guru). This system of education which aims at the all-round development of the disciple is called the *Gurukulam* system of education and is one of the best methods of teaching. The *Sishya* helps the *Guru* and his wife in the daily chores and simultaneously gains knowledge from the *Guru*. It is a residential training-cum-teaching method.

The teaching in the ashram is not like the modern teaching in the classroom where all the students are taught the same subjects by the teacher in the same manner for the same period. The *Guru* tailors the lessons depending on the attitude, aptitude, and mental nature of the *sishya*. The teaching is at a leisurely pace depending on how the student is able to grasp the knowledge. He is not stressed to learn his lessons in a fixed period of time. Some Sishyas complete their education quickly in a matter of seven to ten years, whereas others may take longer. It is said that Adi Sankaracharya completed his education with his *Guru Bhagavad Pada* in three years' time which is the shortest interval cited. *Bhagavan Sri Krishna* is said to have completed his education in *Guru Sandeepani's Ashram* in sixty-four days!

**"Why do people say that we have to respect and prostrate before a guru?" Jaya wanted to know.**

In Hinduism, the *Gurus* are held in high esteem. The verse runs thus,

गुरुर्ब्रह्मा गुरुर्विष्णु गुरुर्देवो महेश्वरः

गुरु साक्षात परब्रह्मा तस्मै श्रीगुरवे नमः

*Guru Brahma Guru Vishnu Guru Devo Maheshwaraha*

*Guru Saakshaat Para Brahma Tasmai Sri Gurave Namaha*

It means, *"Guru is the Creator (Brahma), Guru is the Preserver(Vishnu), Guru Deva is the Destroyer (Maheshwara). Guru is the absolute (singular) Bhagavan himself. Salutations to that Sri Guru."*

This sloka emphasises that the *Guru* is above all and hence we must prostrate before him and revere him. Respect, reverence, and humility shown to the *Guru* are the main characteristics of a good sishya. Did you understand this?

[All the three nod their heads].

In fact, if you have read our Puranas, you find that even our *Avatars* like *Sri Rama* and *Sri Krishna* spent time in the *Gurukulam*. *Sri Rama* was mentored by the great Sage *Vasishta* who was the chief priest in King *Dasaratha's* court. *Sri Krishna* stayed at the *Gurukulam* of sage *Sandeepani* and learnt all the skills and scriptures in a short period of 64 days despite being the *Avatar* of *Maha Vishnu*. They set an example for the rest of mankind by being devoted *Sishyas* under their *Gurus*. You must read the *Ramayana* and the *Srimad Bhagavatham* to know more about them.

**"But, grandpa, can a *Guru* be a woman? Or can only men become *Gurus*?" Jaya had a genuine doubt.**

Good question. Women also can be *Gurus* when they have acquired the spiritual knowledge and the wisdom. There are many women who have been *Gurus* in the past, and many are present even now. Sri Sarada Devi, Anandamayi Ma, Sister Nivedita, Mata Amritanandamayi, and many more women are *Gurus* well accepted by the Hindus.

**"What are the duties and responsibilities of a *sishya*?" Vijaya wanted to know.**

In the *Gurukulam* system of education, all *Sishyas* are equal. Sri Krishna lived in the Gurukulam with students drawn from all walks of life. It is here that he developed a deep friendship with *Sudama* a poor brahmin boy and this story is given in the *Srimad Bhagavatham* in detail. The disciple or *sishya* has to be totally dedicated to the *Guru*. Ego has no role in the *Gurukulam*. All disciples are equal in the eyes of the *Guru*. The *sishya* must be humble and ready to perform any task assigned to him by the *Guru*.

He must get up early in the *Brahma muhurta* (4.30 am-6.am). Following his usual ablutions and bath, he should spend time in learning the scriptures. Then he should perform some yogic exercises and meditation. Morning and evening, he should spend time in reciting verses from the Vedas and the mantras which he has learnt from his *Guru*. He ought to live a pious life, not spending time in idle gossip or criticizing others. He is expected to shun perfumes and self-grooming and live a frugal and austere life. He is required to follow all the instructions of his *Guru*.

As the saying goes, '*Early to bed and early to rise, makes one healthy, wealthy and wise*'. The *sishya's* mental power and intellect are honed by this strict disciplined life. In this modern age, students should rise early and spend some time in exercise and meditation. Then the rest of the time in the morning should be spent in studying the lessons before going to school. When one is a student living at home, the parents are their *Gurus*. So, obedience, respect and doing chores for them around the house are also the duties of a student.

Similarly, the student should show respect and reverence to his teachers in schools and colleges. In ancient days the teaching of the *Sishyas* by the *Guru* was done under the shade of the trees in the ashram. Often there would be a sprawling banyan tree in the ashram under which the *Guru* and the *Sishyas* sat and conducted their deliberations and classes.

**"While we are in the subject of *Guru*, Grandpa, what is the difference between a *Guru* and an *Acharya*?" Aditya had a very sensible question.**

A *Guru* is one who guides you in the spiritual path towards the Absolute Truth – the *Brahman*. He shows you the way and tells you how to do it. He is a teacher.

An *Acharya* on the other hand <u>leads by example</u>. He guides and at the same time practices all the austerities and undergoes the same rigors as you. He leads by practice rather than precept. Mahatma Gandhi was an *acharya*. He did not tell people what to do but he set an example by living the life of an ascetic. He lived an austere life thus setting an example to his countrymen. There is a verse in the Bhagavad Gita which exemplifies this beautifully.

यद्यदाचरति श्रेष्ठस्तत्तदेवेतरो जनः ।
स यत्प्रमाणं कुरुते लोकस्तदनुवर्तते ॥ ३-२१॥

Yadyad ācarati śreṣṭha statta devetaro janaḥ<br>
Sa yat pramāṇaṃ kurute lokas tadanu vartate

It means, *"Whatever a great man does, the other men also follow (imitate); whatever he sets up as the standard, the world (people) follows".*

### "Grandpa, you digressed from the main subject of meditation" pointed out Aditya.

Yes, now let us discuss about meditation. Before explaining how to meditate, I will tell you what the advantages are you gain by meditating for even small periods of 15 – 20 minutes once or twice daily. Some of the advantages are:

- Regular meditation decreases the levels of stress hormones – cortisol, in the body thereby reducing stress in us. This leads to a reduction in stress induced illnesses like peptic ulcer, high blood pressure and psychological problems.
- The emotional quotient of the person increases and thereby, he becomes calmer and more collected. He develops empathy and is able to share the pain and sorrow of others.
- By meditating one learns to get rid of one's bad traits and habits, if any, and develop a positive mindset and traits.
- Regular meditation helps to focus on the present and improves the power of concentration. In students, it helps in their studies and learning. An improvement in memory and mental clarity also has been noted. It improves one's power of discrimination.

- Meditation is helpful in tolerating pain and also helps people with problems of addiction.

**Meditation pose**

- During regular meditation, often problems which did not seem to have a solution suddenly get solved. A scientific problem or dilemma or an unsolved concern that had been nagging the mind of an individual may suddenly find an answer during or soon after a session of meditation ; even the apple falling on Newton's head while he was relaxing (meditating) or Kekulé finding the structure of the benzene ring when he was asleep (deep meditation) are some examples. During meditation, the mind connects to the *'Supreme Being'* or *'Universal Consciousness* and conditions our mind to receive ideas from That source.

**"How do we practice meditation, Grandpa?" Jaya seemed impatient. "Where is this described in the scriptures?".**

Meditation has been described in many texts in the scriptures including Patanjali's *Yoga Sutra* about which I have previously told you. But what I am now going to tell you is taken from the *Srimad Bhagavatham.* In the 11th Canto, 14th Chapter of the text, *Bhagavan Sri Krishna* tells his friend and close confidant, *Uddhava* on how meditation should be done. It is also described in the *Bhagavad Gita* by *Bhagavan Sri Krishna* himself to Arjuna.

You must sit in a place which is neither too high nor too low. You can sit on the floor on a mat, a plank of wood or on a blanket. Choose quiet surroundings without auditory or visual distractions. Do not sit on the bare floor. Sit in a comfortable position in a clean place. It is ideal to sit in the *Padmasana* (lotus pose) of yoga. Any pose which does not cause discomfort to you is acceptable. The spine should be erect, and the head, neck and spine should be vertical in the same straight line.

Place your hands on your lap. Concentrate your mind on the tip of your nose. (this does not mean that you look cross-eyed but imagine that you are seeing the tip of your nose). This is done only to prevent your mind from wandering off. It is observed that if you move your eyes, your mind too moves along with it. The eyes may be kept gently closed.

Now, gradually perform *Pranayama*. *Pranayama* is the breathing exercise to calm your mind. It has three steps. The three steps of *Pranayama* – *Poorakam* (inhalation*), *Kumbhaka*m (retention) and *Rechakam* (exhalation) should be done slowly. Close your right nostril with your right thumb and inhale and exhale through the left nostril. Then repeat it through the right nostril by closing the left nostril with your right ring and little fingers together. (keep the index and middle finger flexed). Inhalation should be done in 4 seconds, holding the breath four times that - 16 seconds, and exhalation half that – 8 seconds. The ratio is 4 – 16 – 8. These periods of time can be changed as per the convenience of the person, but the ratio is maintained as such. (1 : 4 : 2). Pranayama may also be done by inhaling through the right nostril and exhaling through the left nostril and then alternating the sides. In the initial stages this can be repeated 5 times with each nostril and gradually increased to 10 or 15 times.

One must practice Pranayama at least twice daily. Along with the breathing exercise, one should repeat the *'Pranava mantra' 'OM'* in one's mind. The ideal time to  perform Pranayama and meditation is during the *Brahma muhurtam* which is between 4.30 am and 6 am in the morning. The atmosphere is still at that time and ambient noise is minimal. It is believed that *Goddess Saraswathi*, the Goddess of Knowledge travels the earth during this *Brahma muhurtam* blessing her devotees.



The practitioner of meditation should then bring the image of the early morning sun into his mind. Imagine your whole mind to be filled with the sun's bright light. Gradually imagine the four armed form of *Bhagavan Vishnu.* Start at the feet and gradually work upwards concentrating your mind on each of his limbs as you work upwards toward his four arms holding the *Sudarshana chakra,* the conch, the mace, and the lotus. Finally bring your mind to focus on his face and fix the image of the *Bhagavan's* face in your mind and gradually your mind should become free of thoughts. Remain in that state for a few minutes and gently open your eyes.

The time taken to meditate can be gradually increased. Meditating for about 20 minutes twice a day will suffice.

What I have described to you is the meditation as described by *Bhagavan Sri Krishna* in the *Srimad Bhagavatham.* There are other methods of meditation also. Transcendental meditation, Chakra meditation,

Kundalini meditation, and Tantra meditation are also practiced. Once again, I would like to stress that meditation should be learnt from a proper *Guru* who initiates you into it.

**"Grandpa, should we repeat any mantra during meditation? Is there any advantage by doing so? " Vijaya had a simple query.**

Ah yes. You can repeat any simple *Mantra* in your mind when you are meditating. This can help your concentration. Let us see the meaning of *Mantra*. (*Man* = mind; *Tra* = to uplift; to release). A *Mantra* will increase awareness and improve the concentration of the individual. Instead of concentrating on an object, one can concentrate on a sound – the *Mantra*. You can choose any mantra. *'Om'*, *'Om Namah Shivaya'*, *'Om Namo Narayanaya'*, *'Om Namo Bhagavathe Vasudevaya'* etc., are some of the *Mantras* which you can repeat during meditation. You can also repeat the *Gayatri mantra* or the *Maha mantra* – *'Hare Rama, Hare Rama....'* You can choose any phrase as the sound for meditation. You can repeat *'So Ham'*, *'Aham Brahmasmi'*, *'Rama Rama'*, *'Narayana'*, or *'Krishna Krishna'*.

Those who are non-Hindus can repeat any phrase or word of their choice. Muslims have the various names for God. They can repeat a name, or they can repeat other phrases which they use in prayer. So can Christians repeat phrases or the names of God or any phrase in praise of the Lord.

**Grandpa, you were mentioning about
'Brahma Muhurta' Aditya wanted to know
more about it.**

Good. The word meaning of *'Brahma muhurta'* is
'Brahma's Time' or the 'Creator's Time'. It is the best time
of the day to indulge in spiritual practice like meditation
and studying the scriptures and contemplating on them.
The time of the day has been divided into *'muhurtas'*.
One *muhurtam* is 48 minutes. The night consists of 15
*muhurtas* (12 hours). The *Brahma muhurtam*
corresponds to two *muhurtas* before sunrise. That will be
$48 \times 2 = 96$ minutes (1 hour and 36 minutes). Assuming
that the sunrises at 6 am, the *Brahma muhurta* is
roughly from 4.30 am to 6 am.

According the *Ashtanga Hridaya* which is an ancient
*Ayurveda* text, waking up daily during the *Brahma
muhurta* increases one's longevity, vitality and helps to
avoid diseases. Scientifically speaking, the pre-dawn
period is said to have plenty of nascent oxygen in the
atmosphere, less pollution, and less noise. It is the ideal
time for spiritual practices like meditation and practising
music and chanting. It is the time when the awareness
level of the mind is very high. The mind is highly
receptive to knowledge during this period as the body
and mind are relaxed and recharged after a night's rest.
The mind is alert, and this is the time when innovative
solutions to many difficult problems pop up in our
minds. Our *Prana* or 'life force energy' is the strongest
during this period which is conducive to spiritual
practice. The Alpha waves in the brain are activated then.
It is the best time for students to study, as comprehension
and assimilation of knowledge during this period is quick
and lasting. Once you begin waking up daily during the

*Brahma Muhurta* you will recognize the tremendous change in you in a very short time.

To rise early at the *Brahma muhurta*, one should go to bed sufficiently early and get a good night's sleep. After rising at 4.30 am, once the ablutions are over, one should meditate for some time. Reading spiritual texts is ideal during this period. The student should introspect what he did the previous day and plan what he wants to do on that day. One should mentally pay obeisance to one's parents, *Guru*, and teachers during the *Brahma muhurta*. Chanting a few slokas is ideal.

One should avoid eating and drinking during this period (except water) and should not do any vigorous exercises or indulge in stressful activities during the *Brahma muhurta*. Using electronic devices like the mobile phone, television or the computer must be avoided. Speaking or reciting loudly is also forbidden. Children, pregnant women, and elderly people are exempted from waking up during the *Brahma muhurta*.

**"Can non-Hindus practice *Pranayama* and meditation? What type of meditation should a person who is not a Hindu do? Obviously, they wouldn't want to meditate on the form of *Bhagavan Vishnu*?" Aditya's logical mind was active again.**

Surely, why not. One need not be a Hindu to practice meditation. If you are a Christian, after *Pranayama*, you can meditate on the form of Jesus on the cross. If you are a Muslim, you can focus on the *Kaaba* or on the crescent of the moon or any other object or symbol of your choice. You can concentrate on the sun or on a flower like the rose or on the flame of a lamp or candle. An atheist too can still concentrate on the sun alone or on the flame of a lamp or candle. The aim is to hold the mind steady and achieve a state where the mind is free of any intrusive thoughts. *Pranayama* is only a breathing exercise and can be practiced by anyone irrespective of religion, caste, or race.

**"Can one sit on a chair to meditate?" Vijaya was inquisitive. "I saw grandma meditating sitting on a chair in her room".**

Sure, there is no harm in sitting on a chair, a divan, or a davenport as you wish. But never lie down and meditate lest you go to sleep and begin to snore. Wherever you sit, Swami Chinmayananda used to say, *"don't sit like a 'question mark', sit like an 'exclamation mark."*

# 9. YOGA

**"What is Yoga, Grandpa?" my father was telling me to join a yoga class during the next holidays" Aditya asked.**

Yoga is an inseparable part of Hinduism. Conversely, do not feel that those who practice yoga are all Hindus, or that only Hindus can practice yoga. The yoga which you are mentioning is only one section of the yoga practice which is called '*Hatha Yoga*' which deals with the physical exercise of the body to improve our strength and flexibility. This is being practiced by more than 20 million practitioners in the United States alone and many more worldwide. That is the extent to which the practice of yoga has spread in the world. Today I shall tell you about Yoga in a bit more detail.

The word '*Yoga*' comes from the Sanskrit word '*yuj*' meaning 'to unite', 'to join' or 'to yoke'. Yoga constitutes a group of physical, mental, and spiritual practices to discipline the mind and the body to ultimately unite it with the *Brahman*. These practices have been present from the *Vedic* periods and have been referenced in the *Rig Veda*. It was Swami Vivekananda who introduced yoga to the West and since then it has caught on in a big way in the West.

*Sage Patanjali* is the father of yoga. His famous compilation, the '*Yoga Sutras*' are the source of yoga – the physical, mental, and spiritual disciplines of yoga.

**"Who was Patanjali?" Vijaya's curiosity was aroused.**

He was a sage credited with the writing of '*Patanjali Yoga Sutra*' - a treatise on Yoga. There is an interesting story about his birth. It is said that *Bhagavan Shiva* was performing his cosmic dance one day and *Bhagavan Vishnu* was appreciating him. *Adi Sesha*, the thousand headed snake on which *Bhagavan Vishnu* rests also wanted to see *Bhagavan Siva's* dance. *Bhagavan Vishnu* told *Adi Sesha* to go to Chidambaram (a place in Tamil Nadu, India) where *Bhagavan Siva* is manifest as *Nataraja* (<u>the King of Dance</u>).

A woman by the name of *Gonika* was praying with folded hands to the Sun God to give her a son when a little snake fell from heaven into her outstretched palms. This snake assumed the form of a baby and was named '*Patanjali*' (*Pata-* <u>to fall</u> ; *Anjali-* <u>to pray with folded palms</u>). Hence sage *Patanjali* is believed to be the incarnation of *Adi Sesha*. He wrote three treatises of which *Yoga Sutras* are the most important. Yoga is restraining the mind from wandering and when the mind is restrained the true Self is revealed.

*Patanjali* advocated the eight-fold path of yoga practice called the 'Ashtanga Yoga' (*Ashta* = <u>eight</u>; *Anga* = <u>limb</u>). The eight paths or limbs described are as follows:

1. **Yama**. (<u>Abstinences</u>) *Yama* is external discipline or <u>discipline of the body</u>. They are the ethical rules or the "don'ts" in Hinduism. The five *Yamas* which are listed by Patanjali are

a. **Ahimsa** (<u>Non-violence</u>, <u>non-injury</u> to all living beings) which means not harming other living beings through thought, word, or action.

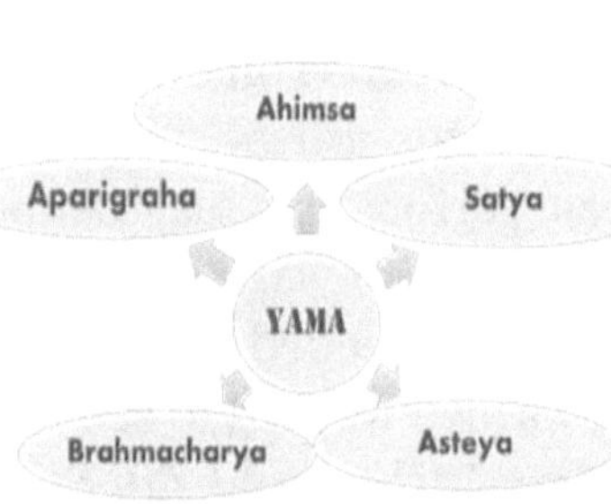


b. **Satya** (<u>Truthfulness</u>) which means being truthful in thought, speech, and action and not uttering lies.

c. **Asteya** (<u>Non-stealing</u>) meaning not stealing the possessions of others.

d. **Brahmacharya** (<u>chastity</u>, <u>sexual restraint</u>) leading a disciplined life by controlling ones desires and keeping the five senses under restraint. It means non-indulgence.

e. **Aparigraha** (<u>Non-Avarice</u>) not being greedy or coveting the possessions of others.

2. **Niyama** (<u>Observances</u>) *Niyamas* are for internal discipline or <u>discipline of the mind</u>. They help

to promote virtuous habits in humans. Five *Niyamas* are listed by Patanjali.

a. ***Soucham*** (<u>Purity</u> or <u>cleanliness</u>). This includes cleanliness of the Body and Mind - of speech and thoughts.

b. ***Santosha*** (<u>Contentment</u>, <u>Satisfaction</u>). The individual should be content with his possessions and circumstances and accept them as they are.

c. ***Tapas*** (<u>Spiritual observance</u>, <u>Self-discipline</u>, <u>Perseverance</u>). It means ascetic practices to achieve spiritual powers.

d. ***Svadhyaya*** (<u>Self-study</u>, study of *Vedas* and other scriptures). The person should have the intense desire to acquire knowledge.

e. ***Ishvara Pranidhana*** (<u>Devotion to God</u>; <u>contemplation on the Brahman</u>). All actions must be surrendered to Him. More about this, we will discuss in *Karma Yoga*.

Each of the Yamas and Niyamas helps in personal growth of the individual and development of his character and personality.

3. ***Asanas*** (<u>Yoga Postures</u>) These are yoga postures for the individual to sit comfortably and concentrate or meditate. The posture should be comfortable and

**Yoga Asanas**

should not cause pain or distress. These are called the *'Hatha Yoga Asanas'* and 84 asanas are described. The asanas are named after birds, animals, trees and other objects or beings in nature like the *Padmasana* (lotus-posture), *Simhasana* (lion) *Bhujangasana* (snake) *Mayurasana* (peacock), *Marjarasana* (cat) etc.

This is the type of yoga that is taking the Western countries by storm under the name of "Yoga" and being taught by practitioners the world over.

4.  ***Pranayama***. (Control of Breath) (*Prana* = breath; *Ayama* = restraint).   After the person assumes a comfortable yogic posture, he endeavors to control his breath. We have discussed this previously under the topic on *Meditation*. There are many modifications to this under various names and eight types of *Pranayama* are described. It is always advisable to learn these techniques under the guidance of a properly trained teacher of yoga.

5.  ***Pratyahara***. (Withdrawal of the senses)
This does not mean simply closing the eyes or plugging the ears to avoid seeing or hearing but is much more than that. It the conscious withdrawal of the mind from the sensory objects and turning the mind inward. This is the step that moves the mind from the external world to the internal world.

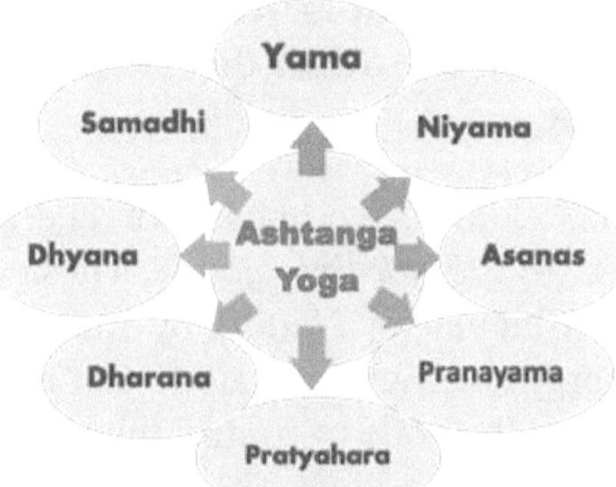



6. ***Dharana***. (<u>Concentration</u>). The mind is fixed on a single object or *mantra* or image. Any image would do. One has to focus on it. It can be the image of an idol of God, a flower, or a flame. Another method is to concentrate on one's breathing – inhalation and exhalation. Yet another method is to concentrate on the tip of the nose or a point between the eyebrows (not being cross-eyed). This is mainly to prevent the mind from entertaining thoughts or shifting from one thought to another. *Dharana* is the training of the mind to meditate.

7. ***Dhyana***. (<u>Meditation</u>). Contemplating on that object or image or mantra that one decides on *Dharana,* is *Dhyana* or <u>meditation</u>. If one has concentrated on a particular subject, then *Dhyana* is contemplating on that subject or object from all aspects.

8. ***Samadhi*** (<u>Union</u>; <u>Trance</u>). This is the state called the '*thoughtless state of mind*'. The person is one with the *Brahman* and is in a transcendental state of consciousness when everything around him seems to disappear. He feels intense bliss. He feels an ecstatic awareness of the Self and the Universal Consciousness.

**"Grandpa, what is 'Kundalini Yoga' I read this name the other day from a book" asks Aditya.**

Our body is composed of <u>energy channels</u> according to *Kundalini yoga*. These are called '*Naadis*" (Singular – *Naadi*) by the ancient seers. These energy channels are said to run from the brain to all parts of the body to control them. There are said to be 72,000 such *Naadis*. The concentrated energy is believed to be located at the base of the spine in the form of a <u>coiled snake</u> (*Kundalini*). When this energy is 'awakened' by yogic practices, it is said to rise up towards the brain through the <u>spinal cord</u> (*Sushumna Naadi*). There are some focal energy centers in the spinal cord along which this energy rises. These centers are called '*Chakras*'. The word '*Chakra*' means '<u>wheel</u>' or '<u>circle</u>'.

There are seven *Chakras* in this route of the *Kundalini,* and they are named from below upwards as *Muladhara* (<u>root</u>; <u>base of spine</u>), *Svadhisthana* (<u>sacral</u>), *Manipura* (<u>solar</u> <u>plexus</u>), *Anahata* (<u>heart</u>), *Vishuddha* (<u>throat</u>), *Ajna* (<u>between the eyebrows</u>; <u>Third eye</u>) and *Sahasrara* (<u>crown of the head</u>).

These centers of energy are present along the spine and yogic practices like meditation and pranayama stimulate and activate these centers so that the individual becomes aware of his inner energy and potential. It is said to open up hitherto unknown mental faculties. However, it is cautioned that these practices should be undertaken only under the guidance of an expert teacher or *Guru*.  They should not practice by oneself or be taught by half-baked charlatans.

**"Then what about *Bhakti* yoga, *Jnana* yoga and *Karma* yoga about which I have heard when I went for a discourse about the *Bhagavad Gita* by a Swamiji"** was the question posed by Vijaya.

What we described so far under the *Yoga sutras* of *Patanjali* is called 'Raja Yoga'. (*Raja* means, 'Chief', 'King' or 'the best kind').

There are three other types of yoga called the *Trimarga* (three paths) which are mentioned in the *Bhagavad Gita* by *Bhagavan Krishna* while advising Arjuna. They are the *Bhakti yoga, Karma yoga* and the *Jnana yoga*. I will briefly touch upon them now.

*Vedanta* says that man's suffering, sorrows, and problems arise from three main sources. They are:

- *Adhyathmikam* – Those that <u>arise from the body</u> like ailments, pain.
- *Adhibhouthikam* – Those that <u>arise from our material possessions</u> like our wealth, house, car, jewelry etc., or by our attachment to them.
- *Adhideivikam* – Those that <u>arise from people</u> connected to us like our family, relatives, friends, etc. Also, from natural calamities like floods, earthquake, fire etc.

The main aim or goal of a human being according to Hinduism is to attain the Supreme Truth called *Brahman*. Attaining self-realization, one learns to get over the above threefold causes of our miseries and distresses in life. Dedicating and surrendering ourselves to the *Supreme Brahman* gives us a sense of detachment and develops in us a mind filled with *Sama Buddhi* (equanimity) and *Vivekam* (power of discrimination). When these two qualities develop in us, we tend to accept the *Dvandvas* (opposites) in life with equanimity.

For attaining this state of mind, man must follow certain paths in his goal towards perfection. These paths have been called the Paths of Yoga. Depending on the type of person, his mindset, and capacities, each one can choose the path to follow. Thus, a Three-fold path has been described and this is clearly elaborated by *Bhagavan Sri Krishna* in the *Bhagavad Gita* in his advice to Arjuna. We will discuss them in brief.

1. ***Karma Yoga*** (Path of Action).    This is the *'path of selfless action'*. An 'action' is whatever we do with our body or mind. It can be done through our mind (thoughts) or body (speech or deed). Any action is called *'Karma'*. Man cannot live without action. The very breathing which goes on automatically in our body is also *Karma*. Eating, playing, walking, exercising, working hard, or doing anything is *Karma*. Actions done for others like helping a person, giving alms to the needy or providing food to the hungry is also *Karma*.

The directive of *Karma* yoga is 'selfless' action and dedicating all actions to the Supreme Being or

*Brahman* or God, without attaching ourselves to the result of our actions. Whatever we do, we mentally dedicate the fruits of the action to God. That does not mean that you should not accept a reward or remuneration for what you do. *The remuneration or reward alone should not be the reason for your action.*

I will illustrate this with an example. You help a friend in need without expecting anything in return. That is 'selfless action'. You should not expect your friend to return the favor or hold you in his debt for what you have done. When a student studies for the examination, he should put in all his sincere effort to do the best he can and perform well. But the worry or anxiety about the result should not hinder the action of writing the examination. Do not fill your mind with what the result of your action is going to be, just do whatever you have to do *sincerely, honestly, and wholeheartedly* dedicating the result to God. Be ready to accept the result, whatever it might be. The result will take care of itself and you will get what you deserve. That is *Karma Yoga.*

There are many people who strive in society and do a lot of *Seva* (<u>social service</u>), without expecting anything in return. Take the example of Mother Teresa or Albert Schweitzer. They did not work for rewards. Mother Teresa did not aspire for the Nobel prize when she looked after the poor and the destitute. All of them did their work as a dedication to God. Mahatma Gandhi worked tirelessly for gaining independence for India from the shackles of the British rule. He was a *Karma Yogi.* He did not expect anything in return. He never hankered after political gains or positions even after gaining independence for India.

We will discuss more about *Karma* and the role it plays in our lives and destiny at a later date.

Describing *Karma Yoga, Bhagavan Sri Krishna* says in the *Bhagavad Gita,*

कर्मण्ये वाधिकारस्ते मा फलेषु कदाचन।
मा कर्मफलहेतु भूर्मा ते सङ्गोऽस्त्व कर्मणि॥ २-४७

*Karmanye vadhikaraste Ma Phaleshu Kadachana,*
*Ma Karmaphala heturbhurma Te Sangostvakarmani*

The meaning of the verse is *"You have the right to work only but never to its fruits. Let not the fruits of action be your motive, nor let your attachment be to inaction".*

2. ***Bhakti Yoga*** (<u>Path of Devotion</u>)

*Bhakti* means '<u>devotion</u>' or '<u>love</u>'. *Bhakti* is divine love for the God who is omnipotent and omniscient. On a broader plane, it is love and devotion extending to all of God's creations, animals, and humans alike. It is total surrender to the *Bhagavan*. Whatever be the method you adopt – meditation, *japa*, singing his praise, chanting slokas, worshiping him through *Pooja*, whatever it might be, it is the uncompromising love for the Divine that defines *Bhakti Yoga*. It does not mean that one must follow the Hindu Gods to develop *Bhakti Yoga*. Any object of worship is enough for one to practice of *Bhakti Yoga*. A Christian can be devoted to his Divine Lord Jesus and so can a Muslim. That is also *Bhakti.*

To develop *Bhakti,* there are nine different practices that are recommended in the scriptures.

**138**

These have been beautifully explained in the *Srimad Bhagavatham* by the child prince *Prahlada*, son of *Hiranyakashipu*, the *asura* king. They are:

i.      **Shravanam** – "Listening". Listening to the scriptures and the mythological stories of the Gods thereby developing *Bhakti*. This is the method that grandmothers employ to inculcate devotion in the minds of kids from early childhood.

ii.      **Kirtanam** – "Singing". Singing devotional songs and *bhajans* in praise of the Gods. This can be done individually in the comfort of one's home or in groups in temples or in a congregation.

iii.      **Smaranam** – "Constantly Remembering". Remembering the divine form always. Thinking constantly of *Bhagavan Sri Krishna* or *Rama* or *Siva* according to  our devotion. This can be done whatever activity we are engaged in. The womenfolk of Hindu households used to constantly sing the Gods' praise while doing their daily chores like milking the cow, churning curd, washing clothes, or singing a lullaby.

iv.      **Padasevanam** – "Service at His feet". Service at the feet of God is also *Karma* yoga or selfless service. Whatever we do, is dedicated to the Divine.

v.      **Archanam** – "Ritual Worship". This is the ritual worship through *Poojas* or *homams* (offering into the fire). This holds good for rituals of other religions too.

vi.      **Vandanam** – "Prostration at His feet". The prostration before the Divine. When visiting temples, devotees prostrate before the deity to indicate total surrender of themselves to the divine. The kneeling of the Christians in church is also such an action. The *Namaaz* of Muslims is also an example of *Vandanam*.

vii.    ***Dasyam*** - "Unquestioning Devotion". One considers himself or herself as the servant of the

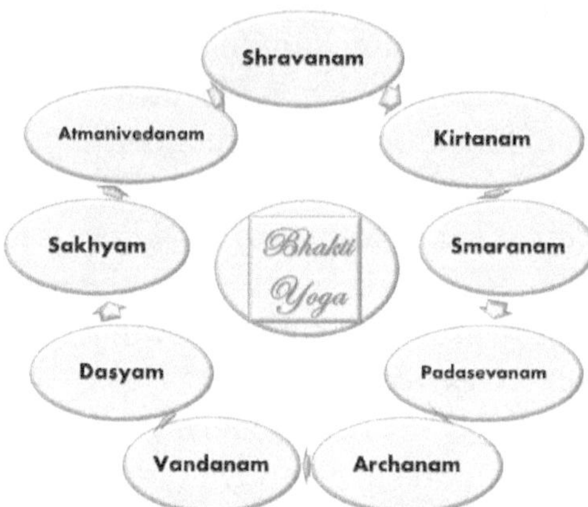


*Bhagavan* and does everything in His service. Surrendering one's ego to God all acts of service are dedicated to him.

viii.    ***Sakhyam*** – "Friendship".   Here the devotee considers God as his mate or friend and does everything for gaining His affection. It is like the friendship between *Bhagavan Sri Krishna* and *Sudama* described in the *Srimad Bhagavatham*.

ix.    ***Atmanivedanam*** - "Self-Offering". The complete surrender of the self to the *Bhagavan* is the final act of total surrender to the Divine. *"I totally yield to You"* – is the feeling of the devotee.


3.    ***Jnana Yoga***. (Path of Knowledge or Wisdom).   The learner in *Jnana* yoga strives to understand his true self. 'Who am I' is the question he poses to himself and through deliberation and contemplation understands that he is the *Brahman*. He realizes that  he and *Brahman* are one and the

same. This knowledge is attained with the help of a *Guru* through reflection and meditation. He recognizes the presence of the *Brahman* in all living beings and life forms.

Swami Vivekananda succinctly said about the *Jnana* yoga, *"God manifested himself on earth in the form of living creatures."* *Jnana* yoga is described in great detail in chapter 4 of the *Bhagavad Gita.*

*Jnana* yoga is the most difficult path of the three yoga *margas* (<u>paths</u>). The seeker must meditate and find out the true knowledge for himself. He has to experience the *oneness* with the Brahman, which only a few are able to do. The devotee is enlightened as to his true nature when he pursues the path of knowledge. This needs the help of a *Guru* who reveals the secrets in the *Vedas* and *Upanishads* to the pupil and makes him understand his true self, which is the ultimate knowledge of 'Who am I?"

# 10. DHARMA

**"Grandpa, what is the meaning of Hindu *Dharma*? What are its implications?" Aditya was the one who initiated the discussion every day.**

The word meaning of '*Dharma*' is 'that which holds' or 'that which supports'. It is very difficult to find an exact word in English equivalent to *Dharma*. It has been variously and loosely translated as 'duty', 'righteousness', 'merit', 'conduct', and 'religious duty'

The *Vedas* are the ultimate authority for *Dharma*. The word is derived from the Sanskrit root "*Dhri*" which means 'to support' or 'to maintain'. *Dharma* is necessary to prevent dissipating tendencies in society. *Dharma* is said to be the heart of Hindu Philosophy. The inflections of meaning of the word *Dharma* also change depending on the context where it is applied or mentioned in the scriptures.

The categories of divisions where *Dharma* is applicable can be as follows. The meaning of the word *Dharma* also changes according to the context in which it is used. Let us see some of these categories and elaborate them one by one. Note that the shades of meaning of the word '*Dharma*' varies with each category.

i.    The **Purusharthas** – *Dharma, Artha, Kama,* and *Moksha.*   These are the *objectives* (<u>dharma</u>) in the life of a Hindu.

ii.    The **Ashrama Dharma** – *Brahmachari, Grihastha, Vanaprastha* and *Sannyasa.* These are called the '*Chaturasrama*' (<u>Four Ashramas</u>). These are the four stages in the life of a Hindu and his *duties* (<u>dharma</u>)during these stages.

iii.    The **Varna Dharma** – *Brahmin, Kshatriya, Vaisya,* and *Sudra.* These are the socioeconomic classification of society according to their qualities and calling and their *characteristics* (<u>dharma</u>) depending on their *Varna.*

iv.    The **Yuga Dharma** – *Satya Yuga, Tretha Yuga, Dvapara Yuga* and *Kali Yuga.* The values and *mindset* (<u>dharma</u>) of people in the four *Yugas* are different and these are called *Yuga Dharma.*

We will go into details of these presently.

**"Grandpa, explain to us each of these in detail. What are Purushartas?" Jaya wanted details.**

***Purushartas*** are the <u>goals</u> or <u>aspirations</u> in the life of a person. They literally mean '<u>objectives of</u>

man'. The word 'man' here denotes human beings, both men and women.  Let us briefly discuss them. The *Purushartas* are four in number as mentioned previously and we will discuss them one by one.

1.     ***Dharma*** here indicates the <u>Moral values</u> in life. It is the most important of the four. The other three *Purushartas* are pursued acting within the framework of *Dharma* without violating its principles. They are the principles of righteousness, proper moral conduct according to the laid down tenets, performing one's duties as laid down according to the stage of one's life and living a virtuous life. Deviating from the *Dharma* way of life is called *Adharma* (<u>immoral</u> ; <u>sinful</u>).

The *Dharma* or duties of a person are variable depending on the person and the circumstances. It differs according to one's place in society, one's occupation, one's *Varna* and one's age.  A doctor may prescribe different medicines for different patients depending on the need and the disease which he is treating. Similarly, *Dharma* also changes accordingly. *Dharma* or rules are also different for women compared to men. It also differs depending on the stage of one's life, whether one is a student, householder, retired or a sannyasi. But the basic values and morals like nonviolence, non-stealing,, cleanliness, control of the senses etc., which have been proposed by *Patanjali* in his *Yoga sutra* are common for every Hindu irrespective of his status, stage, age, or occupation. We will discuss these points subsequently.

2. ***Artha*** indicates the <u>Material values</u> in life and pursuit of activities that lead to material gains like wealth and prosperity. Activities needed to earn a

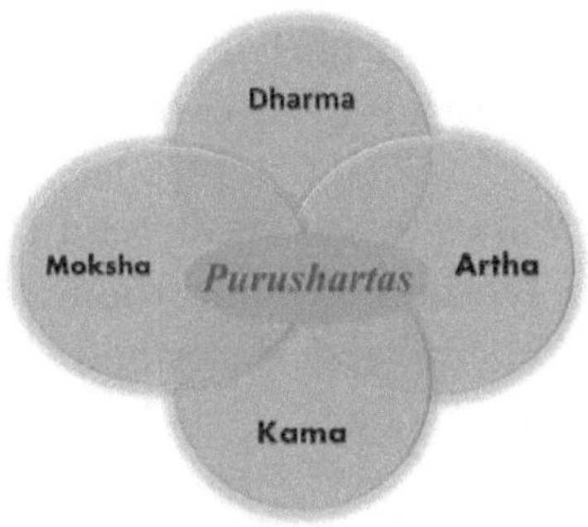


living, pursuing a career, and becoming prosperous are all justified in the pursuit of *Artha*. But it is ordained that all acquisition of wealth and prosperity should be only through means which are *Dharmic* like honesty, non-violence, non-stealing etc. Man is permitted to earn wealth and progress materially staying within the boundaries of *Dharma*. Owning wealth and achieving prosperity is *not* denied in Hindu philosophy.

3. ***Kama*** indicates the <u>Psychological values</u> like seeking what one desires, one's passion, pursuit of pleasure of the senses, and love. Again, all these are to be achieved without straying from the laws of *Dharma* and following the values and morals laid down in the scriptures. Thus, the pleasures of life may be pursued by anyone as long as he does not digress from the path of *Dharma*.

4. ***Moksha*** indicates the <u>Spiritual values</u> which is liberation of the soul from the <u>eternal cycle of birth and death</u> or *Samsara* through self-knowledge and self-realization. This is the ultimate aim or goal in the life of every Hindu.

Thus, all activities are focused on attaining these four main objectives in life. These activities have been categorized into two called ***Pravrtti*** and ***Nivrtti***. *Pravrtti* denotes all actions performed in the world for <u>material gains</u>. Hence, *Artha* and *Kama* come under the *Pravrtti* actions.

*Nivrtti* on the other hand denotes actions performed for <u>self-realization</u> and liberation of the soul. Hence, *Moksha* is a result of *Nivrtti* action.

All these four *Purushartas* have been studied and analyzed in detail by the sages and the ways and means of achieving them are described in our scriptures. Some of these texts are:

The *Yoga Sutras* of Patanjali, the *Manu Smriti*, *Narada Smriti* and the *Thirukural* - which is written in the Tamil language. They are all texts delineating the rules of *Dharma* to be followed and laws laid down therein.

Rules of politics, economics, administration and wealth management are discussed in the texts *Artha Sastra* by Kautilya, *Kamandakiya Nitisara*, *Brihaspati Sutra*, and *Sukra Niti*. These give extensive descriptions on how <u>wealth</u> (*Artha*) should be acquired, increased, and shared. I am mentioning these names only to give you an insight into the volume of literature available. You should endeavour to study these later when time permits.

The pursuit of pleasure, love, emotions and erotic aspects of life are discussed in texts like the *Kama Sutra* by Vatsyayana, *Ratirahasya*, *Jayamangala*, *Smaradipika*, *Ratimanjari*, *Ratiratnapradipika*, and *Ananga Ranga*. These texts are for the study of *Kama*.

The
*Upanishads, Vivekachudamani, Bhagavad Gita*, and
the sastras on Yoga are the treatises which discuss
elaborately the practices to attain *Moksha*
(liberation).

The ten virtues enunciated by *Patanjali* in his
*Yoga sutra* need to be recapitulated at this juncture.
They are *Satya, Brahmacharya, Asteya, Aparigraha,
Ahimsa, Saucha, Santosha, Tapas, Svadhyaya* and
*Ishvara Pranidhana*. We have already discussed
these.

**"Grandpa, can you tell us briefly about
'Ashrama Dharma' which you said is
important for Hindus. What does it
mean?" Aditya asked.**

Good. Now that you have understood the
*Purushartas*, let us briefly understand what *Ashrama
Dharmas* are. They are really the four stages in the life
of an individual. They are also called the
*Chaturasrama.* (*Chathur* = four ; *Ashramas* = stage)
The duties of the person in each *Ashrama* is different.
We will discuss each one separately.

i.     The ***Brahmacharya*** is the first
*Ashrama* and is also called the 'stage of the student'.
Literally, the word means 'following the path of
Brahman'.   This starts with the *Upanayanam*
ceremony when the student is initiated into the *Vedic*
scriptures. In the modern day, it means the period
when the student is actively involved in his studies.
This is the time that the student ardently devotes to
studies without any external distractions. The student

follows a strict life of discipline, celibacy, and self-restraint during this period.

During the days of studentship, the disciple lives with the *Guru* in his *Gurukulam* in a purely residential status. The *Guru* (<u>teacher</u>) is both God and guardian to the student in the days when he is in the

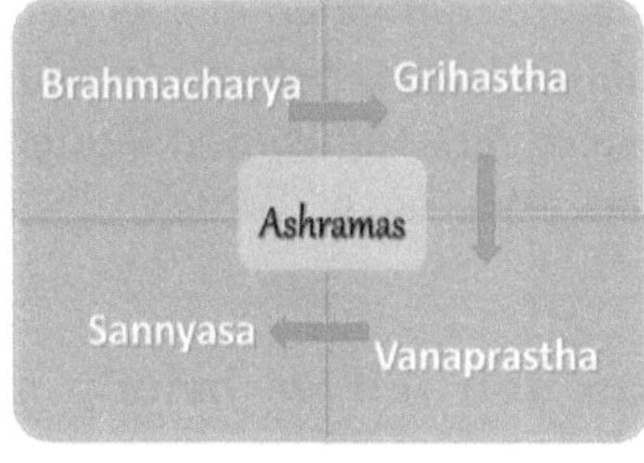


*Ashram* with the *Guru* and fellow disciples. This stage usually continued for 12 years but could vary from 9 years to 36 years as per *Manu Smrithi* depending on the scholastic capacity of the student. The *Guru* is highly revered by the students and no disrespect was shown to him at any time. A strict disciplined and austere life is expected to be led by the students. The students learn to cultivate moral excellence and spiritual values during this period and avoid all sorts of pleasures. The *Guru* teaches them all the scriptures and ensures that the students under his tutelage develop the knowledge and practical skills to face the life ahead in the external world.

When the period of *Gurukulam* training is over, the student can return to his home to his parents. But before leaving there is a 'graduation ceremony' where the student is called upon to demonstrate his knowledge and skills to an assemblage. Following this the student presents the *Guru* with gifts or 'fees' for his long training, in the form of gold, land, cows, grains, parasol, footwear, fruits, vegetables, or any other stuff according to the capacity of the student.

The value or cost of the offering hardly matters. It is the reverence and dedication with which the <u>disciple</u> (*sishya*) presents this to the *Guru* which is important. This is called the '*Guru Dakshina*' (*Dakshina* = <u>fees</u> ; <u>honorarium</u> ; <u>donation</u>).

The *Guru* then blesses the student, and the student then leaves the *Gurukulam* to go back to his parents to enter the next stage of his life which is that of a *Grihastha*. The *Brahmacharya Ashrama* is usually over by the age of 25 when the student is an adult.

In the modern age, the *Brahmachari* can be equated with the student life of a person when he acquires knowledge or learns a skill and achieves academic brilliance. During his school and college years, the student's focus should be on studies alone and not on other distractions. Usually, the studies are completed by the age of 25, except in certain professions like Medicine or some disciplines of engineering or technology. After completing his studies, when the student enters an employment, he becomes a *Grihastha*.

ii.     The **Grihastha** is the next stage. The student or *Brahmachari* who returns from the *Gurukulam* is now an adult ready to take on the responsibilities of adulthood and raise a family. *Grihastha* means '<u>householder</u>'. (*Griha* = <u>home</u> ; <u>house</u>). The *Grihastha Ashrama* is considered to be the most important of the four *Ashramas*. The *Grihastha*, as he is addressed, marries, and raises a family. He has manifold duties, to look after his wife and children, care for his elderly parents, earn a living, and care for the members of the other three *Ashramas* and the society. Charity and social service are essential requirements of a *Grihastha*. This is the *Ashrama* in which he simultaneously pursues material pleasures and spiritual practices on a daily basis. All this is done within the boundaries of the prescribed *Dharma* and *Vedic* laws.

The *Grihastha* is called upon to perform the 'Pancha Maha yagnas (<u>five</u> <u>great</u> <u>sacrifices</u>) daily. They are the *Brahma yajna, Deva yajna, Pitru yajna, Bhuta yajna* and *Athithi yajna* or *Manushya yajna.* We will discuss this later in more detail.

It is during the *Grihasthasrama* that an individual simultaneously pursues the four *Purushartas* of *Dharma, Artha, Kama,* and *Moksha.* The first three are given importance during this stage and the last one – *Moksha* is not pursued with as much intensity as in the next two stages.

The *Grihastha* performs all his activities dedicating all the results to God in a selfless manner. This does not mean that he should not accept remuneration for his services or profession. But the reward or remuneration will not be his *primary aim* when he renders any service to another individual or society. A *Grihastha* never 'demands' remuneration for his services. This is the type of *Karma* yoga which the *Grihastha* practices during his family life. All his actions are dedicated to the Supreme *Brahman.*

The *Grihastha* period is usually said to be about twenty five years till the individual reaches the age of 50 or till his grandson is born.

iii.     The **Vanaprastha** stage, which begins around the age of 50 is said to last till about the age of 74. The word 'Vanaprastha' literally means, '<u>retiring to the forest</u>'. (Vana = <u>jungle</u> ; <u>forest</u> : Prastha = <u>going</u>). The householder is then called the Vanaprastha. This is the stage when the individual hands over the responsibilities to his children and retires to the solitude of the forest. Gradually withdrawing from the material world, assuming only the position of an advisor to the family, he leaves the day to day management of the household to his children. The *Manu Smriti* says that when a person's hair turns gray, when his skin begins to wrinkle and he has spent time with his grandsons, it is time for him to retire to the solitude of the jungle renouncing his responsibilities. He should detach himself from the earthly world of possessions and pleasure.

Usually in ancient days, the *Vanaprastha* moved to the hermitage of a sage near the jungle. He built a cabin or cottage in the premises of the hermitage (*Ashram*) and spent the rest of his *Vanaprastha* life in the *ashram* of the sage. He lived the life of an ascetic shunning the pleasures of life and living on the fruits and vegetables gathered from the forest. He devoted more of his time to spiritual practices and strove towards the fourth *Purushartha* – *Moksha*. He became more detached and secluded as time progressed. His family – sons and grandchildren visited him from time to time, to seek his advice and blessings but he avoided any active involvement in their matters. He led life in a purely advisory capacity.

In ancient days even kings have been seen to enter the stage of *Vanaprastha* and retire to the solitude of the forest after coronating their successor as king. The *Puranas* mention the instances of the *Pandavas* in *Mahabharata* and *Sri Rama* in *Ramayana* accepting *Vanaprastha* after crowning their children or grandchildren as kings.

In the modern day, this sort of living in the 'jungle' is not possible, but the concept of *Vanaprastha* is being eminently followed by the Hindus. Often, the wife also accompanies the husband in *Vanaprastha*. In the modern day, the equivalent of this is the aged living in gated communities or 'retirement' homes. This is a concept which is increasingly becoming popular in India and in most Western cultures too. The person can become a *Vanaprastha* even while living with his sons and grandchildren in the same home. It is his mindset that changes to detach itself from responsibilities and interferences in the family matters. These are totally handed over to the children and the *Vanaprastha* spends his time meditating and reading the scriptures or going on pilgrimages to various temples and holy places. He is accompanied by his wife in his pilgrimages and spiritual practices.

iv.     ***Sannyasa Ashrama*** is the fourth stage of life where the individual totally renounces all material pleasures and lives the life of an ascetic. It is after the age of 75. The literary meaning of the word *Sannyasa* is 'purification of everything'. He is called a *Sannyasi*. Women who reach this stage are called <u>Sannyasins</u>. *Sannyasis* have totally renounced all material pleasures, and their aim is only the fourth *Purushartha* which is *Moksha*. They spend their whole time in spiritual practices, meditation, *Japam* (constantly repeating a holy name, *mantra* or prayer) etc. They do not own any material possessions and avoid emotional attachments. Often the *sannyasi* moves from place to place as he has no permanent abode. He leads a simple life devoid of any pleasures.

Many *sannyasis* often wear saffron or white clothes to distinguish themselves from those in the previous three *Ashramas*. But this is not a mandatory requirement. The mental make-up of a sannyasi is more important than his attire. It is perfectly possible to live in the midst of this modern world with the mentality of a *Sannyasi*. Adi Sankaracharya in his *Bhaja Govindam* has aptly summarized this in the couplet:

जटिलो मुण्डी लुञ्छित केशः, काषायाम्बर बहुकृतवेषः।<br>पश्यन्नपि च न पश्यति मूढः, उदर निमित्तं बहुकृत वेषः ॥१४॥

*Jatilo mundi luñchitakesa kasayambarabahukrtavesa,*

*Pasyannapi cana pasyati mudha, udaranimittam bahukritha vesam.*

It means, *"One ascetic may have matted hair, one may have a shaven head, one may have hair plucked out one by one, one may be in in ochre robes – all these are distracted ones who, though seeing, do not see. These are different disguises are only for their belly's sake"*.

This only goes to emphasize the fact that it is not the external appearance of the sannyasi that is important, but his inner mindset, attitude, conduct and his intense desire to achieve self-realization are important.

In the modern age, the *Sannyasi* life is not easy for every *Vanaprastha*. When a person retires from all his official activities and relegates all his properties and possessions to his children, he technically is a *Sannyasi* – one without any material possessions. In old age when a person is not able to effectively manage his finances and his possessions, he should relinquish his authority to his heirs.

I am sure that you have now got a general idea of the four *Ashramas* in the life of a Hindu when he goes through these stages of life. Actually, this is a very practical way to lead one's life without any friction and strife in the society or in the relationships within the family. It is also  shows that we should  hand over responsibility to the younger generation and assume an advisory role when we reach a certain stage in life.

**"Grandpa, what are the types of *Karmas* or duties that a Hindu is called upon to do during his spiritual journey?" Jaya asked.**

Yes sure, we will discuss that now. Four types of *Vaidika Karmas* (*Vaidika* = according to Vedas) are described.

i.      ***Nitya Karmas*** – These are actions or obligatory *Karmas* that we have to perform daily. They are spiritual in nature. The *Sandyavandanam, Japam, Pooja, Namasankeertanam* etc., come under this category.

ii.      ***Naimittika Karmas*** – These are ones performed on special occasions. The *Karmas* performed on birthdays, the obsequies on the death of a person, the *Upanayanam* ceremony, the naming of a child, the wedding rituals are all *Naimittika Karmas*. The *Poojas* done on days like the *Navaratri*, *Saraswathi Pooja*, *Lakshmi Pooja* are all such *Karmas*.

iii. ***Kamya Karmas*** – These are performed when one needs <u>to fulfill one's desires</u>. These are not obligatory and failing to observe them is not considered a sin or against tradition. The *Yajna* named *Putrakameshti* done by a couple for obtaining a child, or the *Yajna* for Varuna, the God of rains for heavy showers for agriculture or *Yajnas* for overall prosperity of the community or society fall under this category.

iv. ***Prayaschitta Karma*** – (*Prayaschittam* = <u>repentance</u> ; <u>atonement</u>)These are performed when the individual has gone against *Dharma,* and these are done as a repentance. It is well known that to err is human. These *Karmas* as done as atonement for the sins one has committed knowingly or inadvertently. These *Karmas* can be in the form of charity done as an expiation for the sins committed, fasting on specific days, going on a pilgrimage to temples or performing special *Poojas* or *Homams*.

The above are the four types of *Karmas* which a Hindu usually resorts to. In addition, we should also be aware that there are *Karmas* which are forbidden by our scriptures like stealing, greed, coveting another' wealth, consuming alcohol and killing. These are all called '***Nishiddha Karmas***' (*Nishiddha* = <u>prohibited</u>).

Actions of *Karma yoga* where the person performs selfless action without any desire for the results or reward are termed '***Nishkama Karmas***'

*(Nishkama = <u>selfless</u>)*. These two terms are mentioned here only for completion to understand the various types of Karmas.

**"Well, Grandpa, you told us that you will elaborate on the '*Pancha Maha Yajnas*' of the *Grihastha*"** Aditya reminded me.

Now, coming to our discussion of the *Pancha Maha Yajnas*. These are <u>five</u> obligatory *Karmas* a Hindu is expected to perform daily. They come under the *Nitya Karmas*. Hence these must be done daily.

1.    ***Brahma yajna*** is also called *Rishi yajna*. It is the obligatory duty of learning and teaching the religious texts. Every householder should spend some time daily learning the scriptures and teaching them to the next generation. This would include his children who should be taught by him from an early age.

2.    ***Deva yajna*** is the offering of ghee into the *Homam* or *Agni* (<u>fire</u>). It includes the daily

chanting of various *bhajans* and songs in praise of the Gods. The *Vishnu Sahasranamam, Lalitha Sahasranamam,* and *Hanuman Chalisa* are examples of worship in *Deva yajna*. *Sahasranamam* means '<u>thousand names</u>'. Chanting the thousand names of God is an important part of worship for the Hindu.

3. ***Pithru yajna*** are done for our parents and ancestors. As long as they are alive, taking care of our parents with love and affection is part of this *yajna*. Offerings to ancestors done on every <u>New moon day</u> (*Amavasya*) and on days of their <u>death anniversary</u> (*Shraddha*) are important. In addition, daily offering of water to the *Pithrus* (<u>ancestors</u>) during the *Sandyavandanam* is part of the *Pithru yajna*.

4. ***Bhoota yajna*** (*Bhoota* = <u>living beings</u>) is feeding and taking care of animals and birds. Hindus often rear cows in their homes. These are looked after with affection like their own children.

**Kolam**

They are fed and worshipped on special occasions. Daily, after cooking food at home, some food is offered to the birds by placing a ladleful of cooked rice outside the home. Many Hindu women do this. The tradition of drawing *Kolam* (<u>designs</u>) in front of the house in the morning with rice flour is to feed the insects like ants. Milk is offered in front of snake pits for the snakes to feed on. During summer months, small trays or vessels filled with water are left outside the homes for birds to quench their thirst.

5. ***Manushya*** or ***Manava yajna*** (*Manava* = <u>human</u>) is taking care of fellow human beings. This includes feeding the needy, providing clothes, shelter, being hospitable towards <u>guests</u> (*Athithi yajna*), giving alms to the poor and other charitable activities.

These are the five yajnas which are important daily in the life of a Hindu. Even in this modern age, most Hindus perform these five yajnas in a modest manner according to their convenience and ability.

**"There are two more *Dharmas* which you have not told us about" Vijaya was not the one to forget.**

Yes. I have not told you about the *Yuga Dharma* and the *Varna Dharma*. I will now tell you about the **Yuga Dharma**.

Time, in Hindu scriptures is divided into *Yugas (Yuga* = age of mankind*)*. Each *Yuga* comprises many thousands of years. There are four *Yugas* described and they occur cyclically. The four yugas are named *Satya yuga (Krita) , Tretha yuga, Dvapara yuga* and *Kali yuga.*

The characteristics of the *Yugas* and the *Dharma* in each are different as people, their character and behaviour  also change during the yugas. Let us see this in brief.

The **Satya yuga** is also called the **Krita yuga**. *Tapas* or austerity was given importance in this *yuga. Contemplation and meditation* were the methods to reach the *Brahman*. Rules in society were very strict and people were very pious, straightforward and *Dharmic*.

During the next *yuga* which is the **Tretha yuga**, there was a slight decline in morality and ethics of man. In this age, importance was given to *Jnana* or knowledge. *Yajna and sacrifice* were considered as the method of pursuit towards self-realization during this yuga.

The third yuga was the **Dvapara yuga**. *Yajnas and Pooja* were the methods applied in worship and the *Dharma* declined further.

The fourth yuga is the **Kali yuga** in which we are living at present. The *Kali yuga* is said to be one where the maximum decline in *Dharma* occurs. People will become selfish, family traditions and relationships will dissipate, there will be an overall decline in culture. Money and material possessions will be man's main aim in life, cleanliness and purity will decrease, arrogance will increase, and man will resort to any misdeed for money. Power, lust, and greed will rule the roost. There will be an all-round deterioration in moral standards and ethics. *Yajnas* and *Poojas* will decrease. The only way to salvation in *Kali yuga* is through *Namajapam* (chanting the names of the deity) and *Bhajans*.

These are the *Yuga dharmas* and the various modes of worship which are prescribed in the various *Yugas*. We will learn more about the *Yugas* when we discuss the *Concept of Time in Hinduism*.

We will discuss the *Varna Dharma* or *Varna Ashrama* on another day.

# 11.  KARMA AND REINCARNATION

**"Grandpa, you have referred to the word *'Karma'* many times previously. Can you tell us more about it? What is its meaning, what are its implications and why is *Karma* important in our life?" Aditya was the one to ask such intelligent questions.**

*Karma* is a word used in Hinduism to explain the universal principle of *cause and effect*. You must have heard of the saying 'what goes around, comes around' or 'as you sow, so shall you reap'. *Karma* in summary means the same thing. But its implications are much deeper.

First let us see what we mean by *Karma*. You can see the word 'Karma' being used very loosely now a days by many in the Western world and even in some movies and TV shows, perhaps without knowing its true meaning. *Karma* is the '*effect*' that runs across multitude of births and reincarnations of the soul. As we have discussed earlier, we have a soul and a physical body. The <u>soul</u> or *Atman* or *Jeevatma* as it is variably named is a part of that Universal Consciousness that we call as the *Brahman*. Just like the *Brahman* is eternal, the *Atman* or soul is also eternal and indestructible. The Bhagavad Gita says, *"fire cannot burn it, knife cannot cleave it, air cannot dry it and water cannot wet it."* The immortality of the soul is emphasized in our religion. Our scriptures give a very elegant allegorical example for the connection between the *Brahman* and the *Atman*. When a lamp is lit inside a pot of clay and the pot has hundreds of holes of various dimensions in it, you will find light glowing through all these holes with different levels brightness depending on the size of the holes. But all this light is essentially part of the single brilliant lamp which shines inside the pot. The lamp is *Brahman* and the rays of light emanating from the holes are the individual souls. So, in truth we are all *'spiritual beings'* adorning a human body in this birth and, in the next birth we will come back with another new body. This is reincarnation.

The word meaning of *'Karma'* is '<u>action</u>'. It arises from the Sanskrit word *'Kri'* which means '<u>to do</u>'. The *Karma* or action can be in *Thought, Word, and Deed*. In other words, even thinking ill of someone or something is considered bad *Karma*. Similarly speaking ill of someone or hurting a person with harsh words is also considered bad *Karma*. Physical violence undoubtedly is the worst form of *Karma*. One has to bear the consequences of all these three types of *Karma*. One has to face the reaction to all actions – be it good or bad. It will boomerang upon us. Similarly, kind words, kind and lofty thoughts and helpful and good actions constitute good Karma.

**"What is the meaning of Reincarnation?" little Vijaya was curious.**

The word 'Reincarnation' means 'entering the flesh again' [carnem = flesh, meat (L)]. Reincarnation is called *'Punarjanmam'* in Sanskrit. It means 'to be born again'. Hindus believe in reincarnation. So do Buddhists, Jains, and Sikhs. The ancient Egyptians and Greeks believed in reincarnation. Plato and Socrates believed in reincarnation as is evident in their works. The native indigenous population of the Americas and Australia also believe in reincarnation of the soul.

**"Who keeps track of these *Karma* in a person's life?" Vijaya's query was logical.**

The *Karmas* that one does, leave impressions on the soul of the person and these are recorded like your computer records all details in a hard disc or chip. Analyzing *Karma* further, it can be categorized into three types:

i.      The first is called the *'Sanchita Karma'*. It is the accumulated sum total of the Karmas of all our past lives waiting to be exhausted, endured or resolved. It is like the money that you have accumulated and deposited in the bank as fixed or term deposits. It needs to be used up to the last penny before you can be declared free from rebirth. At present we have no control over this.

ii.     The second is called the *'Prarabdha Karma'* which is that portion of the *Sanchita Karma* which you are already experiencing in the present life. Very loosely stated, it can be translated to mean 'Fate'.

It is like the amount present in your 'current account' (checking account) that you are spending at now. We have no control over this also.

iii.      The third is called the **Kriyamana Karma** or **Agami Karma** which is the *Karma* that we are at present doing in this life. This is the only *Karma* which can shape our future destiny and over which we have a control. Whereas we cannot change our *Sanchita* or *Prarabdha Karmas,* we can alter our present *Karma* by taking care to be *Dharmic* in this life. The *Kriyamana Karma* is like the money you are depositing in your bank account in the present, for future use.

So, what we do now in the present life will determine our future in this life and our future lives. Invariably, we have to be reborn to exhaust our *Sanchita Karmas* of our previous lives and what we accumulate in our present lives. This cycle goes on till we totally  exhaust all our *Karmas*. In other words, till our 'bank balance' becomes 'zero'. This <u>cycle of birth and rebirth</u> is called '*Samsara*' in Hinduism and indicates the innumerable births we have taken previously and the many that are yet to be accomplished.

Our next life will depend on what we do in our present life and on what we have done in our previous lives. In our present life, if we are righteous, honest, truthful, and non-violent, helping others, and acting selflessly, we can expect a better life in our future reincarnation. But if a person is wicked, selfish, greedy, uncharitable, and evil, then we can expect an equally dreadful life for him in the future reincarnations. A man who lives and behaves like an animal in this life may be born as an animal in his next life. What we do in our present life decides what we will be in our future reincarnations.

**"Why are some born poor and others rich? Why are some suffering from diseases and others are healthy? Why is there so much diversity and inequality in God's creations?" Jaya was doubtful.**

Grandpa nodded. 'True. We find that people are different. What we are in this life is conditioned by what we were in our previous lives. If we have physically wounded anyone in our past life, we can expect physical harm in this life from someone else. If we have hurt someone with our harsh words, we can expect insults and abuse  from others in this life. This is an inevitable cause and effect relationship. The diseases, poverty and suffering in this life is also a reflection of our past *Sanchita Karmas*.

**"Grandpa, you talked about good and bad actions. Can you elaborate them further? What do you mean by them?"  Aditya wanted to know.**

Actions itself can be of three types. They are called *Karma*, *Akarma* and *Vikarma*. I will explain them in detail.

*Karma* or '<u>action</u>' is the prescribed action for each one according to his stage in life. It is also an individual's *duty*. For a student like you the prescribed *Karma* is studying and acquiring knowledge. A householder's *Karma* is to look after his family and parents, earn a living and serve the society. A doctor's *karma* is to treat his patients. A king's *karma* is to ensure the welfare of his subjects and so on. All these should be done as per the prescribed *Dharma* not going against the laws laid down in the scriptures. *Karma* is the <u>obligatory duty</u> of everyone.

**Akarma** is '<u>inaction</u>'. Not doing one's duties is *akarma*. A householder not looking after his family, a student not interested in his studies or a doctor not treating his patients is *akarma*. In other words, *akarma* is <u>neglecting one's duties</u>.

**Vikarma** is '<u>wrongful action</u>' or doing actions which are <u>forbidden</u>. A householder who engages in actions which are not expected of him like stealing or gambling. These are actions forbidden by the laws of the land and by religion. It is *Vikarma*. Actions which directly or indirectly cause harm to others are also *Vikarma*. A government servant who indulges in corrupt practices and bribery, a politician who acts inimical to society and his subjects is doing *Vikarma*.

These are the three types of actions. *Akarma* and *Vikarma* are bad *Karmas* which add to your negative *Sanchita karma* whereas the *Karma* according to *Dharma* is the positive *Karma* which is the 'good *Karma*'.

**"Does God punish us thus for our bad and evil *Karmas*?" Vijaya, the youngest among the three seemed to be apprehensive of the consequences of such actions.**

Grandpa smiled. No. you are wrong. God or *Brahman,* whatever name we say, does not interfere with our *Karmas* or its consequences. *We decide our own fate.* Our fate is in *our* hands only. God never decides our fate. He never punishes us. We punish ourselves through our *Karmas.* God is impartial. He equitably presides over the universe. Really, there is nothing called *"Fate".* It is all our *Karma* or our *Prarabdha Karma* which we experience as our fate.

Similarly, we say that one person in 'lucky' or another is 'unlucky'. Luck has nothing to do with it. What you call 'luck' is your good *Sanchita Karma* in your past acting through the *Prarabdha Karma* today. You might have done some very good deed in the past which is boomeranging on you as 'good luck'. So is  bad luck.

**"Do our Gods who took *avatar* as humans have the same law of *Karma* applicable to them? Or are they exempt from the *Sanchita Karmas* like some of our politicians who get impunity even if they commit illegal actions?" Aditya asked with a mischievous twinkle in his eye.**

No one is immune to the consequences of their *Karmas.* When Gods incarnate on earth in human form, they have to face the results of their *Karmas* just like us humans. When *Sri Rama,* hidden behind a tree surreptitiously killed *Vali,* the monkey king, his *Sanchita Karma* followed him in his next *avatar* as *Sri Krishna. Sri Krishna* was killed by the arrow of a hunter when he was resting under a tree in the forest. That is how *Bhagavan Sri Krishna's avatar* ended.

In the *Ramayana*, king *Dasaratha* inadvertently killed a young *Rishi* in the forest mistaking the sound while he was filling his pot with water from the river for that of an elephant drinking water. The king had to die in the absence of all his four sons. It was the result of his *Karma*. *Sita* had abused *Lakshmana* in the forest when she heard *Sri Rama's* apparent voice shouting in distress when he went in search of the golden deer. She had to undergo mental torture for a year in the captivity of *Ravana*. So, you see that even the Gods in mythology were no exception to the results of their *Karma*.

Each person is born with a different bundle of *Sanchita Karmas* according to his or her previous actions. That is why we see that in the same family, the brothers and sisters have different talents, character, and mindset even though the parents are the same and they grow up under similar circumstances at home. Even twins have different characteristics.

**"What is the evidence that reincarnation occurs? We do not remember our previous births" Vijaya asked smiling.**

Very true. We do not remember what we were in our previous lives. We could have been humans. We could also have been animals, birds, or reptiles in some of our previous lives. The attitude and behaviour of some individuals endorses this, Grandpa said laughing.

You have seen that many children have inexplicable talents. There are definite examples of children who are mathematical prodigies from early life. Other children may be very talented in music from an early age. Another child may be an artist and begins drawing even from a very tender age. We have seen many children aged six and seven who could recite slokas from the *Bhagavad Gita* memorizing it very quickly. These inborn talents, as we call them, are really the carried over impressions and memory from our previous births.  The examples are numerous. Some children in the same family are born with a spiritual bent of mind, they learn the slokas and the mantras very easily whereas their brother may be a total atheist!  Haven't you  noticed this in society? Even twins do not share the same talents and character.

All these are indirect evidences that we carry the <u>tendencies</u> of our previous  Karmas which our rishis called '*Vasanas*' when we are born in this world. The subtle body or the Astral body which is the soul that   exists after death carries these <u>tendencies</u> (*Vasanas*) and <u>impressions</u> (*Samskaras*) into the next birth. A child with music in his veins from  childhood could be a reincarnation of a famous musician. A child artist could be a reincarnation of a famous artist of a past generation, and so on.

Research is also going on in scientific circles regarding reincarnation. There are many well documented instances where children have recalled their previous birth. Have you yourself not felt a déjà vu when you visit a place for the first time? It gives you an eerie feeling that you have been there before, even though you are sure that you haven't been there. It could be that it is from a lingering memory from one of your previous births.

Brian L Weiss, a psychiatrist in Miami, Florida in the United States has written his experiences regarding regression therapy under hypnosis in his book, *"Many Lives, Many Masters"* where he has described many cases where his patients recalled past lives under hypnosis. Read the book. It will be available in your library.

**"When does this cycle end?" Aditya wanted to know. "When will we stop reincarnating?"**

A good question, grandpa answered. Your cycle of *Samsara* will end when your *Sanchita Karmas* are all exhausted. Good *Karmas* lead to reincarnation in higher spheres of life. A virtuous person evolves to a higher state in his next life. This process goes on. As I said previously, it is till your 'bank balance' of *Karmas* becomes zero. That state is called *Moksha*. It is also called by other names like *Kaivalya*, *Mukti* or *Nirvana*. The soul which has exhausted all its *Sanchita Karmas* or *Vasanas* becomes one with the *Brahman*. It merges with the Universal Consciousness. This is the ultimate goal of man and every Hindu strives towards this goal.

**"Is killing another human being an evil *Karma*? If so, how can you justify a soldier who kills the enemy in war?" Aditya's questions were always logical.**

In describing *Karma Yoga*, I told you about selfless action. The <u>motive</u> or <u>intent</u> of the action is most important. A soldier who kills the enemy soldier in a war does it to defend his country and not for his selfish gains. Here the intent is safeguarding the interest of one's country. But if the same soldier kills anyone in times of peace, he is punished for his crime. So also, a surgeon amputates the leg of a patient to cure the patient and save his life. Cutting off a person's leg is a sinful act in any other circumstance. But when the surgeon does it with a good intent, it becomes a positive *Karma*. The surgeon may cause pain when he does this, but that is not done with ill will. You can quote numerous such examples. When your mom punished you for a misdeed, it was with a good intention. This is what *Bhagavan Sri Krishna* has said in the *Bhagavad Gita* where He encourages Arjuna to fight and annihilate his enemies as it was part of his *Dharma* to do so.

The motive and intent behind one's action justifies the action which apparently may look like a cruel one. It is ordained in all religions that you should not speak lies. So also, in Hinduism. But our scriptures clearly say that lies told to save a life or to save oneself in times of distress are not considered bad Karma.

Even good actions which are selfish or done with an intent for some gain for us are *Karmas* which bind us. For example, a person helping the poor for advertising himself as a philanthropist is not good *Karma*. Charity without expecting anything in return is only the true good *Karma*.

**"So, finally, grandpa, what can we do to avoid reincarnation and exhaust our Karmas?" Aditya asked.**

You may remember all that we discussed previously regarding the *Yamas* and *Niyamas* and the need to live an austere life of righteousness. This is called *Dharma*. The good qualities which we described previously like non-violence, non-thieving, austerity in thought, speech and action are ways to make our lives more positive and exhaust our Karmas. By living such a life, you perform good *Kriyamana Karmas* and ultimately exhaust your *Sanchita Karmas*. In addition, constantly fixing your mind on the *Brahman*, constant meditation, devotion, and total surrender to Him are the means for one to exhaust his *Karmas* and get relieved from the *Samsara* cycle of birth and reincarnation.

By doing selfless work, you do not get tied to *Karma* but become free of it. Each time a soul is reborn, it gets closer and closer to the *Brahman*. When one lives according to the natural laws proclaimed by Hinduism, one gets more and more perfect with each reincarnation. Ultimately the time comes when all your Karmas are exhausted, and you no longer need to be reborn. After many such soul purifying *Punarjanmams*, you become one with the Supreme. That is the state of *Moksha* or <u>Salvation</u> or <u>Liberation</u> of the soul.

Hence, you find that the ultimate goal of a Hindu's life to attain <u>Moksha</u> and get freedom from <u>Samsara</u> – the cycle of rebirths. A Hindu does not strive to reach 'heaven' by his good deeds. Heaven and hell are but temporary stopovers in the eternal journey of the soul towards salvation.

# 12. MYTHOLOGY

**"What is Hindu mythology? What are the important ones and why are they so numerous? What is the purpose of all these mythological stories? Frankly, some of them seem outright ridiculous!" the critical mind of Aditya was always skeptical.**

Grandpa laughed loudly. Well said, my boy. Mythologies are integral parts of all religions. They can be called *'concretized philosophy'*. For the common folk to understand them, the complicated abstract and ethical ideas of Hindu philosophy are made simple and presented as easily understandable stories for the common folk. The stories are both entertaining and thought-provoking. Often history and mythology are intermingled and many characters in history find a place in mythology too. Our myths have simple stories which instill truths and morals into the listeners. Children are always fascinated by stories, at the same time imbibe the subtle morals that are woven into these stories. Many of the mythological stories also offer solutions to the day to day problems of man. Many of the characters in the myths like Rama, Krishna, Sita, Lakshmana, Hanuman, Duryodhana, Ravana etc., teach us what is good and what is bad. The listeners tend to emulate the characteristics of the heroes and heroines in the myths and avoid those of the villainous characters.

We have already mentioned the *Itihasas* and the *Puranas*. These are all mythological legends rife with philosophical truths and assertions. The myths in these *Puranas* and *Itihasas* are the basis for the dances and dramas in Hindu culture like the *Bharata Natyam, Kathakali, Yaksha Gana,* and many other forms of theatre. Many dramas, serials and movies are staged based on these myths. Most of these myths narrate the conflict between good and evil and the victory of good over evil. Indirectly, this impresses upon the minds of children and the common folk that evil ways always end in anguish  and righteousness always wins in the end.

**"Grandpa, can you tell us in brief about some of the common mythological compositions that we should read?" Vijaya, the youngest, loved stories.**

The two great epics or *Itihasas* are *Ramayana* and *Mahabharata*. The *Puranas* are legends or myths based on various Gods, demigods or sages and translate the philosophical teachings of our *Vedas* and *Upanishads* into understandable legends and stories for the common man. There are 18 main Puranas and 18 more called *Upa Puranas* (<u>Secondary Puranas</u>).

***Ramayana***:      This is the most popular of the *Itihasas*. The literal word meaning of 'Ramayana' is 'journey of Rama'. It deals with the story of Rama the prince of Ayodhya, who has to leave his kingdom and be exiled to the forest for 14 years, to fulfill the promise given to his father. In the forest, his wife Sita is abducted by Ravana, the *asura* King of Sri Lanka. With the help of the monkey king Sugriva and his simian army, Rama builds a causeway across the ocean into Sri Lanka, defeats and kills Ravana and retrieves Sita. He returns to his kingdom and is coronated the king of Ayodhya.

The story describes Rama as the 'Uttama Purusha' (ideal man) whose virtues of honesty, straightforwardness, attachment to his wife, filial devotion and fraternal  affections endear him to the reader. Sita is the paragon of virtue, a devoted wife, and an obedient daughter in law.

***Mahabharata***:      This is the story of a war between two clans of cousins – the *Pandavas* five in number and the *Kauravas* numbering one hundred. It is the fight for the kingdom and speaks of the enmity between the cousins. The story culminates in an eighteen day war in which most of those on the *Kaurava* side are killed and *Pandavas* emerge victorious in the war and claim the kingdom. *Bhagavan Sri Krishna* plays a major role in this narrative. The *Mahabharata* is the epic in which the famous *Bhagavad Gita* is expounded by *Bhagavan Sri Krishna* who volunteers as the charioteer of Arjuna, the third of the *Pandavas*.

The epic is rife with many small parables which bring out the problems faced by us in day to day life and offer solutions on how to overcome them. So much so, the Mahabharata has come to be called the *'Fifth Veda'*.

The grand sire Bhishma who is the great-grandfather of both the *Pandavas* and *Kauravas* fights on the side of the *Kauravas* as he is tied down by loyalty to them. On his death bed, Bhishma advises the *Pandavas* on various aspects of politics, administration, financial management and many other practical matters which stands good even today.

The above two epics are a must-read for every Hindu and should be read by every child. The *Ramayana* and the *Mahabharata* have been abridged and written in English by  Sri C. Rajagopalachari (Rajaji) who was the first Indian Governor General of free India. It is a book for children to read. It is available in every library and bookstore.

***The Puranas***:    These are 18 in number and are based on the myths of the Gods. Each one deals with a particular God like *Vishnu Purana, Shiva Purana, Skanda Purana, Ganesha Purana, Garuda Purana* etc.

***Srimad Bhagavatham***:      It is also called the *Bhagavatha Purana* and deals with the *Avatars* (incarnations) of Maha Vishnu. The most important incarnation of *Maha Vishnu* is *Bhagavan Sri Krishna* and his legend is dealt with in detail in the *Srimad Bhagavatham*. In addition, the concept of

God and the creation of the Universe and the human race are all dealt with in this great work.

The story of *Bhagavatham* starts with the story of King Parikshith who is the grandson of Arjuna the third of the Pandavas. King Parikshith is the only surviving scion of the Pandava dynasty after the great *Mahabharata* war. He  is cursed by a sage while hunting in the forest that he will be fatally bitten by the serpent king *Takshaka* in seven days' time. Seeing his imminent death, the king renounces his kingdom and observes penance in the shores of the river Yamuna. During this seven day period, Sage Suka, who is the son of Sage Vyasa narrates the *Srimad Bhagavatham* to the king.

This is also a book which is read by every devout Hindu. It not only describes the mythology but is sprinkled with gems of truth and philosophy throughout the text. The concept of the *Brahman* is elaborated in the book. Exhaustive and abridged versions of this great work are available in most Indian languages. The English translation is available world over.

Children, you must familiarize yourself with these three major mythological works and understand the stories and the underlying philosophies. Reading these three books will give you a reasonable knowledge about Hinduism. There is a lot to be learnt from them. We will discuss more about some mythological stories as we go along.

**"What about the *Bhagavad Gita*, grandpa, you did not mention about it" Jaya was persistent.**

The *Bhagavad Gita*, as I already told you is part of the *Mahabharata* epic. It comprises 700 verses (couplets) and is divided into 18 chapters. It is the most important spiritual text of the Hindus and is a

**Sri Krishna advising the Bhagavad Gita to Arjuna**

text which guides man on living wisely and virtuously along the path of *Dharma*. It is *Bhagavan Sri Krishna's* advice to Arjuna in the battlefield. Just before commencement of the great *Mahabharata* war, Arjuna feels depressed on seeing his relatives arrayed against him in the battlefield and refuses to fight. *Bhagavan Sri Krishna* in his inimitable manner puts forth arguments on why Arjuna should fight and ultimately convinces him to take up arms against the foe.

It is really the advice to every one of us how to face the problems in our life, how to overcome sorrow, how to overcome stress, how to manage and harness our emotions and passions; in short it is a treatise on how to be successful in life. The *Bhagavad Gita* is a text that has found favor with the leaders of Management and is being taught in Management Schools in various parts of the world.

Various commentaries on the *Bhagavad Gita* are available and have been read widely and translated extensively. English versions abound in literature. Many have commented on the greatness of the Gita.

Swami Vivekananda has commented thus, *"The Bhagavad Geetha is a bouquet composed of the beautiful flowers of spiritual truths collected from the Upanishads"*

*"The Geetha is one of the clearest and most comprehensive summaries of the Perennial Philosophy ever to have been done. Hence its enduring value, not only for Indians, but for all mankind.... The Bhagavad Geeta is perhaps the most systematic spiritual statement of the Perennial Philosophy"*, said Aldous Huxley, the famous English novelist.

The *Bhagavad Gita* is a text that can be studied and practically applied in our lives by people of any religion. It is not a text confined to Hindus. Applying the principles and tenets expounded in the Gita makes a person be a better human. It helps a Christian become a better Christian and a Muslim, a better Muslim.

Children, you should read the *Bhagavad Gita* which is available in simple language and assimilate and abide by its teachings in your life. It will help you in your studies and increase your focus and power of concentration. 'The Bhagavad Gita for Children' written by the Late Swami Chinmayananda is available in all stores must be read by every child.

# 13. AVATARS

**"Grandpa, what is the meaning of *Avatar*? Can you tell us about the *avatars* of *Bhagavan Vishnu*?" as usual it was Aditya who initiated the discussion.**

One of the basic concepts in Hinduism is that God descends on earth when there is an upsurge of evil in the world, and the pious and the devoted are at peril. The word '*Avatar*' means '<u>descent</u>' in Sanskrit. God descends on earth in the form a human or any other being for upkeeping goodness on earth. *Avatars* are not described in the *Vedas* but are described in the *Puranas*. *Avatars* are the personification of the *Brahman* or the Supreme Consciousness. This is called the *Saguna Brahman* (<u>embodied</u> Brahman).

Generally, when we speak of an *Avatar*, we imply the *Avatars* of *Bhagavan Vishnu*. But you must understand that there are *Avatars* described in the *Puranas* for other deities also like Siva, Brahma, Ganesha, Devi etc. *Bhagavan Vishnu* has stated the he takes *Avatars* to establish and upkeep *Dharma* on earth. This is exemplified in the famous sloka in the Bhagavad Gita which runs thus:

यदा यदा हि धर्मस्य ग्लानिर्भवति भारत ।
अभ्युत्थानमधर्मस्य तदात्मानं सृजाम्यहम् ॥४-७॥

परित्राणाय साधूनां विनाशाय च दुष्कृताम् ।
धर्मसंस्थापनार्थाय सम्भवामि युगे युगे ॥४-८॥

*Yada yada hi dharmasya glanirbhavati bharata |*
*Abhythanamadharmasya tadatmanam srijamyaham ||*

*Paritranaya sadhunam vinashaya cha dushkritam |*
*Dharmasamsthapanarthaya sambhavami yuge yuge ||*

It means, *"Whenever there is decay of righteousness, O Bharata,*

*And there is increase of unrighteousness, then I Myself come forth ; (4:7)*

*For the protection of the good and for the destruction of evildoers,*

*For the sake of firmly establishing righteousness, I am born from age to age".(4:8)*

**"We have heard that there are ten *Avatars* of Bhagavan Vishnu. Is that all? Are there anymore?" Jaya wanted to know.**

The ten *Avatars* of Bhagavan Vishnu described are the most important ones. But in total there are twenty-two *Avatars* of *Bhagavan Vishnu*. The word '*Vishnu*' itself means 'All-Pervasive'. It is said that there are still many more which are described in the *Puranas*. I will give you the names of the 22 *Avatars* first and then elaborate the ten important ones later. These 22 *Avatars* are described in the *Srimad Bhagavatham*.

The twenty -two *Avatars* described are:

| | |
|---|---|
| Sanal Kumaras | Narasimha Avatar (man-lion) |
| Varaha Avatar (Boar) | Dhanvantari Avatar |
| Narada Avatar | Vamana Avatar |
| Nara Narayana Avatar | Parasurama Avatar |
| Kapila Avatar | Veda Vyasa Avatar |
| Dattatreya Rishi | Rama Avatar |
| Yajna Avatar | Balarama Avatar |
| Rishabha Avatar | Krishna Avatar |
| Prithu Avatar | Matsya Avatar (Giant Fish |
| Kurma Avatar (Tortoise) | Buddha Avatar |
| | Kalki Avatar |
| Mohini Avatar | |

The *Avatars* incarnate whenever there is a crisis in the universe and evil outweighs goodness. *Bhagavan Vishnu* descends on earth to set things right. Some of these *Avatars* are said to be '*Amsha*'

*Avatars* (*Amsha* = <u>partial</u>) where they last for only a short while on earth and return when the task in completed. *Sri Rama* and *Sri Krishna* lived a full life on earth from birth to death. *Sri Krishna* was the only *Avatar* which represented the Supreme Consciousness in toto and hence he is the only deity considered as a *Poorna Avatar. (Poorna* = <u>complete</u>). Even *Sri Rama* was only a *Ardha* (<u>half</u>) *Avatar.* Even though the ten important Avatars are described in the *Srimad Bhagavatham* in order from the *Matsya Avatar* to *Kalki Avatar* in an order according to the evolutionary theory, these really occurred in a different sequence. But for clarity's sake, I will tell you in brief the ten essential *Avatars* of *Bhagavan Vishnu.*

1) ***Matsya Avatar.*** There are two occasions when *Bhagavan Maha Vishnu* assumed the *Avatar* of a gigantic fish. The first was to retrieve the *Vedas* from an *asura* called *Hayagriva* who stole the *Vedas* from *Brahma.* The second occasion was to save King *Satyavrata* and the *Rishis* from a disastrous deluge where the king was told to carry all living beings and plant seeds in a gargantuan boat and was guided to safety by the gigantic fish. This story which was written in Hindu *Puranas* centuries ago bears close resemblance to the description of the great flood and the story of Noah's Ark in Christianity.

2) ***Kurma Avatar.*** When the *devas* and *asuras* churned the milky ocean to obtain the *Amrita* or <u>nectar</u> which sustained life, the mountain named *Mandara* was used as the churning-stick and the snake *Vasuki* as the rope. *Bhagavan Vishnu* assumed the *Kurma Avatar* (<u>tortoise</u>) to support the

mountain on its back to prevent it from sinking into the milky ocean.

3) ***Varaha Avatar***.   *Bhagavan Vishnu* assumed the form of a *Varaham* (<u>boar</u>) to rescue the earth from sinking into the sea. The earth was snatched by an asura named *Hiranyaksha* who was slayed by the *Varaham*, and the earth retrieved and placed in its appropriate position in the universe.

4) ***Narasimha Avatar***.   *Bhagavan Vishnu* assumed the form of a *Narasimha* (<u>half-man half-lion</u>; *Nara* = <u>man</u> ; *Simha* = <u>lion</u>) to save his devotee, the young boy Prahlada from his tyrannical father, the asura King *Hiranyaksha*.

5) ***Vamana Avatar***.   When the asura king *Mahabali* became arrogant and wanted to usurp *Indra's* throne in heaven. *Bhagavan Vishnu* assumed the *Avatar* of a young *Brahmachari, Vamana* and exiled *Mahabali* to the netherworld called *Suthala* (not *Paathala*) where he was permitted to rule as king. Mahabali, who was  a straightforward king and a devotee of *Bhagavan Vishnu*  had to be banished only because he had turned arrogant. *Bhagavan Vishnu* wanted to quell his arrogance and humble him.

6) ***Parasurama Avatar***.   The *Kshatriya* kings of the time became arrogant and unruly and killed the sage *Jamadagni*. His son sage *Parasurama*, the axe-wielding brahmin was *Bhagavan Vishnu's* next *Avatar* who annihilated the *Kshatriya* kings.

7) ***Rama Avatar***.     *Sri Rama*, the hero of the epic *Ramayana* was the prince of *Ayodhya* whose wife Sita was abducted by the emperor of Sri Lanka, *Ravana*. *Sri Rama* with the help of the monkey-king Sugriva and his simian army, slayed *Ravana,* and retrieved *Sita*.

8) ***Balarama Avatar***.    *Balarama* was the elder brother of *Sri Krishna*. Though he is mentioned as one of the ten *Avatars*, he was described as the incarnation of *Ananta*, the thousand headed snake on which *Bhagavan Vishnu* rests.

9) ***Krishna Avatar***.    *Sri Krishna Avatar* is a *Poorna Avatar* where he lived the life of a human being and set an example to establish *Dharma* in society. He is famed by the rendition of the *Bhagavad Gita* to Arjuna in the battlefield prior to the *Mahabharata* war.

10) ***Kalki Avatar***.     This is a future *Avatar* which is predicted to occur at the end of *Kali yuga* (present age). *Bhagavan Vishnu* will incarnate in future to fight evil and establish *Dharma* in the universe.

A word about the ten Avatars. Some consider *Gautama Buddha* as an *Avatar* instead of *Balarama*. It makes no difference. I would suggest that you read a summarised version of the *Srimad Bhagavatham* to understand these *Avatars* in detail. Later on, you can read the whole *Srimad Bhagavatham* in original which is available in many Indian languages and in English. It usually runs into many volumes as there are elaborate commentaries of the original Sanskrit text.

**"Grandpa, you said that other Gods also have *Avatars*. Can you tell us about them too?" Vijaya had her doubts.**

Yes, *Avatars* have also been described for *Bhagavan Siva*. I will briefly name some of them here. Nineteen Avatars of Siva are described in *Siva Purana*. Some of them are *Pipalaada, Nandi, Veerbhadra, Sharabha, Ashwatthama, Bhairava, Durvasa, Grihapathi, Vrishabha,* and *Hanuman,* are some of the *Avatars* of *Bhagavan Siva*.

*Valmiki, Sukra, Brihaspati, Kashyapa, Vyasa, Khat* and *Kalidasa* are mentioned as *Avatars* of *Bhagavan Brahma*.

*Kaali, Sati, Parvathi, Durga, Annapurna, Kaushiki,* and *Bhramari* are described as some of the *Avatars* of *Devi* or *Shakthi*.

*Mohotkata, Mayūreśvara, Gajanana* and *Dhumraketu* are the four *Avatars* of *Bhagavan Ganesha* described in *Ganesha Purana*. Few more are described.

**"How does *Bhagavan Vishnu* or any other God come to my help when I am in a crisis or dire need of help? Will an *Avatar* come and  help me?" Vijaya in all her innocence wanted to know.**

Grandpa laughed aloud. That is a good question. Sure dear, He will come to your help if you are devoted to Him wholeheartedly. In the modern day you cannot expect *Bhagavan Vishnu* or any other God like *Ganesha, Siva,* or *Devi* to come in person to help you in their Divine form. Have you read my short stories in the two books which I wrote for you and presented to you. The books *"Tell Me a Story, Grandpa"* and *"Grandpa, Tell Me More Stories"*?

[The children nod in acquiescence].

In that there are many stories where God does help people in distress. He does it  by sending someone to help you when you need it. Or God gives you the intellect to solve a problem or overcome a difficulty. Occasionally, when you are struggling to find a solution to a problem in life, suddenly you find that an easy and practical solution pops into your head. Where do you think this thought comes from? It is the Universal Consciousness about which we have been talking all this time which gives you that solution. Have you not faced a situation, where you have been wrestling with a problem, not knowing what to do and suddenly, a new idea snaps in your head? Who put the idea in your head? When you make an erroneous decision, or if you do something which is wrong and against the rules, something inside you, an inner voice,  keeps nagging you that what you are doing is 'not right'. Have you not felt these many times before?  You may call this "intuition"  or "hunch" and many a time you may be correct. Yes, this is God telling you from inside that you are making a mistake.

There was a devastating flood in the state of Kerala in India in 2018, the likes of which had not been seen in recent years. The government resources were stretched to the limit and the government could not access the remote areas of the state where people were stranded in homes surrounded by ten to fifteen feet of water. Many people were stranded on the roofs and terraces of their homes. And then suddenly the whole fishermen community in the shores of Kerala sprang into action. They commandeered all their boats and soon the roads in Kerala were teeming with boats traveling in all directions and gathering stranded residents from the remotest inaccessible areas and guiding them to the relief camps and areas of safety thus averting a major disaster. Hundreds of lives were saved. Who do you think put this idea into the heads of the fishermen to perform this selfless service?

In the same state of Kerala, in Calicut city in August 2020, there was an air crash in the international airport in the middle of the night when it was raining heavily. The aircraft hit the runway, skidded off the tarmac on to the road in the nearby village and broke into two. Immediately, from all over, residents of the village converged on the site of the mishap in large numbers and despite the pouring rain, helped to save many of the victims. Who do you think asked the residents in that village to help the air crash victims?

When you were suddenly ill at school, your teacher immediately gave you first aid, didn't she? God was helping you through your teacher. When a dog chased you on the road the other day, did not a stranger come to your help and chase it away and carry you to safety? God was helping you through that stranger. All this is because, you think of God daily, do your *japa* and *bhajans* and follow the morals and principles which we have so far discussed.

So don't expect God to come to you in his resplendent four-armed form with the Conch, Sudarshana chakra etc., he will reach you through someone or through a sensible thought or an idea which suddenly appears in your mind. He is always there to help you in numerous ways. Unfortunately, many people do not realize this aspect of the Divine.

That is how God helps us solve our problems and face the crises in our lives. The only requisite for this is your unflinching devotion and surrender to Him.

# 14. VARNA ASHRAMA & CASTE SYSTEM

**"What are the *Varna Ashramas* or the *Varna Dharma*?"** Aditya was the first to pose the question as a continuation of our previous discussion on various *Dharmas*. **"You said you'd discuss it later."**

We will discuss in brief the background regarding the '*Varna Ashramas*' or *Varna* System of Hinduism. According to the *Vedas*, society was divided into four classes. These groups or classes was called the '*Varnas*'. They were the *Brahmanas, Kshatriyas, Vaisyas,* and the *Sudras*. The literal word meaning of the word '*Varna*' is '<u>color</u>'. This, however, has nothing to do with the complexion of the individuals. This social structure was based on the individual's occupation, duty, and other characteristics. <u>*It was not based on birth or heredity of the individual*</u>. But as is seen today, in ancient times also, occupations often ran in families, a priest's son continued the same profession, or a carpenter's son acquired the skills as a carpenter from his father and a businessman's son continued his father's business. As this continued, this system tended to become a hereditary classification rather than a  purely occupational one. The word '*Jathi*' (<u>caste</u>) was affixed to these divisions. The Europeans who came to India named this as the '*Caste system*' and today it has acquired the notoriety that comes with the name.

The reference to this four-class system is mentioned in the *Purusha Sooktham* which is the chant in the *Rig Veda* about the *Brahman*. All the four *Varnas* have arisen from the *Brahman*, says the *Purusha Sooktham*. The *Brahman* is personified as '*Purusha*' (<u>person</u>). The *Brahmanas* were said to arise from the head of the Brahman. The *Kshatriyas* arose from the arms, the *Vaisyas* from the thighs and the *Sudras* from the feet. This only allegorically means that the *Brahmanas* used their *head* (<u>intellectuals</u> ; thinkers), the *Kshatriyas* their *arms* (power ; strength -the <u>warriors</u>), the *Vaisyas legs*  (travel, - <u>businessmen</u>) and the *Sudras feet* (work - <u>service</u>) in their professions.  It was more of a vocational segregation rather than a genealogical designation.

The **Brahmanas** (<u>Brahmins</u>) often worked as priests, teachers, *Gurus* and *Acharyas* and were often employed in the courts of the kings as advisors to the king and royalty. They were in professions like teaching, the spread of knowledge, and worship. They practiced austerity and had high moral and ethical standards. They possessed wisdom and were called upon to perform the *Yajnas* and the rituals for the other classes and for the betterment of the community. They were given the task of promoting and teaching the *Vedas* to their protégés.

The *Brahmanas* are those who exhibit the _mode of Goodness_. In the modern day, the *Brahmana* community can be equated with the teachers, scientists, advisors to the government, the decision-makers in a corporate world like the CXOs etc. they represent the intellectuals in society.

The **Kshatriyas** (warriors ; administrators) had qualities of strength, courage, valor, leadership qualities  and resources at their command. They obtained advice from the *Brahmanas*. The *Kshatriyas* are with the preponderant _mode of Passion_ intermingled with the modes of goodness. They were in administration and management and in the olden days were kings and warriors. Most of the kings were *Kshatriyas*. They involved themselves in the welfare of the people and the defense of the country. They were the law makers and law enforcers. In today's world we can equate them with the politicians, the army personnel, the judiciary, the police, and the civil administrators.

The **Vaisyas** (businessmen) were the 'wealth-generators' or the business class. Their main vocation was agriculture, trade, and cattle rearing. They provided the provisions needed for the other three classes. They generated wealth for the country and the king. In today's circumstances, they can be compared to the businessmen and the corporate sector. They too combined the _modes of passion and goodness_, but to a variable extent.

The **Sudras** (workers) were the working class who served the other classes. They were the workers, the artisans, the carpenters, the masons, the farmers, the laborers and so on. The *Sudras* predominantly exhibited the <u>*mode of Ignorance*</u>. Hence, they were more skilful than wise. They form the working or labour class and the skilled workers in society. In today's world they can be compared to the service sector and the workforce in the country who carry out the orders of various sections in society like the clerks in the government service, the laborers, the construction workers, the plumbers, the farmers, the service providers etc.

Thus, these divisions were based on the intellectual capacity and vocations of the individual and **_not_** <u>on their birth</u>, but as is known, many vocations tend to run in families and thus in a way the *Varna* system tended to become family based.

In the *Bhagavad Gita* Sri Krishna categorically says regarding the *Varna* system,

चातुर्वर्ण्यं मया सृष्टं गुणकर्मविभागशः ।
तस्य कर्तारमपि मां विद्ध्य कर्तारमव्ययम् ॥ 4 - 13 ॥

*Chātur-varṇyaṁ mayā sṛṣṭaṁ*

*Guṇa-karma-vibhāgaśaḥ*

*Tasya kartāram api māṁ*

*Viddhy akartāram avyayam . (BG 4.13)*

It means, *"The four-fold system of Varnas was created by Me according to divisions of Guna (<u>quality</u>) and karma (<u>work</u>). Although I am the creator of this system, you should know that I am* *immutable and akarta (<u>the non-doer</u>), and I am NOT the direct instigator."*

This clearly shows that it was the <u>quality</u> (*Guna*) and <u>work</u> (*Karma*) which delineated one's *Varna* (<u>caste</u>) and not birth or lineage. The word '*caste*' was introduced by the Europeans. The word is derived from the Portuguese word '*casta*' meaning "<u>race</u>, <u>lineage</u> *or* <u>breed</u>". Hence, the word '*caste*' is not an Indian word.

It was during the Mughal era in India that the caste system came into prominence. This was followed by the British era when they appointed Christians and Hindus belonging to the upper castes to their administrative service. The modern concept of the caste system based on *birth* is the due to the malfeasance of the Mughals and the British. The British incorporated the caste system into their governance. When India gained independence and formulated its own policies the "*reservation*" system for castes was introduced for government employment and in higher education with a view to the uplifting of the lower classes. It was done with the good intention of uplifting the lower castes. But now it has turned into a Frankenstein monster promoting caste politics, caste vote banks, caste-based violence, leading to more discrimination.

In ancient India, the *Varna* system was an exemplary hierarchical socio-economic governance structure and was the backbone of society. Furthermore, these classes were not rigid, water-tight compartments. One could shift from one class to another depending on one's character, conduct and vocation. Indian *Vedic* history is thus rife with examples of individuals changing from one class (*Varna*) to another due to changes in their character and occupation. Ratnakaran, who was a hunter (*Sudra*) with tireless effort, spiritually transformed himself into Sage *Valmiki* (*Brahmana*) who later wrote the great epic the *Ramayana*. Sage Vyasa (*Brahmana*) was born to a fisherwoman (*Sudra*). Sage *Parasurama* (*Brahmana*) and *Guru Dronacharya* (*Brahmana*) became warriors (*Kshatriya*) due to their nature and occupation. Sage *Viswamithra* (*Brahmana*) was originally a *Kshatriya* king and by virtue of his penance and learning became a *Brahmana.* There are also instances where *Brahmanas* and *Kshatriyas* owing to their impropriety and evil ways led the life of *Sudras*.

Thus, the interchange of *Varnas* was **not** impossible nor banned in *Vedic* society. All the sages are held in high esteem because of their *mode of goodness* and their teachings to society. Their previous *Varna Ashrama* is not held against them. This in reality is the *Varna* system propounded in the *Vedas*. Unfortunately, it has been misunderstood by the present generation and misconstrued by our administrators.

Remember that in society all the four Varnas should live in harmony, and no one is indispensable. A carpenter, plumber or barber is equally important as a teacher, a doctor, a politician or an engineer. Each one is proficient in his own way and his services are equally important to society.

Also, *untouchability* was not a part of the Varna classification. The only requisite was 'cleanliness' (*Soucham*) which was occasionally lacking in the lower classes. This later formed the basis of *untouchability* and was taken advantage of by the political bosses. If you read the *'Rudram'* which is a chant from the *Yajur Veda* where the God Siva is extolled, you will find phrases like *'Thou art the master and the servant, the potter, the carpenter, the maker of chariots, the blacksmith, the hunter, the fisherman etc'*. This only goes to show that God was recognized as present in every human being irrespective of his status in society.

I hope I have made my point of view clear to you.

**"You mentioned the words *'Guna'* and *'Karma'* when you were quoting *Sri Krishna* from the *Bhagavad Gita*; we understand what *Karma* is. Tell us what Guna is. Can you elaborate this further?" Jaya wanted to know.**

The word meaning of *'Guna'* is 'quality', 'attribute' or 'property'. There are three gunas which are called *'Triguna' (Tri* = three*)*. These properties or qualities are present in everything in nature in the living and the non-living inanimate objects.

These are called **Sattva** (goodness, calmness,), **Rajas** (passion, activity) and **Tamas** (ignorance, inertia, laziness). According to Hindu philosophy, all three are present in all beings and things in the world – both animate and inanimate. *But* _the proportion of each of these Gunas may differ_. When the word '*Guna*' is used to describe a human being, it means <u>character</u>, <u>behaviour</u>, or his <u>psychological makeup</u>. All three Gunas are present in a person in different proportions. A person can have a predominant *Sattvic, Rajasic* or *Tamasic Guna*.

- *Sattva Guna* is one of positivity, calmness, purity, virtue, balance of mind, knowledge, and goodness.

- *Rajas* is a *Guna* of passion, restlessness, activity, egoism, and self-centredness.

- *Tamas* is a *Guna* of ignorance, inertia , negativity, laziness, imbalance, impurity, violence, and inactivity.

In every person, these *Gunas* are present in various proportions. A *Sattvic* person is one who exhibits good qualities, calmness, knowledge, and virtues like honesty, sincerity, non-violence etc. *Sattvic* quality is predominant in *Brahmanas* (Brahmins). That does not mean that he has no *Rajasic* or *Tamasic* qualities, though the proportion of these are minimal and overshadowed by the positive *Sattvic* qualities.

A *Rajasic* person predominantly exhibits more of passion, courage, and activity. He is egoistic, restless, and a go-getter. This quality is seen more in the *Kshatriyas* and *Vaisyas*. However, they do exhibit *Sattvic* and *Tamasic* qualities also to a small extent.

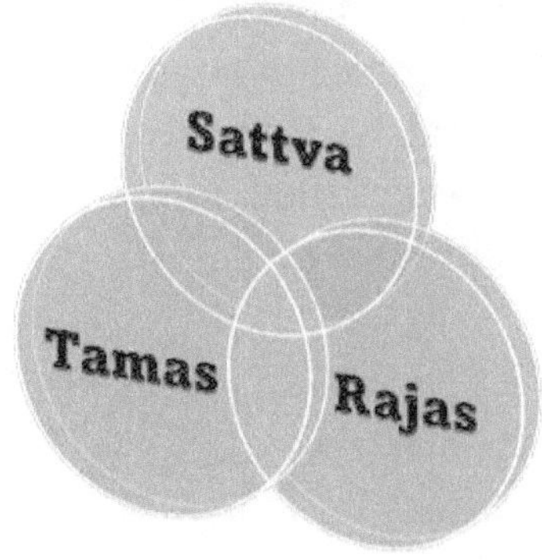


A *Tamasic* person exhibits more of laziness, apathy, depression, ignorance, lethargy, negative tendencies, and guilt. *Sudras* are said to have more of this *Guna*. But they too exhibit some amount of *Sattvic* and *Rajasic* qualities. The mode of goodness is not entirely absent in them.

These three *Gunas* can also be seen in everything in the world. Think of the food you eat – it can be *Sattvic*, *Rajasic* or *Tamasic*. (We will discuss this on another occasion when we discuss '*Diet in Hinduism*'). It can be seen in animals and birds too. Once you begin analyzing the characteristic of each animal and bird, you can classify them into these three types. Think of a cow and a lion and tell me which would be called *Sattvic* and which *Rajasic*?

You can extrapolate these *Gunas* to other areas like the Movies you watch, the Music you listen to, the friends you keep company with, the places you visit or the websites you browse on your computer. All these can be *Sattvic*, *Rajasic* or *Tamasic*. Try to do this yourself and analyze the various things in life. You will be surprised by the result! Take this as a simple exercise for yourself and try to classify the things around you into these three subgroups. Even inanimate objects like metals – gold, silver, iron and tin can correspondingly be classified. Plants and trees too can be similarly classified.

# 15. DIET AND VEGETARIANISM

**"Grandpa, are all Hindus vegetarians? Is there any advantage of being a vegetarian in the spiritual journey?" Aditya was the first to broach a new topic.**

The spiritual benefits of a vegetarian diet have been well brought out in the Hindu scriptures. Many of the scriptures extol the virtues of vegetarianism and decry meat-eating. Contrary to western beliefs all Hindus are not vegetarians. The number of Hindus who are vegetarians varies region wise. However, those who are non-vegetarian consume meat and fish only on occasions or on certain days. Their staple diet is vegetarian composed of rice, wheat, *dal* (lentils), beans, vegetables, and fruits. By far, the Brahmins are vegetarians whereas the other classes are not necessarily vegetarians. Similarly, the priests and sannyasis are strict vegetarians.

In a country like India where nearly 80% are Hindus, only about 30% are vegetarian by conservative estimates. A country like India, however, is one with the maximum number of vegetarians. Western countries are now increasingly adopting vegetarianism both for health and spiritual purposes. An extreme group of vegetarians call themselves 'Vegans' as they do not consume any animal products including milk, cheese, butter, or curd.

The diet of the Hindu as per the scriptures is mainly vegetarian. This is because of the concept of *Ahimsa* (<u>non-violence</u>) and compassion towards all living beings which prohibits the killing of animals or birds for food. Thus, the contemporary Hindu has a predominantly vegetarian diet. The main diet is lacto-vegetarian including a vegetarian diet with milk and its derivatives. Eggs, meat, and fish are not eaten. Some pious, conservative Hindus who are strict vegetarians also shun foods like garlic, onion, cinnamon, and seasonings which are considered the main ingredients of non-vegetarian food.

Animal sacrifice has been known in Hinduism from ancient times when the sacrificial animals were consumed after offering them the to the Gods. Many of our *Puranas* bear testimony to this. These practices have almost disappeared in the modern Hindu society. This endorses the fact that many of the practices mentioned in the ancient *Smritis* change with time. Anecdotal narrations are available in the *Puranas* and *Itihasas* that the ancient Hindus consumed meat. But in the same breath, the concept of *Ahimsa* is upheld and the need to avoid meat is mentioned. *Kshatriyas* and *Vaisyas* are permitted to consume meat as their professions needed them to be non-vegetarians. They needed the energy and the strength for their pursuits.

**"Grandpa, you said that food can be *Saatvic*, *Rajasic* or *Tamasic*. Will you elaborate on this?" Jaya wanted to know.**

Yes, let me tell you about the three subdivisions of food itself into *Sattvic*, *Rajasic* and *Tamasic*.

Going back into our ancient scriptures, the role of food in the behaviour of humans has been mentioned in the Hindu texts. The *Bhagavad Gita* has classified mankind into three types based on their behaviour, the *Sattvic*, *Rajasic* and the *Tamasic*. These have already been discussed.

The food eaten by the *Sattvic* persons promotes good qualities like, empathy, contentment, righteousness, cleanliness, and a good nature in them. Their food is clean, wholesome and freshly cooked. Foods like fruits, vegetables, milk, nuts etc., are said to be *Sattvic* in nature and the consumer's behaviour is conditioned by these foods. Chapter 17 of the *Bhagavad Gita* discusses this in great detail.

Foods having a strong flavour, pungent taste, bitter, sour, highly spicy, and hot, are called *Rajasic* foods and inculcate *Rajasic* behaviour in the eater like, passion, aggressiveness, restlessness, anger and over activity. These foods sometimes create uncontrollable energies in them leading to impetuousness and violence.

Foods cooked more than three hours previously (stale food), spoilt food, food with pungent or foul smell, foods left overnight, fermented foods (like liquors) are all said to be *Tamasic*. A person of *Tamasic* character does not have the intellectual capacity to discriminate between right and wrong. Their behaviour is not cultured or may even be barbaric. They are given to bouts of anger, rage, jealousy, violence and such vile and negative emotions. Idleness, dullness, recklessness etc., are their characteristics.

Thus, we see that even more than 5000 years ago, when the *Bhagavad Gita* was written, it was known that food alters human behaviour and that one's attitude and actions are to a great extent conditioned by the food that one consumes.

**"As a doctor, Grandpa, do you have anything to say about effect of vegetarianism on health?" Jaya wanted an answer.**

Good question. Yes, vegetarianism is a definitely a healthy lifestyle and many diseases which you see with non-vegetarianism are avoidable by being vegetarian. Diseases of the gut like Colon cancer and Diverticulosis are less common in vegetarians. Heart disease is also less in vegetarians than in non-vegetarians. Lifestyle diseases are also less in them.

The human brain is one of the most complex structures in the whole universe. The human gut is populated with trillions of microbes which are useful and live a symbiotic existence within us. These are collectively called the *"Microbiota"*. These microbes are nourished by the food we consume while they in turn help us in a variety of ways including helping optimal brain development and functioning. These microbes produce numerous neurochemicals on which we are dependent. They help in food processing, digestion of complex indigestible polysaccharides, synthesis of vitamins and inhibition of pathogens. Many complex carbohydrates like dietary fibers can be digested and then fermented by the microbes in the large intestines into short chain fatty acids which have significant actions on the brain.

It is proposed that the total weight of the microbes in the human gut is almost equal to the weight of the human brain. Normally the colonization of the gut occurs during and after childbirth. These microbes play an important role in brain development. The microbial composition of the gut in the child is determined by many factors like antibiotic use, environmental factors and maternal microbiota. By the age of two to five, the child's microbiota resembles that of the adult.

Some of the chemicals produced by these microbes which are absorbed by the gut, play an important role in memory and learning. Dementia in the elderly also may be due to the changing microbiota in them. Many studies have shown that the microbes within the gut can interact with the human brain and alter the behaviour of the patient. It has been found that the gut microbiota in children with Autism Spectrum Disorders is different from that of a normal child. A "Western Diet" high in carbohydrates and processed food may have a great impact on gut microbiota. A pure vegetarian diet has been found to be associated with a reduction in potentially pathological microbes in the gut whereas a high fat diet may change the microbes that could lead to increased risk of inflammation.

It is now well known that organisms in the gut can alter human behaviour. Some foods when ingested produce health benefits in psychiatric disorders. These are foods containing live strains of gut friendly bacteria. Fiber rich food also promote the growth of useful bacteria in the gut.

So, children, you can see that food can also alter human behaviour according to modern science. This was proposed by our sages millennia ago by careful observation and analysis of human behaviour and its relation to food.

From this itself you can deduce that for a person who is spiritually inclined, the vegetarian diet is the ideal as it tends to render his behaviour and character more *Sattvic* and thus promote the good qualities and values that have been laid down by the *Vedas*.

**"Wow, Grandpa, you have blended science and Hinduism and given us a rational explanation of vegetarianism in Hinduism. That was quite a nice information for us.**

**"What is the role of fasting in Hinduism?" Vijaya's innocent question brought a smile to my lips. "Grandma fasts on many days a month quoting various auspicious days and occasions as a reason."**

Fasting is not confined to Hinduism. Christians fast during the period they call as *'Lent'* and Muslims fast during daytime in the month of *Ramadan*. Fasting in Hinduism (and in other religions too) is an act of spiritualism to purify both the mind and the body, thus achieving the blessings of the Divine. Fasting essentially means giving up food / drink for a variable period of time.

Fasting has both spiritual and physical benefits and is a form of austerity in Hinduism. Fasting gives rest to the digestive system, helps to reduce weight, helps to decrease toxins and eliminate them from the body, reduce fat and cholesterol and improve the overall health of the individual. It is also helpful for diabetic patients as it helps to improve insulin sensitivity and improves the control of blood sugar. However, the diabetic should be careful regarding his medications when he is fasting. It also helps to improve the mental health of a person by improving self-esteem, self-discipline, and self-confidence. It imposes restrictions on the mind and the body.

On the spiritual front fasting is a sacrifice to the Divine or God. By giving up food we express our devotion to God and symbolically offer our submission to Him. Fasting fosters a bond between man and God. Fasting helps to control one's mind, one's senses and emotions thereby improves the character and conduct of man. It  is also undertaken as a part of many religious rituals and festivals. Fasting prior to the <u>death anniversary</u> of our ancestors (*Shraddha*), fasting on *Siva Ratri*, *Navaratri*, and *Janmashtami* is undertaken. Fasting is a sort of *tapas* (<u>penance</u>) in Hinduism. It  is also undertaken as a form of penance or expiation for any sins which may have been committed (*Prayaschittam*= atonement).

In Ayurveda, it is stated, "लंघनं परम् औषधं" (***Langhanam parama aushadham***) which means '*fasting is the best medicine*'. Fasting which is prescribed in Hinduism is also of various types. Not consuming food and water for a specific period or on certain auspicious days, fasting for part of the day for a fixed number of days, partaking of only one particular type of vegetarian food for a set number of days or eating only one meal a day which is called '*Orikkal*' (once) are some of the methods of fasting in Hinduism.  Some fast on specific days in a month. The eleventh day after the new moon (*Amavasya*) or full moon (*Poornima*) is called '*Ekadashi*'. Many Hindus fast on that day. Others may fast on specific weekdays. Fasting on Mondays is followed by the devotees of *Siva*, Thursdays by devotees of *Vishnu* and Saturdays for *Sastha*. Some individuals undertake fasting by avoiding rice and wheat on these days. They consume only milk and fruits on that day.

Certain rituals demand that the couple who are performing them fast till the whole ritual is over. This is true for the marriage rituals, certain *Yajnas* and *Poojas*. Fasting is prescribed in the *Srimad Bhagavatham which says, "If, because of disease or old age one is not able to perform his prescribed duties for advancement in spiritual consciousness or study of the Vedas, he should practice fasting, not taking any food.*" (7-12:23).

Breaking the fast is also done in different ways. Holy water consecrated after a pooja with *Tulsi* (holy

Basil) leaves are taken to break the fast. Others offer milk or rice pudding (*Paayasam*) to the deity as *Nivedyam* and take it as *Prasadam* to break the fast. Some go to the temple and take a sip of holy water (*Theertham*) offered by the priest to break the fast. Following this light food is taken. Non vegetarian food is never taken during or after the fasting.

# 16. ARTS AND HINDUISM

**"Grandpa, what do you have to say about the arts in Hinduism?" Aditya was the first to ask a question.**

A very good question, dear, began Grandpa. Hinduism describes 64 arts. The word *'Kalà'* is used in Hinduism to mean the performing arts. I will mention a few of them here. May be, we can discuss a few of them briefly. One must understand that in Hinduism, Art and Culture are closely interwoven and art is also a part of the spiritual experience.

Let us name some of these arts. In the ancient texts, sage *Vatsyayana* has listed the 64 arts which are said to make a person perfect. Some of the names of these arts in Sanskrit are *Geeta* (music), *Natya* (dancing), *Vadya* (playing musical instruments), *Alekhya* (painting), *Suchi Vaya karma* (needlework), *Vastu vidya* (sculpturing), *Kesha Marjana kausala* (hair dressing), *Samvachya* (art of conversation), *Pustaka vachana* (art of reciting books from memory), and so on.

Let us see a few of them. The dances *Bharata Natyam* (Tamil Nadu), *Kuchi pudi* (Andhra Pradesh), *Mohiniyattam* and *Kathakali* (Kerala), *Yaksha Gana* (Karnataka), and *Kathak* (North India) are all art forms based on Hindu traditions from different regions of India. According to Hinduism, the whole universe is composed of vibrations with its innate rhythm which is called '*Laya*'. Art is considered to be divine in Hinduism and there is a rhythm to everything in the universe which also includes the biological rhythm of the human body. Dance and music are but expressions of that rhythm used to attain spiritual bliss. Most of the dance forms in Hinduism have the *Puranas* or *Itihasas* as the central theme. *Bhagavan Siva* is called '*Nataraja*' the 'king of dance'. Dance evokes a spiritual feeling in both the performer and the perceiver.

As an example, we will see a few facts regarding *Bharata Natyam* which is the most popular dance form in Hinduism. It is a very complex dance form steeped in Hindu culture and religious symbolism. The artist has to learn how to express emotions in his/her face during the dance. There are nine emotions described and are called the *Navarasas* (nine emotions). They are *Sringaram* (love), *Haasyam* (comedy), *Raudram* (rage), *Kaarunyam* (compassion), *Bibhatsam* (aversion), *Bhayanakam* (horror), *Veeram* (courage), *Adhbhutam* (wonder) and *Shantam* (peace). The artist also uses various *Mudras* (hand gestures) and symbols with his/her hands to convey different meanings. The artist develops the ability to express the nine different emotions in his/her face during the dance. The name *Bharata Natyam* comes from the name of sage

*Bharata* who wrote the *Natya Sastra* (<u>science of dance</u>) from which *Bharata Natyam* originated.

**"Is architecture also part art in Hinduism?" Jaya asked.**

The architecture seen in the temples, the beautiful sculptures and the ornamental pillars in the temples are works of art that bear testimony to the rich heritage of Hinduism. *Bhagavan Nataraja* in Hinduism is the deity who represents the cosmic dance. Everything in the universe from the macro like the stars and the planets to the micro like the electrons in the atom are in a constant state of flux which is the cosmic dance that has been envisioned by our sages.

The cosmic dance of *Bhagavan Siva* is symbolized in the *Nataraja* idol. This cosmic dance represents the cycle of creation and destruction. The small <u>drum</u> called *Damaru* in his right upper hand represents sound vibrations which is the origin of creation and the fire in his left upper hand represents destruction or dissolution. He dances on

**Nataraja**

the back of a dwarf demon who is named *Apasmaraka* (<u>ignorance</u>). *Bhagavan Nataraja* suppresses and overcomes the ignorance in us and gives us realization regarding the cycle of birth and death. The ring of flames which surrounds Nataraja represents the cycle of birth and death - creation and destruction. His right hand shows the *Abhaya mudra* (<u>symbol of fearlessness</u>) and the other points to the raised foot indicating that we have to rise above ignorance to know the Omniscient *Brahman*.

**"What about musical instruments and the mural paintings in the walls of the temples?" Vijaya did not want to be left out.**

Instrumental music like the *Veena, Violin, Flute, Tambura, Nadaswaram* and the various types of percussion instruments are all testimony to the art that flourished in ancient India and is still being practiced and promoted in India. Art and Hinduism are so intricately connected to each other that one cannot be separated from the other. Hence every art form has a religious connotation built into it. The pluralism of Hinduism is also seen in all its art forms.

Similar to the dance forms, the paintings of ancient Hindu artists in the murals of temples and other structures indicate the thriving arts of the era. The paintings often depict the Hindu Gods and Goddesses as described in the *Puranas* and *Itihasas*. The art of painting was well described and the making and mixing of different colored paints from natural sources like minerals and plants has been well known to our ancient seers. The drawings of *Kolam* (<u>designs drawn with rice flour</u>) in front of homes and on the walls and the *Rangoli* in North India are also art forms that every Hindu housewife is an expert at.

**"What about music, Grandpa?" Jaya asked. She was learning *Carnatic music* of late.**

The name *'Carnatic'* comes from the Sanskrit word *'Karnataka'* (<u>traditional</u>). It also means '<u>pleasing to the ear</u>' (*Karna* = <u>ear</u> ; *Ata* = <u>pleasing</u> ; <u>haunting</u>) The seven notes of *Sa, Ri, Ga, Ma, Pa, Dha, Ni* are called the *'Saptha Svaras'* (Saptha = <u>seven</u>; Svara = <u>note</u>) and are akin to the notes *Do, Re, Mi, Fa, So, La,* and *Ti* in English. Metaphorically they are used to represent the sounds of animals or birds. Thus, they are named **Sa**djam = peacock. **Rishabham** (bull), **Ga**ndharam (ram), **Madhyamam** (crane), **Panchamam** (cuckoo), **Dhai**vatam (horse) and **Ni**shadam (elephant). *Carnatic music* is based on these seven notes and so are the instrumental music compositions. Carnatic music has an elevating effect both on the singer and the listener and raises a person to the highest level of spiritual ecstasy.

# 17. SCIENCE AND HINDUISM

**"Grandpa, tell us a few things about whether Science and Hinduism are compatible with each other. I always thought that religion and science were contradictory to each other" as usual Aditya was the first to choose a topic for the day.**

The belief that Hinduism is a mystical religion which is concerned only with idolatry and spiritual principles is totally wrong. Spanning more than 5000 years, Hinduism has been a fountainhead of scientific thought and practices. The famous French Nobel Laureate Romain Rolland has observed that *"Religious faith in the case of Hindus has never been allowed to run counter to scientific laws."*

The famous physicist and 'father of the atom bomb' Julius R Oppenheimer said, *"What we shall find in Modern Physics is an exemplification, an encouragement and a refinement of old Hindu wisdom."*

*"When I read the Bhagavad Gita and reflect about how God created this universe, everything else seems so superfluous. I have made the Bhagavad Gita as the main source of my inspiration and guide for the purpose of scientific investigation and formation of my theories"*, said the famous German-born theoretical physicist Albert Einstein.

Hinduism has touched upon almost all the sections of science. Science is the search for knowledge and our ancestors have been at the forefront of this exploration. In Hinduism, religion was never opposed to science. Almost all branches of science have been described in various texts in Hindu Literature. We will see them briefly.

The word *'science'* is derived from the Latin word *'scire'* meaning 'to know'. Our *Vedas* also mean 'knowledge'. With *religion*, our sages propounded the philosophies for people to follow and understand the *values of life*. With *science*, they attempted to solve the *problems and challenges of life* to survive and search solutions to the mysteries of the universe. Thus, their exploration was both into the outer world (*Nature*) and the inner world of man (*Mind*). Thus, whereas religion provided the emotional support needed for man through the values and morals that it proffered, science gave the intellectual support by providing solutions to day to day problems face by him. Thus, you will find that Hinduism never opposed science. *Religion* and *science* formed the two sides of the same coin.

The *Vedas* encompass all fields of knowledge, both spiritual and material. The *Upavedas*

(<u>supplementary Vedas</u>) which are part of the *Vedas* deal with many scientific aspects and thoughts. Giving examples, the *Ayurveda* deals with health and wellness, *Dhanurveda* with the science of war, archery, tactical military formation and the like, *Artha sastra* deals with statecraft, management, and administration, *Sthapatya Veda* deals with architecture, and so on.

**Architecture** called *Vaastu Sastra* is the science of architecture described in the *Vedas*. Elaborate details regarding the construction of buildings, towns and temples are explained. A simple glance at the temple architecture, especially in South and Central India will give you an idea of the advanced architecture of ancient times. The sculptures that adorn the temples bear ample testimony to the advanced knowledge of our ancestors. Building gigantic structures without any modern equipment that man uses today is proof enough of the greatness of ancient architectural knowledge.

**Medical knowledge** was also far advanced. The *Charaka Samhita* of *Ayurveda* gives a detailed account of medicines, dosage, their administration etc. There is a mention in the texts about cataract extraction, plastic surgery for repair of the defects of the nose, simple surgical techniques, dental extraction, setting of fractured bones and many other similar medical procedures. Often science was blended with religion. *Dhanvantari,* an *Avatar* of *Bhagavan Vishnu* is worshipped as the God of medicine and health by Hindus.

Indian **Mathematics** was known from as early as 1200 BCE. *Aryabhata, Varahamihira, Brahmagupta* and *Bhaskara* were well known mathematicians. Many complex mathematical problems have been solved by the ancient sages in the *Vedic* texts. *Vedic* mathematics is attracting the interest of mathematicians world over. Many complex problems have been solved using *Vedic* mathematics. The concept of 'zero' and the decimal system were elaborated in India by the sages. Trigonometry and Calculus were discovered as a part of the *Jyothisha sastra* (Astronomy & Astrology). The *Sulba Sutras* described the construction of the fire-altars for homams. These were constructed in definite geometrical patterns of circles, squares, rectangles, and triangles with the same area to definite specifications. This was possible by the advanced geometrical calculations which the sages made.

The *Vaisheshika darsanam* by Rishi *Kaanad* described Gravity and Laws of Motion. The art of computing time was evolved in ancient India. The

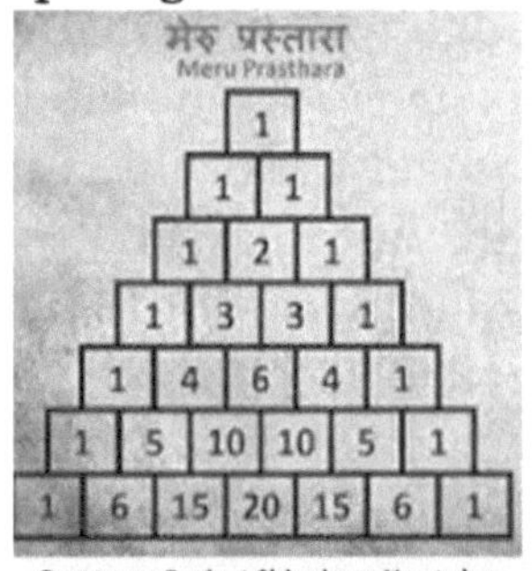

Courtesy : Project Shivoham-You tube

meridian for the calculation ran through Ujjain in North India. Many theorems in geometry were explained in the ancient texts including what is known today as the Pythagorean theorem. Another important mathematical model is the algorithms on supercomputing which have been described by sage *Pingala*. It is called '*Meru Prastara*' and is a construct of numbers in a triangular pyramidal fashion. In modern mathematics it is called the *Pascal's triangle*, but it was described as by sage *Pingala* possibly in 2nd century BC. These bear witness to the fact that mathematics was advanced in ancient India and many of the sages were expert at it.

### "Were Anatomy and Biology known to our ancestors, Grandpa?" Jaya was curious.

Yes, definitely. An elaborate description of the growth of the human fetus in the womb from the beginning of fertilization of the egg is given in *Siva Puranam, Garba Upanishad,* and *Garuda Puranam.* '*Garba*' means '<u>pregnancy</u>'. Descriptions regarding the metabolism in the human body have also been described. The fetus when it is fully grown in the mother's womb is said to feel tortured and it has been described that the fetus remembers its previous life. But at birth this memory is totally erased.

**Modern medical science** agrees that by 18 weeks, the human fetus in the womb can hear sounds and responds to sounds and noises by 24 weeks. In the *Puranas* there are at least two instances where this has been described. Arjuna was talking to his wife Subhadra who was pregnant with their son, *Abhimanyu.* Arjuna was describing the method to breach a tactical formation of the army called the *Chakra Vyuham* (<u>spiral formation).</u> The child in the womb heard this and later in war *Abhimanyu* could recall this and fight the war to breach that formation. Similarly, sage Narada was extolling the virtues and the benefits of devotion to *Bhagavan Maha Vishnu* to the wife of asura king *Hiranyakashipu* and the boy *Prahlada* in her womb heard this and became an ardent devotee of *Maha Vishnu* from birth. These are mentioned in the *Mahabharata* and *Srimad Bhagavatham*.

**"What about Physics?" Aditya wanted to know about his favorite subject.**

Details of elements and earth's gravity have been described in the ancient texts named the *Dravya Sutra*. The word used for gravity is '*Gurutva*'. The atom has been described by the ancient sages as the '*Paramanu*' and has been described in the ancient texts as '*the smallest single indivisible unit of matter*'. The atom has been described as spherical in structure.

**Metallurgy**, which is the science of metals, has been described in detail and the process of extracting metals from ores has been elaborated. The extracting of copper, gold, and silver and the making of alloys has been described in the ancient texts. Our seers have enumerated that the path to prosperity is through '*Prayoga*' (experiment). Many of the Hindu sages who practiced spirituality and were *Gurus* doubled up as scientists too and discovered many scientific truths and contributed them to the world.

**Astronomy** was also far advanced in ancient India and is described in many of the Hindu texts. We have already discussed the origin of creation and the Big Bang theory. The *Pushpaka Vimana* is an aircraft that is described in the Ramayana, said to be owned by *Ravana* the emperor of Sri Lanka. Other *Vimanas* also have been described in the *Srimad Bhagavatham* in different sections. In another instance, the sage *Kardaman* and his wife *Devahuti* are described as spending time in a '*climate controlled elaborately equipped*' *Vimana* traveling to the Himalayas and around world. The word "*Vimanam*" is used for aircraft in Sanskrit. This goes to show that the ancient Hindus were aware of the possibilities of air travel. In another instance, *Srimad Bhagavatham* mentions that King *Chitraketu* was traveling over the Himalayas in his *Vimanam* when he saw *Bhagavan Siva* and *Parvathy* seated in Mount Kailas.

The All Pervasive *Nirguna Brahman* (formless consciousness) in Hinduism is described as a repository of knowledge from which the humans derive their knowledge. Knowledge is widely present in the Universe is what the Hindu scriptures declare. It is akin to the '*cloud*' in the Internet of today where we are able to tap into the knowledge in the '*cloud*' with the help of our computers. Ancient sages tapped into this knowledge using the power of their mind through contemplation and meditation.

Unfortunately, many of these truths were not known to the world or have been "rediscovered" by the European scientists who are credited with all these discoveries. You, children must read more about these scientific facts and discoveries in Hinduism and understand them for yourself.

# 18. CONCEPT OF TIME

**"What are the various concepts regarding time in Hinduism. Have the sages described time in its greatest dimension and in its minutest form?" Aditya set the ball rolling with his first question.**

Yes, my dears. The concept of Time has been very clearly and elaborately described in our scriptures by our sages who have made accurate calculations. The *Vedas, Manu Smriti, Vishnu Purana, Mahabharatha* etc., have described the details regarding <u>time</u> or *'Kaala'* as per Hindu religion. The ancient scriptures have given a very definite and clear concept about time. Carl Sagan, the famous astronomer has called Hinduism *"as the only religion whose time scale for the universe matches the billions of years documented by modern science."* Hinduism also believes that the time durations vary for different worlds as described in various scriptures. Also, they described different time frames for the Gods and other celestial beings and the *Pithrus* (ancestors) whose souls dwell in an astral plane in different 'worlds' till the next rebirth.

Before discussing about time in Hinduism, let me say a few words regarding the origin of the universe and its relation to time. The scriptures also describe millions of universes – "*Akhila Kodi Brahmandam*" – (*Akhila* = <u>multitude</u>; *Kodi* = <u>10 million</u>; *Brahmandam* = <u>universe</u>). Hindus believed there are many universes out there which are populated by many spiritual beings. In the *Srimad Bhagavatham*, the earth has been described as a 'globe' (*Bhoogolam* = <u>globe</u>; <u>spherical</u>). This was done long before Europeans 'discovered' that the earth was round.

The creation of the universe according to Hindu scriptures is from the expansion of a single small '*Hiranyagarbha*' (<u>golden egg</u>) (*Hiranya* = <u>golden</u>; *garbha* = <u>womb</u>: <u>egg</u>). This was the seed of creation. In the beginning it was darkness all around. Then the Universal *Brahman* arose of its own accord. This is called *Swayambhu* (<u>self-born</u> ; <u>created by its own accord</u>). From This arose the *Hiranyagarbha*. The *Hiranyagarbha* then began to expand and multiply to create the whole universe which we see today. The five elements arose from the primeval soul or *Brahman*. *Akash* (<u>Space</u> or <u>ether</u>) arose first. It gave rise to *Vayu* (<u>air</u>) which in turn gave rise to *Agni* (<u>fire</u>). Fire in turn produced *Apa* (<u>water</u>) and from water arose *Prithvi* (<u>earth</u> or <u>solid</u>). The process of creation has been elaborately described in the *Srimad Bhagavatham*. It is a must-read for every Hindu.

Just as the expansion of the universe is described in the scriptures closely akin to the 'Big Bang' theory expounded by the astronomers, the dissolution of the universe is also described as '*Pralaya*' in the scriptures. *Pralaya* literally means 'dissolution'. One *Chathur yuga* (*Chathur* = four ; *Yuga* = age ; epoch) comprises totally the four *yugas* - namely, *Satya, Tretha, Dvapara* and *Kali yugas*. A thousand such *Chathur Yugas* (ages) form one *Kalpa*. At the end of one *Kalpa,* the whole universe dissolves and returns to its original state. This is called the *Brahma Pralayam* (dissolution by Brahma). Cosmologists declare that the universe is still expanding. It is predicted that at the end of this expansion will come the 'Big Crunch' when the universe will start to contract and condense into a super-hot and super dense single unit. This is consistent with what is described in the Hindu scriptures as *Pralaya* where the universe is dissolved at the end of a cycle of 1000 yugas or a *Kalpa*.

The whole universe thus follows a rhythm, or a cycle called '*Rita*' by our ancestors. In the universe, there is a cosmic cycle for everything. In the human being, we see the biorhythm which is also a diurnal cycle. There is the yearly seasonal cycle for the earth, the cycle of birth and death for the living beings and a cycle or orbit for all the heavenly bodies. Only, the length of the cycles vary from single day to months to years to *Yugas* to *Kalpas*. Even time has been described as cyclical and not linear.

**"So, what is the role of the Gods, Brahma, Vishnu and Siva in these cycles?" Jaya had a pertinent question.**

This cycle of <u>Creation</u>, <u>Continuation</u> and <u>Dissolution</u> is called '*Srishti*', '*Sthithi*' and '*Laya*'. The *Trinity – Brahma, Vishnu* and *Siva* are given the functions of these three as per Hindu Mythology. But for a moment do not forget that all of them are manifestations of the one and only Universal Consciousness, the *Brahman.*

At this juncture, I want you to understand that the word '*Brahman*' and '*Brahma*' are not the same. *Bhagavan Brahma* is the name of the God, one of the trinity, who is concerned with creation. *Brahman* is the name given to the Universal Formless Consciousness.

*Bhagavan Brahma* is given the portfolio of <u>creation</u>. Bhagavan *Vishnu* preserves the created beings and objects thus providing sustenance. His main function is <u>maintenance</u>. *Siva* is entrusted with the <u>dissolution</u> or destruction. These three are but essential features of creation. What is created must be maintained properly and then to sustain creation, the old ones need to be destroyed. This holds true be it with living beings including man or buildings or any structures in nature. Trees have to be destroyed for new ones to grow, mountains may crumble for changes to occur, flowers have to be destroyed for fruits to develop. It is part of the cosmic cycle. Birth and death are also a part of this cycle. And "Time" is said to control these cycles.

**"Wow, grandpa, this is mind blowing. Just imagine that our ancestors have described all this without having access to telescopes and computers!" Vijaya's eyes were round**

**with surprise. "But then, tell us how many years is one *yuga*."**

Yes, now let us look at some awesome astronomical numbers.

One *Kalpa* is said to be <u>one day</u> for *Bhagavan Brahma* (A 12-hour day). According to the *Vishnu Purana*, one *Kalpa* is equal to <u>4.32 billion human years</u>. As we said earlier, each *Kalpa* is divided into 1000 *Chathur yugas* or *Maha yugas*. Each *Maha yuga* is divided into four yugas – *Satya (Krita), Tretha, Dvapara* and *Kali* yugas.

At the end of one *Kalpa*, *Pralaya* occurs and everything 'dissolves'. This *Pralaya* continues for another *Kalpa* (4.32 billion years) which is the night for *Brahma*. Thus, a total of 8.64 billion years forms a 24-hour day for Brahma. Thirty such days form a month for Brahma. Twelve such months form a year and 100 years is the life time of a Brahma.

Let us now see the duration of each of these yugas. The years are mentioned in human years.

The *Satya yuga* (*Krita yuga*) runs for 1,728,000 years, *Tretha yuga* for 1,296,000 years, *Dvapara yuga* for 864,000 years and *Kali yuga* for 432,000 years. At present we are in *Kali yuga* which began approximately 5200 years ago. Seventy-one *Maha yugas* constitute a *Manvantara*. Each *Manvantara* is said to be ruled by one *Manu*. A *Manu* is the ruler of the earth or the head of a dynasty during the *Manvantara*. The present *Manvantara* is called

*Vaivasvata Manvantara* ruled by the *Manu* called *Vaivasvata Manu*.

*Brahma* has a life for <u>100 Kalpas</u>. So, imagine the staggering number of years in the life of Brahma (311.04 trillion years of man). One year for man is equal to one day for the *Devas*. Thirty days for humans is equal to one day for the *Pithrus*. The bright fortnight (after the new moon) is the day time and the dark fortnight (after the full moon) is their night time. That is why on every *Amavasya* (<u>new moon day</u>), the *Pithrus* are remembered and given their food and water by humans. This <u>offering for the *Pithrus*</u> is called *Tharpanam*.

This goes to show that our ancestors were aware that the concept of time was different in different worlds as today scientists have discovered that the days and nights are different for different planets and in different locations in the universe.

**"Oh my!" exclaimed Vijaya, "How many zeros will that be in Brahma's life? You told us about the whopping number of years described in our scriptures, but what about the time for humans? What has been said about the calculation of time for man?"**

I will tell you in brief what the smallest unit of time is described in the scriptures that denotes time for us humans and then describe its various multiples.

- *Paramanu* is the smallest unit of time described in the scriptures and corresponds to 16.8

microseconds. It is described as the time taken for sunlight to cross a single speck of dust.

- Two *Paramanu* make an *Anu* (33.7 microsecond).
- Three *Anu* together form one *Trasarenu*. (101 microseconds).
- Three *Trasarenu* form one *Truti* (304 microseconds).
- One hundred *Trutis* form one *Vedha* (30 milliseconds).
- Three *Vedhas* form one *Lava* (91 milliseconds).
- Three *Lavas* form one *Nimisha*, which is equal to one blinking of the eye (0.273 seconds).
- Three *Nimishas* form one *Kshana* (0.82 second).
- Five *Kshanas* form one *Kashta* (4.1 seconds).
- Fifteen *Kashtas* make one *Laghu* (1.6 minute).
- Fifteen *Laghus* form one *Nadika* (24 minutes).
- Two *Nadikas* form one *Muhurta* (48 minutes).
- Seven and half Muhurtas constitute one *Yaama*.
- One *Yaama* is 6 hours. Each day has 4 *Yaamas* each – night and day. This is called *Ahorathram* (24 hours).
- Thirty *Ahorathrams* constitute a *Masa* (month).
- Two *Masas* constitute one Rithu (season)

- Three Rithus (6 months) constitute one *Ayana.*

- Two *Ayanas* constitute one *Varsha* (year). The Ayanas are named *Uttarayanam* (January to July) and *Dakshinayanam* (August-January) -six months each, corresponding to the movement of the sun to the North and South respectively.

Each month is also divided into two *Pakshas* (fortnight). There are 15 *Thithi* for the 15 days of the fortnight and they have different names as *Prathama, Dwitiya, Tritiya, Chathurthi* corresponding to the first, second, third, fourth day, and so on.

I hope I have not confused you with all the names and times. All this is only for your information about the greatness of Hinduism and the vast knowledge contained in our ancient scriptures. It also substantiates how efficiently our sages have classified and documented the knowledge that they acquired. But suffice it to say that our ancestors had divided and classified time from the mega ages like the *Kalpa* to the microsecond or *Paramanu* level. Such was there wisdom and foresight. We should be proud of that legacy.

**"That was mind-boggling" exclaimed Aditya, "Imagine that our sages calculated the gross dimensions of time in millions of years and minutest division in milli-seconds! It is unbelievable!".**

# 19. DEATH AND REINCARNATION

**"Grandpa, we are almost at the end of our holiday season and will be returning to our schools soon. As a final summing up can you tell us about 'Death' and what happens to a person after death" Aditya was curious about death. "How do we reincarnate after death?"**

Before we go into this discussion, I would like to remind you to refresh the thoughts in your mind about the discussion we had on *'Karma and Reincarnation'*. But I will briefly touch upon these concepts again.

Our ancient sages were baffled by two things in Nature. One was death and the other was the various natural disasters like floods, lightning, thunder, rain, earthquakes and so on. This set them inquiring and this lead to various revelations about the nature of these phenomena.

The revelations to the sages about the law of *Karma* gave them an insight into the concept of reincarnation. They recognized the immortality of the soul and the *Brahman*. They realized that the soul in all living beings is the same and is only a reflection of the Absolute Consciousness which is called 'God' in various religions. *Karma* was recognized as the '*Law of Action*' which governs the life of an individual. The basic concept of this law is that *every action is followed by an equal reaction*. If we hurt another individual or any living being with our thought, word, or deed, it is bound to boomerang on us. This may not occur immediately, or in this life but could be carried over to the next life. Thus, our actions are stored as impressions in our soul and the results of these must be faced and endured in our future lives. For this the soul has to reincarnate repeatedly.

It has been beautifully explained in the Bhagavad Gita in the sloka –

वासांसि जीर्णानि यथा विहाय
नवानि गृह्णाति नरोऽपराणि ।
तथा शरीराणि विहाय जीर्णा-
न्यन्यानि संयाति नवानि देही ॥ २-२२ ॥

*Vāsāṃsi jīrṇāni yathā vihāya*
*Navāni gṛhṇāti naro'parāṇi*
*Tathā śarīrāṇi vihāya jīrṇā-*
*Nyanyāni saṃyāti navāni dehī* (2:22)

It means - *Just as a man casts off his worn out clothes and puts on new ones, so also the embodied-Self casts off its worn out bodies and enters new bodies.*

Death is called '*Mrityu*' in Sanskrit. The God of Death is called *Yama raja* or *Dharmaraja* (king of Dharma). He is also named '*Kaala*' which means 'time'. The body dies because of diseases or old age. But the soul does not perish but lives on. The soul leaves the body through the top of the head (fontanelle) in the pious, righteous and *Sattvic* individuals. In the *Rajasic* it leaves through the eyes or the mouth, whereas in those who have done evil deeds and have been *Tamasic*, the soul leaves through the lower orifices.

After leaving the mortal body, the soul or *Jeevatma* lives in a subtle 'astral body' in the *Devaloka* (astral world) temporarily till its rebirth. When it is time for rebirth, the soul descends to *Bhuloka* (earth) to reincarnate into another body. While in the astral body, all the stored (*Sanchita*) karmas, the emotions, the experiences both good and bad continue and when the soul reincarnates in a new body, these experiences persist as *Vasanas* and the accumulated *Karmas* persist as the *Sanchita Karma* which we have discussed already.

**"What is the concept of Heaven and Hell in Hinduism? Do they exist at all? Can a soul be damned eternally to Hell or assigned to Heaven permanently?" Jaya had a pertinent question.**

According to the Hindu Puranas there are 14 astral worlds. They are respectively the seven upper worlds namely, *Bhuh, Bhuvah, Suvah, Mahah, Janah, Tapah* and *Satyam*. *Bhuh* is the earth where we humans and other livings beings exist. The other six are higher worlds.

There are seven nether worlds namely, *Atala, Vitala, Suthala, Rasatala, Talatala, Mahatala* and *Patala*. The *Patala* is the lowest astral world where the evil and wicked souls repair to after death to seek reparation for their misdeeds on earth.

The *Suvah* is the world where the righteous and the pious are lodged temporarily till they reincarnate on earth. The higher worlds – the *Janah, Tapah* and *Satya loka (Brahma loka)* are where the realized souls reach to merge with the *Brahman*. They do not have rebirth after that. This is the concept of the Heavens and Hell in Hinduism.

It is to be remembered that those going to the higher worlds enjoy the pleasures there for a brief period before reincarnating on earth and those going to the nether worlds, undergo atonement for their misdeeds on earth, and are again reborn in our world. In the nether worlds, these souls undergo retribution for their evil deeds and various types of punishment are meted out to them. This is given in detail in the *Garuda Purana. Neither of them stay in these worlds permanently.* Thus, there is no concept of a 'permanent Heaven' or an 'eternal damnation in Hell' in Hinduism. Every soul has to ultimately return to earth to exhaust its *Sanchita Karma*.

Each soul, after it has undergone the chastening in the nether worlds or enjoyed the pleasures of the higher worlds is ready for reincarnation. The soul is minute and subtle. It is atomic in size and said to  return to the earth in the drops of rain. It seeps into the earth and is either absorbed by the trees or consumed by animals or man. These enter the bodies of animals or man and according to their *Karma* are reborn as animals or humans. The subtle soul thus entering the woman's body settles in the egg in her womb and grows into an embryo and thus starts another cycle of reincarnation.

In *Puranas* and *Itihasas*, however, the concept of the pleasures of *Heaven* and the requitals in *Hell* are described for the benefit of the masses to steer them into the righteous and ethical path of behaviour and conduct during their lifetime. Abstruse philosophical concepts are easily delivered to the common folk through stories and parables assimilable to the common folk. The punishments meted out to the evil souls described in the *Puranas* are more symbolic than authentic.

The *Garuda Purana, Srimad Bhagavatham* and *Mahabharata* give vivid descriptions of Heaven and Hell for the common folk to understand their significance. It is described with a view to instill awe of God and the need to practice *Dharma*, in the minds of the devotees.

**"Why do we cremate the dead? Why do we have the elaborate rituals for so many days? What is its implication?" Vijaya had her share of questions.**

As we said in the beginning, the earthly body composed of the *Pancha Bhutas* (<u>five elements</u>) returns to the elements on death of the human body and the *Atman* or soul returns to the origin from where it came. The soul takes on many births and death (*Samsaras*) before reaching its ultimate goal – the *Brahman*. A person could have gone through millions of births and deaths. The gross physical body which is destructible is cremated because, once the soul leaves the body permanently, it cannot reenter it.

It is believed that the soul which leaves the body tries  to re-enter the body unsuccessfully, and hovers above the physical dead body for some time. That is why the dead body of a Hindu is cremated as early as possible – within three hours of death. After cremation there are rituals which help the soul to traverse its path towards the astral plane - towards the *Devaloka or Pithru loka*. On each day of the funeral rites, <u>balls of cooked rice mixed with ghee and black sesame seeds</u> called *Pinda* are offered to the dead individual's soul. It is believed that by the tenth day, soul which has left the body, but still hovering in the surroundings is transformed into a whole astral body with all the features of the dead person. Then it is given a 'farewell' into the astral world or *Devaloka* or *Pithru loka* where it dwells till the next birth.

The travel to the *Pithru loka* takes approximately a year and the soul is fed by the food and water offered by the son every month for the next twelve months. The first anniversary of death is elaborately conducted with rituals for three days when the departed soul reaches the destination in *Devaloka (Pithru loka)*. It is believed that souls which have done evil deeds against the laws of *Dharma* during their lifetime on earth undergo the rigors of requital before reaching the final destination, the *Pithru loka* This is described in detail in the *Garuda Purana* and *Matsya Purana*.

After death, the body is placed on the plain floor on the ground with the head facing south as the body now belongs to the *earth,*. It is bathed with *water*, which is another of the elements and later confined to flames or *Agni* (*fire*) which is the ultimate purifier. The body is dressed in traditional clothes and covered with a length of cloth (shroud). Bodies of women with their husbands alive are draped in a red shroud and widows in a white one. Men are shrouded with a white cloth. They are carried to the cremation ground in a ladder-like bier which is usually made of a combustible material like dry bamboos.

The body along with the bier is placed on a funeral pyre which is lit by the eldest son of the deceased. If the person has no son, a brother, or a close relative whose father is no more may perform the last rites. One or two days after the cremation, the ashes are collected in an earthen pot and immersed in a flowing water body like a river or in the sea. This ritual is called the *Sanjayanam* (<u>collection of ashes</u>). To immerse the ashes in the *Ganges* is supposed to be ideal. Scattering the ashes in mountains like the Himalayas though has been done is not an acceptable Hindu tradition. These rituals differ slightly from region to region depending on the subsects of Hindus.

The mourning period lasts for 13 to 16 days among different subsects of Hindus. The last day is when relatives and friends who have come to mourn the departed are invited for a feast after an elaborate *Pooja* is performed to appease the <u>planetary Gods</u>

(*Navagrahas*). During the fortnight when the family is in mourning, they do not go out of the home or visit temples or attend any functions outside.

**"Why are these rituals so elaborate and why seclude the family of the deceased for a fortnight from going out or attending other functions?" Vijaya wanted to know.**

Well, Looking at these funeral rites from the view point of a physician, I have always felt that this was a sort of self-imposed quarantine for the family. In the olden days, diseases, especially the infectious diseases like small pox, tuberculosis, diarrhea, plague, and various other infectious diseases were the prime reason for death of individuals. Hence, quarantining the whole family for two weeks was a very effective way of preventing the spread of the infection in the community. Everyone who had touched the dead body and taken part in the cremation rituals or visited the home of the deceased to offer condolences, had to take a shower before re-entering their own homes. Furthermore, nobody except close relatives would visit the family for the two weeks except for offering their condolences. This was another method of containing the infection. Cremating the body was also an efficient method of sanitization. The whole house had to be cleaned well after the body is removed for cremation. The *Homam* or fire sacrifice done on the final day of the obsequies along with burning of incense is a sort of fumigation of the whole house.

**"What is '*Moksha*', Grandpa?", was Aditya's next question.**

*Moksha* means <u>liberation</u> from the <u>cycle of birth or death</u> – <u>Samsara</u>. The soul which is repeatedly reborn exhausts its *Karmas* after multitudes of births. In each birth, the soul incarnates in a better human body and lives according to the righteous principles of *Dharma*. Ultimately it reaches a stage when it has no more *Sanchita Karmas* to exhaust, and it reaches perfection and becomes one with the Supreme Consciousness. That state is called *Moksha* or <u>salvation</u>. It is also called *Nirvana* or *Kaivalya*.

However, if the person has been very wicked and malicious during his lifetime living contrary to the dictates of *Dharma*, or if he dies with the thought of material possessions in his mind or if he has taken his own life (suicide), it is believed that he will reincarnate as a lower form of an animal or a still lower living being and must work up the ladder of spiritual evolution.

The story of king *Bharatha* who during his *Vanaprastha* period became attached to a little deer which he rescued from the clutches of a lion and affectionately reared is told in the *Srimad Bhagavatham*. On his deathbed, *Bharatha* could think of nothing but what would happen to the deer on his death, and he died thinking of the deer. Ultimately, he was reborn as a deer. But in his reincarnation as a deer, he retained the memory of his previous birth and was constantly thinking of *Bhagavan Vishnu*. In the subsequent birth he was reborn as a brahmin called *Jada Bharatha*.

The story goes to show that one's thoughts in the last days of life can mold one's future reincarnation. That is the reason why the last two stages in the life of a person are designated as *Vanaprastha* and *Sannyasa* when one is expected to relinquish all attachment to material possessions and family relationships and constantly be in the contemplation of God.

**"Do Hindus believe in ghosts, Grandpa", Vijaya asked rather apprehensively as she always shunned horror movies and stories of ghosts.**

Yes, *Puranas* and *Srimad Bhagavatham* also mentions about ghosts. In Sanskrit they are called '*Bhutas*'. It is believed that these are restless souls or spirits of humans who have died in certain circumstances and are unable to transmigrate to the *Devaloka*. This can be due to violent deaths or unnatural deaths like suicide, extreme attachments to worldly possessions or people or unsettled matters during life. If their progeny do not perform the funeral rites needed for the metempsychosis of the souls, they end up as *Bhutas*. The *Bhutas* (<u>ghosts</u>) are said to haunt certain places and live in certain trees in the forests. As souls are immortal and cannot be destroyed, there are certain rituals especially described in the *Atharva Veda* which exorcise these spirits and send them into the realm of the *Pithru loka* thus granting them the chance to be reborn.

**"Is there superstition in Hinduism?", Aditya had a question based on logic.**

A superstition is an irrational belief based on an unnatural or ominous event or occurrence.  It has no logical basis and will not stand scientific scrutiny. But do not confuse mythology with superstition. At times the dividing line between superstition and religious beliefs may be tenuous and hence such beliefs have to be handled gently.

Some of the superstitions are harmless and others may be perilous. Some of the harmless ones are - a crow cawing near the kitchen indicates the arrivals of guests, a black cat crossing one's path symbolizes ill luck, an itchy right palm means you will get money that day and an itch in the left palm denotes expenditure. Twitching of the left eye in a woman presages good luck whereas in a man it bodes ill luck.

At the same time the animal sacrifices and the practice of *Sati* in olden days where the wives jumped into the funeral pyres of their husbands were cruel practices of superstition. They are dangerous superstitions which need to be condemned.

There are some superstitions that are found to be sensible. I have been told by elders that cutting one's nails at dusk brings ill luck. Probably in the days before electricity was available, when the oil lamps were lit at dusk and nails were cut with scissors, cutting nails for fear of injuring one's fingertips was a 'preventive' superstition. During an eclipse, one is cautioned not to venture out doors. This has no scientific basis as such. But two things struck me as sensible. One should never look at the sun directly during a solar eclipse as it can cause damage to the macula of the retina – it is called *'eclipse blindness'*. Secondly, solar eclipse causes a sudden decrease in the sun's rays and an apparent feeling of dusk or sunset.

It is found that reptiles and other poisonous creatures come out from their burrows apparently thinking that it is nightfall. This could be dangerous for persons who walk barefoot outside their homes.

The examples are numerous, and it is interesting to study them and attempt to analyze the rationality behind some of these. But never believe in many of the unfounded superstitions and do not develop undue anxiety thinking of impending mishaps. Put your logical mind into action whenever you encounter such superstitions and circumvent them without giving offense to others.

# 20. ADI SHANKARACHARYA & SWAMI VIVEKANANDA

**"Today tell us something about Adi Shankaracharya and Swami Vivekananda as both of them are the *Gurus* who have influenced Hinduism to a great extent in recent times" Aditya was the first to pose a question.**

I will tell you about these great saints of Hinduism for they hold a unique position in Hinduism in modern times. First we will discuss a few things about Adi Shankaracharya.

## Adi Sankaracharya

We have talked about the difference between a *Guru* and an *Acharya* in one of our previous discussions. I hope you remember it. An *Acharya* leads the way and shows you by example rather than just guiding and advising you. That is why Adi Sankara was called *'Shankaracharya'*. He lived in the 8th century CE. He is known for his erudition in Sanskrit and in-depth knowledge of the Vedas and other scriptures. He has written exegesis or commentaries called '*Bhashyams*' in Sanskrit for many of the spiritual texts. He has given excellent commentaries for ten Upanishads and the *Brahma Sutra*. His commentary on the *Bhagavad Gita* is unique and is the basis of *Bhagavad Gita* teaching all over the world. He was the pioneer in advocating the Advaita philosophy and restructuring the *Sannyasa* (<u>Hindu monk</u>) order.

Sankara was born at a time when the country was in a state of confusion due to raging superstitions

**Adi Sankaracharya**

and misinterpretations of the scriptures. He helped to bring an order in methods of worship and interpretation of the scriptures.

Adi Sankara was born in an orthodox Namboodiri brahmin family in a village called Kaladi in Kerala in the year 788 CE. His father Shivaguru died when Sankara was a child. His mother Aryamba brought him up. Even from childhood, Sankara's mind was attracted to spirituality. There is a story about him embracing Sannyasa at an early age. One day when eight-year old Sankara was bathing in the Periyar river in his village, a crocodile attacked him. His mother who was on the banks of the river was horrified and shouted for help. Sankara told his mother that if she agreed to his aspiration to become a Sannyasi, the crocodile would let go off his leg. His mother, out of concern for the child agreed and Sankara was released by the crocodile. Keeping her promise, his mother permitted him to accept Sannyasa and thus  began his journey into spirituality.

Sankara traveled to the banks of the Narmada river on foot and accepted the discipleship of the Guru Govinda Bhagavadpada. He remained in the *Gurukulam* for four years. By the age of twelve, the *Guru* declared that Sankara was adequately knowledgeable to write commentaries for the scriptures. In the next four years, Sankara composed the *Bhashyas* for the *Brahma sutra*, the *Upanishads*, and the *Bhagavad Gita*. The *Guru* blessed Sankara and bade him to travel the country to spread the knowledge of the scriptures to the common people of the country. Sankara began his crusade on foot throughout the length and breadth of India (*Bharat*). This is known as the Sankara '*Digvijayam*' (meaning 'conquest of the four quarters').

The people at that time had different misinterpretations of the scriptures and had been blindly following the ritualistic religious ceremonies ignoring the core philosophy of Hinduism as given in the Vedic texts. Superstition also reigned supreme at the time. Sankara capsulized the whole concept of the Vedas into one Sanskrit verse as :

ब्रह्म सत्यं जगन्मिथ्या जीवो ब्रह्मैव नापरः।

*Brahma Satyam Jagan Mithya, Jeevo Brahmaiva Na Para*

The meaning of this is *"Brahman, Pure Consciousness, is the Absolute Reality. The world is unreal"*.

This was the core of the *'Advaita'* (<u>Non-duality</u>) philosophy propounded by Sankara.

एकं सद्‌ विप्रा बहुधा वदन्ति-

*Ekam Sad Vipra Bahudha Vadanti*

*"The truth is but one, people call it by many names"* is another such aphorism.

From the age of 16 to 32, Shankaracharya travelled the length and breadth of the country challenging various scholars to debates and spreading the philosophy of Advaita and bringing an order to the various modes of worship in the country.

Shankaracharya set up four ashrams in four corners of the country and appointed four disciples in charge of them. These are situated in Sringeri (Karnataka, in South India), Puri (Odisha, in the east), Dwaraka (Gujarat, in the west) and Badrinath (Uttarakhand, in the north).

Apart from the *Bhashyas* (<u>exegesis</u>), he has composed numerous *slokas* and *bhajans*. His *Bhaja Govindam*, which is a simple lyrical verse, is one of the famous *bhajans* among Hindus. Also, other compositions are *Soundarya Lahari, Sivananda Lahari, Nirvana Shalkam, Maneesha Panchakam* and many more. About 300 works are attributed to him, but it is believed that he is not the composer of many of these.

There are many legends connected with Sankara. As a child Sannyasi, he went to beg for alms and reached the house of a poor elderly woman. She was so poor that she had nothing in her house but one gooseberry which she affectionately offered to the young sannyasi. Sankara was so overwhelmed by her hospitality that he immediately composed and sang a *Stotram* (<u>hymn</u>) called the '*Kanakadhara Stotram*' in praise of Goddess Lakshmi (Goddess of wealth). It is said that golden gooseberries showered on the woman's home.

Another legend says that Sankara's mother used to go to the Periyar river  daily to bathe. When she became ill and exhausted, Sankara prayed to *Bhagavan Siva* to help his mother. The next morning, to their surprise, the river had changed its course to flow near their home.

It is said that Sankara was in North India when his mother was on her deathbed. Sankara coming to know of this with his yogic powers reached her bedside immediately and could grant her the divine vision of *Bhagavan Vishnu* before she passed away. As the other brahmins in the society did not help Sankara when his mother passed away, Sankara single handed had a pyre set up and with his yogic powers set it alight by sprinkling some water.

In reality, Adi Shankaracharya did what Veda Vyasa did millennia ago in codifying the *Vedas*. Adi Shankaracharya brought a proper order and organization to the *Sanatana Dharma* and condensed the teachings of the *Vedas* and *Upanishads*  into assimilable entities through his commentaries on the *Upanishads, Brahma Sutra,* and *Bhagavad Gita*. Adi Shankaracharya also organized and structured temple worship in many of the temples in India.

He passed away at the age of 32 in Kedarnath, Uttarakhand in North India. Read more about the biography of this great sage if you are interested.

**"Wow, grandpa, we never knew that there was so much to learn about the great sage Adi Shankaracharya. Now tell us about Swami Vivekananda who lived a couple of centuries ago", Jaya was curious.**

## Swami Vivekananda

Sure, you must learn something about Swami Vivekananda too. When you grow older, you must read his books as they are a repository of knowledge about our ancient scriptures and our Hindu heritage. The works are in English and are easy to understand, so you will have no difficulty in assimilating the knowledge contained in those works. The complete works of Swami Vivekananda have been published in nine volumes and are a goldmine of spiritual information regarding the *Santana Dharma*.

Swami Vivekananda was born on 12th January 1863 in Calcutta (present Kolkata) in North India in a traditional Bengali family. He was christened Narendranath Datta by his parents. Narendra, as he was called, was an avid reader of literature and the traditional Indian scriptures. In college, he learnt Western logic, Western philosophy, and European history. He completed the Bachelor of Arts course in college. Narendra had been blessed with the ability of speed-reading and had an excellent memory. The principal of the college recognized the makings of a genius in him.

There is a legend about the young Narendra. When he was a little boy, while discussing the future career of students, he told his teacher that he wanted to be a coachman to drive a horse-drawn carriage. Hearing this the whole class burst into laughter and his teacher mocked him. Young Narendra came home crying. On hearing this, his mother took him to the *Pooja* room and showed him a picture on the wall. It was one of *Bhagavan Sri Krishna* as the charioteer, advising the *Bhagavad Gita* to Arjuna in the battlefield. "My son, you should become a charioteer like *Sri Krishna* when you grow up and steer the whole world", she said. This inspired the tiny mind of Narendra.

Narendra was spiritually inclined from a young age partly by the influence of his devout

**Swami Vivekananda**

mother. Even as a child he used to meditate regularly. His thoughts were influenced by many great philosophers of his time. His meeting with Ramakrishna Paramahamsa in 1881 was a turning point in his life. After initial reluctance, Narendra accepted Ramakrishna as his *Guru*. After the death of Ramakrishna, Narendra travelled extensively in India meeting many scholars of all religions – Hindus, Muslims, Sikhs, Buddhists, and Christians. He also met *Rajas* (kings), government officials and even low caste Hindus. All this contributed to his spiritual education. It was Maharajah Ajit Singh of Khetri who advised Narendra to accept the name of '*Vivekananda*' (*Viveka* = discriminatory wisdom; *Ananda* = bliss).

Swami Vivekananda's journey to the west began in May 1863 with his visit to cities in Japan, China, Canada, and the United States where he addressed an audience of 7000 in the Parliament of Religions, representing India and Hinduism. He was given a standing ovation. He adapted the Hindu ideas and principles to suit the modern world, and this attracted the west. His advocacy of *Raja Yoga* which is from Patanjali's *Yoga Sutra* attracted the western audience. He travelled extensively in the West giving lectures in various centres and cities.

In 1897 he reached Ceylon (now Sri Lanka) and from there travelled to Calcutta visiting many cities like Madras (Chennai) and Madurai on the way and ultimately reached Calcutta. His lectures in the West were mainly to highlight the great spiritual heritage of Hinduism, whereas his lectures in India were mainly regarding social issues like the hateful casteism, improving the life of people, removing untouchability, promoting scientific temper and industrialization. His speeches were spiritualistic and at the same time patriotic. He wanted to put an end to colonialism in India.

He founded the *Ramakrishna Mission* in Calcutta in May 1897 which was mainly concerned with social service. It was based on the ideals propounded in *Karma Yoga*. The *Ramakrishna Madom*, however, was involved with religious activities. Both are outstanding organizations in India and the rest of the world. Later he established many ashrams in other parts of India and abroad. He made another journey to the west in 1899 and returned to India in 1902.

On 4th of July 1902, while meditating, he breathed his last.

Swami Vivekananda is the author of many articles, letters, and poems. He wrote four classical treatises on *Karma Yoga, Jnana Yoga, Raja Yoga* and *Bhakti Yoga* which are outstanding works on Hindu philosophy. He summed up the whole essential philosophy of India into one simple paragraph as follows:

> *"Each soul is potentially divine. The goal is to manifest this Divinity within by controlling nature, external and internal. Do this either by work, or worship, or mental discipline, or philosophy—by one, or more, or all of these—and be free. This is the whole of religion. Doctrines, or dogmas, or rituals, or books, or temples, or forms, are but secondary details".*

# 21. MISCELLANY

"Well, my children said Grandpa, today is your last day of discussion about Hinduism and I am sure that you have been able to understand most of what we discussed. Do you have any more topics which need to be explained?"

**In unison all the three spoke up, "Grandpa, we have an assortment of miscellaneous questions which we have written down over the last three weeks and we would like to have answers to these questions today."**

"Well, guys go ahead, fire off one by one. I will answer them briefly  and as best as I can."

**"Grandpa, why do we bow and prostrate before our *Guru* and other elders or touch our head to their feet?"  Vijaya wanted to know.**

When a person meets an elder in the family, or a sacred person like a saint, they prostrate before him and touch their heads to his feet. Another way is to touch their feet with your hands and then place your hands on your own head. They also prostrate in temples and at home before the deity in the *Pooja* room. This is a sign of reverence for the person or deity. Men should prostrate completely lying prone with their arms extended in front with the hands folded in prayer. In this pose which is called "*Sashtanga Namaskaram*" (*Sa* = <u>with</u>; *Ashta* = <u>eight</u>; *Anga* = <u>limb</u>; *Namaskaram* = <u>prostration</u> ), the person touches eight parts of his body on the floor (earth) to show his absolute reverence and surrender to the individual or to God. The eight parts of the body, the forehead, two palms, two feet, two knees and chest touch the ground.

Women, however, perform the '*Panchanga Namaskaram*' (*Pancha* = <u>five</u>). Touching only their forehead, two palms and two legs. Their chest and abdomen do not touch the floor.

The head is the seat of the Ego and touching the head to the ground in front of the feet of the *Guru* or God, or touching their feet with our head is an indication of humility and surrendering our ego. Also, the greatest blessing from a *Guru* or God is the *Guru's* or God's feet touching one's head. In the *Puranas* , this happened only to two persons. *Ahalya*, who had been cursed to become a stone assumed her human form and attained salvation when the feet of *Sri Rama* touched the stone. The second instance described is the blessing of King *Mahabali* by *Bhagavan Vishnu* in his incarnation as *Vamana* when he placed his right foot on the king's head blessing him and sending him to rule in *Suthala*. This was indeed a blessing and not a 'punishment' as some ill-informed ignoramuses make it out to be.

**"Why do we worship the Tulasi plant and use its leaves in our *Pooja*?" Vijaya was the next.**

The Tulasi plant called *Ocimum sanctum* is a holy plant for the Hindus. It is also called *Vrinda*. It is a shrub which grows to about two to three feet height but can grow into a tree. The word '*Tulasi*' in Sanskrit means "<u>matchless</u>". The plant is a manifestation of the *Goddess Tulasi* who in turn is an *Avatar* of *Goddess Lakshmi*. Hence Tulasi is also considered a consort of *Bhagavan Vishnu*. There are two types of Tulasi plants – the one with bright green leaves called the '*Rama Tulasi*' and the one with dark leaves with a purplish tinge called the '*Krishna Tulasi*'. The Tulasi leaves have a pleasant scent. There are various legends connected to Tulasi as to how it was declared *Bhagavan Vishnu's* consort.

The Tulasi plant is the center of worship for Hindu women. Most Hindu houses have a small altar

**Tulasi Thara**

called '*Tulasi Thara*' on which a Tulasi plant is grown. This may be in the inner courtyard of the house or in the front of the house facing east. After bathing in the morning, the women folk worship the Tulasi, water it and adorn it with flowers. The *Tulasi Thara* is decorated with *Kolam* (<u>Rangoli</u>).

A lamp is lit and placed on it. The leaves of a Tulasi are used for *Pooja*. It is believed that growing Tulasi plants in the home brings prosperity.

The wood and thick roots of the Tulasi plant are carved into beads and made into a *Japa Mala* (rosary; garland) and used in *Japa* (chanting). Tulasi leaves soaked in water is offered as *Theertham* (holy water) for the devotees in temples. The leaves also have medicinal properties and are used in Ayurveda. A person who is dying is given sips of water with Tulasi leaves in it with the belief that this will help liberate his soul.

**"What are the *Mahavakyas*? You had mentioned it in passing" Jaya wanted to know.**

The *Mahavakyas* mean (*Maha* = great; *Vakya* = aphorism/apothegm/ aphorism) great sayings from the *Upanishads*. The *Mahavakyas* are thus short, pithy sayings taken from the *Upanishads* which explain the Advaita philosophy that the *Atman* and *Brahman* are one. These terse sayings emphasize the fact that the soul in our body is indeed a reflection of the Absolute *Brahman*, which is formless, omniscient, and omnipresent. The whole concept of *Brahman* is capsulized in these aphorisms. The four important Mahavakyas are:

तत् त्वम् असि   *Tat Tvam Asi*   That Thou Art (Chandogya.U)

अहं ब्रह्मास्मि   *Aham Brahmasmi*   *I am Brahman* (Brihadaranyaka U)

प्रज्ञानं ब्रह्म   *Prajnanam Brahma*   Prajñāna is Brahman (Aitareya U)

अयम् आत्मा ब्रह्म   *Ayam Atma Brahma*   This Atman is Brahman (Mandukya U)

All these mean that the *Atman* in us and the *Brahman* are the same. The word *'Prajnanam'* indicates the <u>highest form of wisdom and intelligence</u>. There are more such *Vakyas* in the *Upanishads,* but these are the four important *Mahavakyas.*

**"Grandpa, tell us the tale of the churning of the milky ocean and the symbolism behind it" Vijaya, the little one was always interested in the mythology part.**

The churning of the Milky Ocean named *Ksheera Sagara Mathanam* in Sanskrit (*Ksheera* = <u>milk</u>; *Sagara* = <u>ocean</u>; *Mathanam* = <u>churning</u>) is described in many of our *Puranas* like the *Mahabharatha,* *Vishnu Purana* and *Srimad Bhagavatham.* Let me summarize the story for you.

One day, Indra, the ruler of the heavens was traveling on his elephant, when he met the sage Durvasa on the way. Durvasa gave Indra a garland of divine sweet-smelling flowers. Indra carelessly placed this garland on the head of his elephant. The strong fragrance of the flowers attracted bees, and the buzzing of bees annoyed the elephant which threw the garland to the ground and trampled upon it. On feeling insulted, the sage became enraged and cursed Indra that he and his retinue of *Devas* would become weak and deprived of prosperity and youth.

Immediately, Indra and the Devas became weak and decrepit.

Upon the advice of *Bhagavan Vishnu*, Indra proclaimed a truce with the *Asuras* who had become all powerful and defeated the weak *Devas*. *Bhagavan Vishnu* instructed them to churn the milky ocean from which they could get *Amritam* (ambrosia/nectar) which could give them strength, vitality and restore the lost youthfulness. The *Bhagavan* advised them to use the mountain *Mandara* as the churning stick and the snake *Vasuki* as the rope for churning. The *Asuras* were recruited to help in the churning with a promise that the *Amritam* would be shared with them. Plenty of medicinal herbs and sacred articles were added to the ocean before churning. *Bhagavan Vishnu*, taking the *Avatar* as a giant tortoise (*Kurma Avatar*), supported the mountain on His back to prevent it from sinking into the ocean, and the churning began. The churning yielded an impressive array of sacred items out of the ocean. Some of them are:

- *Halahala*, a deadly poison which threatened to burn up the whole earth was the first to emerge from the ocean. This was immediately consumed by *Bhagavan Siva*, and it lodged in his neck. That gave a blue color to his neck and hence the name '*Neelakandan*' (*Neelam* = blue; *Kantam* = neck) for Siva.
- Subsequently, many precious jewels came out of the ocean.
- *Kamadhenu* or *Surabhi*, the cow that granted any wish emerged and was given to *the Rishis* who required it for obtaining milk, ghee and curd needed for the *Yajnas*.

- *Ucchaisravas*, the seven-headed white horse appeared which Indra, the king of the Heavens wanted to own. But as the *Asura* King *Mahabali* liked to have it, *Bhagavan Vishnu* assigned it to him.

- *Airavata*, the white elephant with four tusks, was given to Indra.

- *Kousthubham*, the most valuable gemstone in the universe was received by *Bhagavan Vishnu* who wore it on his chest.

- *Kalpaka Vriksha*, a wish-granting tree was granted to the *Devas* and was planted in Devaloka.

- The divine *Apsaras* or <u>nymphs</u> were designated by Indra as dancers in Devaloka.

- After this radiating a heavenly glow and dazzling with exquisite jewellery, *Goddess Mahalakshmi* arose out of the milky ocean captivating everyone with her beauty. She espoused *Bhagavan Maha Vishnu* as her consort.

- *Varuni*, the Goddess of wine was given to the *Asuras* with the permission of *Bhagavan Maha Vishnu*.

- *Dhanvantari*, the physician of the Gods finally emerged with a pot containing the *Amritam* for the *Devas*. The *Devas* accepted the *Amritam*.

The story, of course continues saying that a tussle ensued between the *Devas* and the *Asuras* and the *Asuras* snatched the vessel of *Amritam* and ran away with it. Whereupon *Bhagavan Vishnu* appeared in the form of an exquisitely beautiful maiden – *Mohini* and tricked the *Asuras* and distributed the *Amritam* to the *Devas*. Finally, the *Devas* regained their strength, vitality and youth.

The story sounds preposterous and belies logical explanation appearing absurdly fictional. But let us look at the philosophy and allegory behind this. We should understand that most of our mythological stories in the scriptures have great philosophical truths hidden deep within them. Our endeavour should be to understand and imbibe the tenets and morals and not just listen to the fascinating stories.

The ocean is always known as a great repository and source of wealth. Oceans are broad and deep. The *Milky Ocean* represents the *Mind* or *Consciousness* of man which in its depths has many thoughts – good and bad, positive and negative, creative and destructive. These thoughts arise from the *Anthakaranam* which includes the *Manas* (mind), *Ahamkaram* (ego), *Buddhi* (memory) and the *Chittam* (intellect). The whole episode of the churning of the milky ocean echoes the spiritual aspirations of man to attain the highest perfection or *Moksha* which is the central theme of the *Sanatana Dharma*. In the process, the human mind encounters many obstacles which tend to hinder his ascent to perfection or salvation. The 'churning' implies the tough spiritual practices like yoga, meditation, strict discipline, austerities, renunciation, self-control, control of the senses etc., to reach that ultimate goal.

The *Devas* and the *Asuras* are the *gods* and *demons* within us. Our mind has both positive (*Deva*) and negative (*Asura*) tendencies. The gods or *Devas* represent our sense organs and our positive side like goodness, discipline, compassion, non-violence, love, devotion, virtues etc., while the demons or *Asuras* are the negative tendencies like hate, greed, jealousy, violence, anger, evil propensities etc. The *Devas* are the *Sattvic* qualities in an individual whereas the *Asuras* represent the *Rajasic* and *Tamasic* qualities.

The churning epitomizes the smooth integration of the positive and negative qualities (*Devas* and *Asuras*) to achieve proper balance in life and attain *Moksha*. The negative tendencies (*Asuras*) act as deterrents in our journey towards our goal which is immortality (*Amritam*) or *Moksha*. *Amritam* means 'absence of death' or 'deathlessness' or 'immortality'.

The mountain *'Mandara'* denotes 'concentration' (*Man* =mind; *Dhara* = a point) – single pointed mind. Spiritual practice needs a single pointed mind and concentration. *Bhagavan Vishnu* supported the mountain on his back assuming the form of a tortoise. The 'tortoise' represents what has been described as *'Pratyahara'* in *Ashtanga Yoga* – withdrawal of one's five sense organs from the external world to concentrate and meditate on the inner divine nature of man. Just like the tortoise withdraws its head and its four limbs (five organs), we should withdraw our five senses from the external objects. This helps to elevate our mind to higher levels as the *Kurma Avataram* lifted the *Mandara* mountain. *Bhagavan Vishnu* provides the support for the mind when we concentrate and meditate. The tortoise also is said to symbolize our heads with its hard outer skull outside and the soft brain inside which is the seat of the *mind, ego, intellect and memory (Anthakaranam)* which supports all our spiritual pursuits.

The snake *Vasuki* which adorns the neck of *Bhagavan Siva* was used as the rope. This symbolizes the desire and intention for our spiritual achievement. Desire is the driving force behind all our actions, both selfish actions and self-less actions. Thus like the rope churning the ocean, our minds sway between the various desires. The *Asuras* had selfish desires whereas the Devas had desires for the good of the world.

The 'churning' represents the spiritual transformation of the mind to achieve *Moksha* or liberation from the cycles of birth and death. When milk is churned, the cream or butter separates from the milk. Similarly, the churning of the mind with meditation and concentration with the support of *Bhagavan Vishnu* helps us  get rid of the negative impurities in the mind and acquire the pure discriminatory consciousness or '*Amritam*'.

The *Halahala* poison that separated from the ocean symbolizes the quintessence of  all the negative tendencies, evil thoughts, and vile propensities in the mind and the *Vasanas* which are eliminated from our mind by our spiritual practices. *Bhagavan Siva* is symbolized as a *Yogi* who has the power of equanimity and purity in Him. He could swallow the poison as he had the strength to retain it in his neck without being affected by it. Thus, a *Yogi* is not affected by the negative tendencies of the mind. The *Halahala* poison lodged in the <u>neck</u> of Bhagavan Siva. The neck is equidistant between the head and the heart. Thus, the poison or *Vasanas* should neither affect the *head* (mind, and intellect) or the *heart* (emotions and feelings) of the individual.

During spiritual practices and meditation, the yogi may develop many *siddhis* (<u>spiritual</u>, <u>paranormal</u> or <u>magical powers</u>), but one should not be carried away by this as the goal is not the *siddhis*, but ultimate liberation or *Moksha*. The siddhis may act as deterrent in the spiritual path to the ultimate goal of man. These are symbolized by the bewildering array of material and distracting objects that arose out of the milky ocean while churning it.

One of the outcomes of the churning was *Goddess Lakshmi* and she espoused *Bhagavan Vishnu*. Likewise, the *Yogi* who is in the spiritual path should acknowledge that everything in the universe belongs to the supreme *Brahman* and work selflessly and not hanker after material possessions and wealth. *Goddess Lakshmi* represents <u>wealth</u> and <u>prosperity</u>. *Dhanvantari* the Divine Physician likewise symbolizes physical, mental and spiritual health and these are the acquisitions by a person who lives by self-discipline and self-control.

*Mohini*, who appears after the *Amritam* is obtained symbolizes *Maya* (<u>illusion</u>) and the various distractions and delusions which hinder the path to salvation. The *Asuras* fell under the spell of *Mohini* (Maya) and hence did not get to partake in the *Amritam*. The *Devas* who were intent and focussed on obtaining *Amritam* were given to enjoy the benefit of *Amritam*. *Mohini* (*Bhagavan Vishnu*) also saw to it that the *Asuras*, who were always against the path of *Dharma* did not receive the *Amritam* and only the *Devas* who were on the path of *Dharma* received it. The cruel and evil actions of the Asuras made them ineligible and incompetent to receive the *Amritam* due to their evil *Karmas*.

**MAHA VISHNU**

**"Why do our deities have so many arms? And many of these arms hold mortal weapons or other objects. Please explain these to us."** **Aditya was curious to know the answer.**

Let us start with the four arms of *Bhagavan Vishnu*. The four arms represent the four *Purushartas* namely, *Dharma, Artha, Kama* and *Moksha*. The arms also symbolize the four cardinal directions – North, South, East and West. *Bhagavan Vishnu* holds four objects in his four arms. We will see them one by one.

The **conch** held on his left upper hand is called '*Panchajanyam*' and represents sound. Sound vibrations are the source of creation in the universe. The primeval sound '***OHM***' arises when the conch is blown. Moreover, '*Panchajanyam*' (*Pancha* = <u>five</u>; *Janya* = <u>born</u>) represents the five senses and the five elements (earth, fire, water, space and air) which are needed for creation. The conch represents the supreme power of *Brahman* to create and maintain the universe and all objects and living beings in it.

*Bhagavan Vishnu* holds the **Gada** (<u>mace</u>) named '*Koumodaki*' in his left lower hand. The mace indicates *Power*, which is physical, mental and spiritual. The mace within    us should destroy the twin evils of 'laziness' (*Aalasyam*) and 'lack of discrimination' (*Avivekam*). We do not know the inner strength which is present within us which can purify and uplift us by destroying the negative tendencies like the mace smashes objects to smithereens.

In His right lower hand, *Bhagavan Vishnu* holds a **lotus** flower. The lotus is a flower which grows in muddy swamps but rises above the muddy waters and stands tall facing the sun. the lotus symbolizes our mind which opens and attains perfection when facing the sun (*Brahman*). The lotus grows in water, but water does not wet the lotus or its leaves. Man should live in the world like the lotus without getting attached to the material objects in the world. He should be *concerned* but not *attached*. As the doctor feels a "*detached concern*" about his patient, so also one should live in this world with concern towards our kith and kin, friends and well-wishers  but not become overly attached to them or to the mundane and ephemeral material possessions. The lotus also symbolizes *purity, abundance* and *spiritual unfoldment*.

In His right upper hand, he holds the **Sudarshana Chakra**. (*Su* = auspicious/ good ; *Darsanam* = vision/ sight ; *Chakra* = wheel; cycle). It is a spinning discus with multiple spokes. It symbolizes the cycle of birth and death. It also epitomizes the mind which should see only the good things in life (*Sudarshana*). The *Chakra* also symbolizes 'Time' which controls every person's life.

The *Sudarshana Chakra* represents the active mind. *Vishnu* used the *Chakra* to destroy His enemies. Symbolically, the enemies within us are the negative tendencies or the *Asuras* which are destroyed by the *Sudarshana Chakra* by giving us an 'auspicious vision' (*Su-Darsanam*) of the *Brahman*.

The **color** of Bhagavan Vishnu is said to be blue like that of the sky. This represents the cosmic dimensions of the *Absolute Reality*. He is said to sojourn in the *Milky Ocean* which represents *bliss*. The thousand-headed snake – *Ananthan* on the coils of which Bhagavan rests denotes *Time* which is cyclical and eternal. The thousand heads of *Ananthan* represent the infinite divisions of time.

The many arms of our deities are truly symbolic of the multiple tasks that they undertake. You can see that in the symbolism of *Bhagavan Vishnu*, you find that *Creation, Maintenance, Destruction* of enemies (negative tendencies) and uplifting the minds of the devotees all are His functions. This multi-faceted multi-tasking responsibilities of the deities is the reason why many of them are depicted with many arms.

**"In that case, tell us why the *Asura Ravana* in the Ramayana is depicted with ten heads", Vijaya wanted to know.**

*Ravana* or *Dasaanana* as he is called was an *Asura* king who ruled Sri Lanka. He is the villain of the epic *Ramayana* where he abducts Sita, the wife of Sri Rama. *Ravana* was an erudite scholar. He was well versed in the four *Vedas* and the six *Sastras*. *Ravana* was a maestro of the *Veena*, a stringed instrument which is used as accompaniment in Carnatic music. He was also an efficient warrior and a shrewd politician. He has authored books on Hindu Astrology and in *Siddha* system of medicine. His knowledge was so extensive that he was depicted to have ten heads (*Six Sastras + Four Vedas*). His ten heads are also said to symbolize the six vices, *Kama* (<u>lust</u>), *Krodha* (<u>anger</u>), *Moha* (<u>delusion</u>), *Lobha* (<u>greed</u>), *Mada* (<u>pride</u>) and *Matsarya* (<u>jealousy</u>; <u>envy</u>) which filled his four other heads represented by the *Manas*, *Ahamkara*, *Buddhi* and *Chitta* about which we have spoken before. The six vices which affected his mindset set him on the path of self-destruction when he abducted Sita.

*Ravana* and his two brothers represented the three *Gunas* in human nature. *Ravana* with his pride and insatiable lust for power symbolized the *Rajasic Guna* in man. His brother *Kumbha Karna* who was a glutton and slept for six months in a year was the symbol of *Tamasic Guna* and *Vibhishana* who was the pious and righteous of the three represented the *Sattvic* aspect of human nature.

**"Grandpa, what is the meaning of the word 'Advaita'? What does it signify?", Jaya's question was logical after listening to my discussions on Hinduism.**

The word '*Advaita*' in Sanskrit means '<u>without a second</u>'. But it has been represented as '<u>nondualism</u>' – a state of being 'single' and not 'dual'. It means that *Brahman* alone is the true Reality. Everything else is *Maya* or illusion. *"The truth is one, scholars call it by different names*". Everything is a manifestation of that *Brahman*. All the four *Mahavakyas* which we have already discussed indicate the same thing. The *Jeevatma* or the <u>soul</u> in us is but a reflection of the *Brahman*. We are not different from the <u>Brahman</u>. Everything that looks different is but one and the same.

We have four fingers and a thumb – but each one is different from the other, but all are part of the one hand. The hand is part of the arm the arms and the legs are different but are part of the one body. When we go deeper into it, everything in the universe is made of the same basic particle - *the atom*, and if you divide it further you get protons, electrons and neutrons which are common for every living being and non-living things in the universe. Ultimately it boils down to this reality. So too, *Brahman* is the Reality from which everything in the universe has sprung.

We have already talked about Adi Sankaracharya who has popularized the *Advaita* philosophy which was already propounded in the *Vedas* but was misinterpreted by the scholars of his day. He emphasised the fact that *Brahman* and I are one and the same – *Aham Brahmasmi*. The *Brahman* and the Self in me are the same – not different.

Advaita philosophy declares that the world is an illusion. It is perceived only as long as the <u>Self</u> (*Atman*) occupies the body. Once the Atman separates from the body, the world disappears. I know that this is abstract philosophy and little bit difficult to understand, but just imagine what happens when you are put under an anaesthetic agent by the doctor. You no longer perceive the world or any of the objects. Your eye is "alive", but you do not see, your ear is "active", but you cannot hear, your skin is "viable", but you do not feel touch or pain when the surgeon cuts into your skin. Your consciousness is now removed from the world around you. Only when the consciousness is restored does the whole world reappear.

**"Tell us about Creation, Grandpa. How do we learn new things? Where is this knowledge about newer things, scientific inventions and discoveries coming from?" Aditya's questions were always logical and challenging.**

We have touched upon this subject in one of our previous discussions. Still, I will briefly explain. All creations in the universe came from the *Brahman*. From the *Brahman* arose the primeval sound and from that the other elements and so on as we have discussed already. As a functionary of this creation, *Brahman* designated *Bhagavan Brahma*, as the God of Creation. Remember, the *Brahman* and *Bhagavan Brahma* are different.

For creating anything, you need three factors :

- **Desire**, which is called *Iccha Sakthi* (*Iccha* = <u>desire</u>; *Sakthi* = <u>power</u>)
- **Knowledge**, which is called *Jnana Sakthi* (*Jnana* = <u>knowledge</u>)
- **Action**, which is called *Kriya Sakthi* (*Kriya* = <u>action</u>)

**265**

Only when these three are available can anything be created. Take for example, you want to construct a house. You must first possess the **desire** to construct one. But that alone is inadequate. You need the **knowledge**. You must put your knowledge into **action** to build the house. All these three occur in the mind first because, *every creation first occurs in the mind.* You desire for it in your mind, your knowledge then chalks out a plan and you decide on a course of action before embarking on the real construction. All this is needed to concretize your desire to build a house.

Consider making a cup of coffee. First of all,

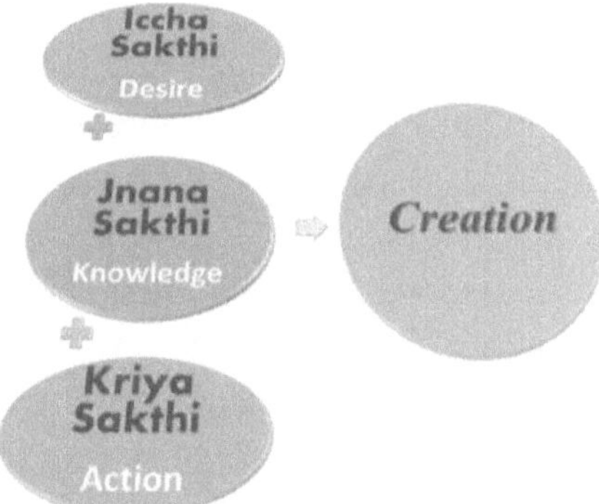


you must have the <u>desire</u> to drink a cup of coffee. You must have the <u>knowledge</u> of how to make coffee. And you must <u>act</u> to procure the ingredients – the coffee powder, milk, sugar and boiling water to make it. Thus, for every creation, you need these three potential requisites. Even having a child first begins as a desire in the minds of the husband and wife.

*Bhagavan Brahma* was empowered with the job of creation and scriptural texts have it that he began creation in earnest after acquiring these three skills of *Iccha, Jnana* and *Kriya Sakthi* by meditating for a long time. At first, he created the elements, then he created the *Anthakaranam* (*Manas, Buddhi, Chittam* and *Ahamkaram.*) Next, he created the five sensory perceptions like the *sight, hearing, smell, touch* and *taste*. Following this, were created the five sense organs and then the five elements in nature combined with all of the above was used in the creation of man and all the living beings on earth.

All the knowledge that is to be known is already there in the cosmos. Man derives this knowledge using his four *Anthakaranams* – *Mind, Memory, Intellect* and *Ego*. The invention of the computer, rocket science, conquest of space, artificial intelligence, marvels of modern medical breakthroughs and all scientific discoveries and inventions have arisen from the deep recesses of the minds of man. And what is that mind? The mind is but a projection of the *Brahman* or the Absolute Universal Consciousness which is the repository of Universal Knowledge. All the knowledge that is yet to come in the world is already there. Man's mind has to draw upon it using his mind and intellect. Wherefrom do you think our ancient sages wrote about mathematics, astronomy, geometry, medicine and other topics which we have already discussed?

**"Grandpa, tell us about *Maya* which you were touching upon in your discussion. What is it? How do we recognize Maya? How do we overcome Maya?" again it was Aditya's turn to pose the question.**

*Maya* in Sanskrit literally means 'illusion' or 'magic' or 'make-believe'. It is the cosmic delusion that makes us believe that what we see as the materialistic world is real. The real nature of the *Self* and the Absolute Self or *Brahman* is shrouded in ignorance by *Maya. Maya* is ignorance. It hides the true nature of the *Brahman* from us.

Man is essentially divine. We are pure, perfect, free and we are the *Brahman.* Our true Self or *Atman* and *Brahman* are one and the same. *We are indeed spiritual beings in a human body.* But do we know it ? No, we are not aware of our true nature due to the camouflage of *Maya* or <u>ignorance</u> that clouds our mind and hides this spiritual truth.

While watching a movie, we see colorful images that keep on changing on the screen, but the screen is fixed, unchanging and white with no variation. But you need the unchanging screen to view the images of the movie. So also, the changing world around us is present in the unchanging Brahman. But we think that our body is real and identify with it. The "I" in me is really the *Self* (*Brahman*), but we falsely believe that "*I*" am the body.

*Maya* is like the cloud that obscures the sun giving the false impression that the sun is absent. The Maya that clouds our mind is the egotism, hatred, anger, ambition, jealousy, envy, lust and the negative emotions which prevent us from recognising the true divine nature of ourselves. Meditation and spiritual practices drive the clouds of *Maya* away and makes the sun of our divine nature shine bright.

Illusion literally means '*something that deceives by producing a false or misleading impression of reality*'. A thick rope on the road at night may appear to the pedestrian as a snake. Once he shines a torchlight on it, the snake disappears, and the rope remains. Illusion is unreality. It is not that the world around us does not exist. It does. But it is not what it appears to be always. That is the *Maya* that shrouds it. The world around us keeps on changing, our experiences change, our perceptions change. What you see as the world may not be what I see as the world. Perceptions of the world changes depending on the person who perceives the world. Maya also means, *"that which is changing and hence spiritually Unreal"*. All ignorance is also called *Maya*.

We give undue importance to our successes, failure, sorrows and sufferings. These are all transitory experiences. *'This too must pass'* is the maxim that we must follow. We should understand that the world around us is what we perceive it as. It is real and tangible, but at the same time it is unreal in the sense that it keeps on changing. It is like the "virtual reality" that you create on the Internet. The dreams that we see when we sleep appear to be absolutely real and vivid as long as we are asleep. But the moment we wake up the whole dream is recognized by us as an illusion created by our brains while we were asleep.

The same world which we see around us can be seen differently by different individuals. the same world that we see today may not be there tomorrow. Our body tomorrow will be different. In our body, every moment there is change occurring. Cells multiply and also get destroyed. The skin sheds constantly to be replaced by new skin. Childhood gives way to youth, youth to middle age which gives way to old age and ultimately to death. All this change is part of the changing world.

**Grandpa, if I cannot change my *Prarabdha* which is the result of my actions in my past lives, then why should I endeavour to change my future by working hard or trying to be virtuous. After all it is my fate to suffer in this life.**

You have got it all wrong. You are having problems, sorrows and suffering in this life due to your past *Sanchita Karma*; I agree. I hope that is clear to you. What you should know is that you cannot change that what has happened already. But you must learn to face it with equanimity or sang froid. The slings and arrows of fortune should not unnerve you. Learn to accept it with calmness. Be it good luck or bad luck, accept both with a balanced mind because you cannot change it. But you can change yourself to accept this with fortitude. So, to face the *Prarabdha*, you need to change yourself.

But you should always attempt to change your present by working positively  towards success, getting your problems solved and moving up the ladder of achievements and accomplishments. Success will definitely reward you then. That is, you are creating altogether a new genre of *Kriyamana Karma* which is going to change not only your future in this life, but also in any future lives you may have. Hence, facing life with composure and accepting success and failure, joy and sorrow, pain and pleasure with equal fortitude is what you should learn to do. But at the same time, you should endeavour to improve your life and circumstances by doing positive karmas so as to make your future secure and bright. That is the secret of karma. *Bhagavan Sri Krishna* explains it thus in the *Bhagavad Gita.*

सुखदुःखे समे कृत्वा लाभालाभौ जयाजयौ |<br>
ततो युद्धाय युज्यस्व नैवं पापमवाप्स्यसि || 2ः38||

*sukha-duḥkhe same kṛitvā lābhālābhau*<br>
*jayājayau*<br>
*tato yuddhāya yujyasva naivaṁ pāpam*<br>
*avāpsyasi*

It means, *"Fight for the sake of duty, treating alike happiness and distress, loss and gain, victory and defeat. Fulfilling your responsibility in this way, you will never incur sin".*

**"Grandpa, does Hinduism mention charity? What is the importance of charity in Hinduism?" Jaya was curious to know.**

*Daanam* (<u>charity</u>) is the sharing of your lawfully earned wealth with the needy and is considered one of the supreme virtues in Hinduism. Charity or *Daanam* helps to reduce the burden of our sins or '*Sanchita Karma*' and elevates us spiritually. Scriptures say that charity, be it food, clothes, money, or materials  should be given only to the needy and deserving. There is no point in giving costly goods or materials to a person who is already well off. Giving food to those who are well fed is not '*Annadaanam*' (*Anna* = <u>food</u>; *Daanam* = <u>donation</u>).

There is an interesting parable about *Karna* who is an important character in the *Mahabharata.*

He was the king of *Anga* and was one of the most philanthropic persons of the time. But he always donated wealth to the needy in the form of gold, silver, land, and other material goods. When he reached heaven after his death, he found that he could not eat food properly and always had indigestion. The God *Yamaraj*, who was in charge of Heaven told *Karna* that he had not given food to the needy - *Annadaanam*, when he was king. He always focused on giving wealth and gold to the poor but had not fed the hungry. So, *Yamaraj*, asked *Karna* to go back to earth and perform *Annadaanam* for one whole fortnight before returning to heaven. Only then did *Karna* get relief from his digestive problem. This story only goes to prove the importance of giving food to the hungry.

Helping a poor student in his studies by paying his fees for school or college is one of the greatest of charities that one can do in modern times. Granting knowledge to someone who has no access to it because of lack of resources is one of the greatest charities that one can do. If you cannot teach a person and share your knowledge, you can at least help him acquire knowledge by helping him financially to acquire the knowledge.

## विद्या धनम् सर्व धनं प्रधानम

*Vidya dhanam sarva dhanath pradhanam*

It means, *'Knowledge is the most important of all types of wealth'*.

A gift or donation given to the wrong person at the wrong time in the wrong place is also of no benefit. Charity should always be given to the deserving person at the proper time and place. Similarly, charity done with an ulterior motive of gaining name and fame bears no fruit. It is a charity for selfish ends. So is charity done expecting some other benefit in return. Real charity, which is said to be *Saatvic*, is that which is done to the person who is in real need of help, without any expectations. As the saying goes, '*do not remember what you give and do not forget what you receive*'.

*Daanam* is also part of many of the rituals and *Yajnas* in Hinduism. During the obsequies rituals after the death a person, various types of *Daanam* are given to assist the safe journey of the soul to the *Pitru lokas*.

**"Grandpa why is the river *Ganga* considered sacred for Hindus?" Vijaya wanted to know.**

The river *Ganga* is named 'Ganges' in English. It is the Hellenic (Greek) version of the name given when Emperor Alexander of Macedonia came to India around 300 BCE. This is similar to the name 'Hindu' which they gave for 'Sindhu'. The Ganges is the longest river in India. It arises from the Himalayas in the *Gangotri* glaciers and ends in the Bay of Bengal. It flows through India and Bangladesh. The *Ganga* is the most sacred river for Hindus and is worshipped as Goddess *Ganga*. Immersing the ashes of a dead person in the *Ganga* is considered to give him *Moksha*. The river is pure and can purify the souls of the departed. Many Hindu households have a small, sealed metallic vessel of *Ganga Jal* (<u>Ganges water</u>) kept in the *Pooja* room. This is given to a person who is dying hoping that a sip of *Ganga Jal* at the end of life will liberate his soul.

The *Ganga* was initially a river in the heavens and descended to earth when king *Bhageeratha* brought it down to earth through rigorous *tapas* (<u>penance</u>) to provide salvation to his 60,000 ancestors who had been burnt to ashes by the curse of sage *Kapila*. This story is given in the *Mahabharata*.

In the *Mahabharata*, the grand sire *Bhishma* was born to King *Shantanu* and Goddess *Ganga*. But *Ganga* left the king with the eighth new-born child due to misunderstanding with the king. She took the boy with her, educated him and taught him all skills needed for a king. Later, when the boy was sixteen, she entrusted the boy to the king and went back to heaven. There are many legends connected with the *Ganga*. You can learn more about these when you read the *Mahabharata* and the *Vishnu Purana*.

**How much of one's wealth should one give as donation or charity according to Hindu texts? Is anything mentioned about this?" Vijaya was curious.**

The wealth earned by an individual should be used for spiritual and material purposes. This was told by Sage *Sukracharya* who was the *Guru* to the *Asuras*. This was mentioned in the context of King *Mahabali* who promised to give *Vamana, Bhagavan Vishnu's Avatar,* whatever the brahmin boy requested as alms.

The sage did not want the king to part with his wealth by giving blanket promises. Whereupon he advised the king as to how much of one's wealth one should give as charity.

The income earned by a person through honest and lawful means should be roughly divided into *five* portions.

One portion should be spent by the person for <u>himself</u> for his own benefit. It should be spent for the upkeep of his own body.

The second portion should be spent for his <u>family</u> whom he is duty bound to take care of.

The third portion should be spent for the <u>future</u>, meaning it should be saved and used for future needs.

The fourth portion should be used for the benefit of <u>society</u> (<u>charity & service</u>) and for giving back to society what society gave him. This included the charitable acts and help rendered to the poor and the needy and included all types of *Daanam*. Thus one-fifth of one's earnings should be spent for charitable purposes.

The fifth portion was to be used for the <u>spiritual upliftment</u> of the individual like going for *Satsangs*, going on pilgrimage to holy places, visiting ashrams for gaining spiritual knowledge etc. In the modern age this would include all the above including sharing one's spiritual knowledge through talks and writings and spending wealth on reading books on spirituality and attending *Satsangs* by scholars and sannyasis.

**"Grandpa, you were mentioning during our discussions that during our visit to the temple or while worshipping at home, one should not ask God for any favors or material benefits. Then what do we worship God for?" Jaya was skeptical.**

I would suggest that you refresh what we discussed when we talked about worship, temple worship and *Poojas*. But your doubt as to what to ask God when you pray is a very practical and extremely important question.

Does your mother want anything from you when she showers her love and affection on you? Do you want anything in return when you share your milk chocolate with your close friend? You adore a movie star and absolutely worship him, don't you? What do you expect from him?

The answer to all this is that it is done without expecting anything in return. So also, is the worship of God. You may be a *Bhakta* (<u>devotee</u>) of *Siva, Krishna, Lakshmi, Vishnu, Hanuman*, or any God. The love, surrender and devotion you show to the deity is important. When you do a *Pooja*, as we have already discussed, we consider the deity as an honored guest in our home and offer our food, hospitality, and praise for Him. Worshipping God is also exactly similar. You do it for your own sake, for the spiritual satisfaction that it gives you, the uplifting emotion that it generates in you. You always seek God's blessing to give you the *'power of discrimination'* (*Viveka Buddhi*) and a *'stable balanced mind'* (*Sthithaprajna*). If you possess these two qualities, you can overcome any adverse situation and face any problem in life. Your devotion or *Bhakti* calms your mind and relieves the tension and stress of life. You develop the firm faith that God is always with you and will look after your welfare through thick and thin.

One should not ask God for material benefits like wealth, promotion in one's job, success in an examination, or solution to your problems. God knows what you need. *God will give you what you deserve, not what you covet.* You should seek His blessings to give you the power and the ability to confront and solve your problems yourself. That is what you should ask for while worshipping God.

**"Does the Hindu pray for others when he prays at home, in the temple or when he conducts a *Pooja*? Or does he pray for himself only?" Aditya wanted to know.**

Yes definitely, when a Hindu worships he does not *"pray"*. The word pray also has meanings like *'petition'*, *'entreat'* and *'beg'*. When a Hindu worships, he includes the whole of mankind in his worship. He seeks the health and well-being of all beings on earth. I will give you a couple of verses that Hindus chant at the end of every *Pooja* or worship, be it at home or the temple.

लोकः समस्ताः सुखिनो भवन्तु)

*Lokah Samastah Sukhino Bhavantu*

**277**

It means, *"May all beings, everywhere in the world, be free and happy"*.

सर्वेशां स्वस्तिर्भवतु ।
सर्वेशां शान्तिर्भवतु ।
सर्वेशां पूर्णंभवतु ।
सर्वेशां मङ्गलंभवतु ।

***Om sarveshaam swastir bhavatu |***
***Sarveshaam shaantir bhavatu |***
***Sarveshaam purnam bhavatu |***
***Sarveshaam mangalam bhavatu |***

It means, *"May there be Well-Being in All, May there be Peace in All, May there be Fulfilment in All, May there be Auspiciousness in All."*

सर्वे भवन्तु सुखिनः
सर्वे सन्तु निरामयाः ।
सर्वे भद्राणि पश्यन्तु
मा कश्चिद्दुःखभाग्भवेत् ।

*Om sarve bhavantu Sukhinah*
*Sarve santu Niramayaah |*
*Sarve bhadraani pashyantu*
*Maa kashcid duhkha Bhaagbhavet |*

It means, *"May all be happy, May all be free from illness, May all see what is auspicious, May no one suffer"*.

ॐ शान्तिः शान्तिः शान्तिः ॥

*Om Shaantih Shaantih Shaantih ||*

It means, "Om, Peace, Peace, Peace." The final chant of *Shanti* or <u>Peace</u> thrice is for emphasis. This is called *"Trivaaram Satyam"* (*Trivaaram* = thrice; *Satyam* = <u>truth</u>). In Hinduism, anything which is chanted thrice is said to come true. The word 'Peace' is chanted thrice to seek Cosmic Peace. Every *Pooja* or *Yajna* ends with this incantation.

Thus, you see that the Hindu priest or common folk do not pray for the uplift of Hindus only. They always pray for the uplift of the whole humanity, not only in India, but all over the world. The chanting encompasses <u>all the living beings on earth, not man alone</u>.

**"Grandpa, you said that one should worship God and not ask for anything in return. But do you think that all devotees or *Bhaktas* are like that?" Vijaya, the little one had her doubts.**

Yes, dear, you are very correct. There are distinct types of *Bhaktas*. They are called the *Arta, Jijnasu, Artharthi,* and *Jnani*. I will briefly explain who they are.

The **Arta** are the distressed group of devotees. They are very devoted to God but seek his blessings to relieve them of their pain and

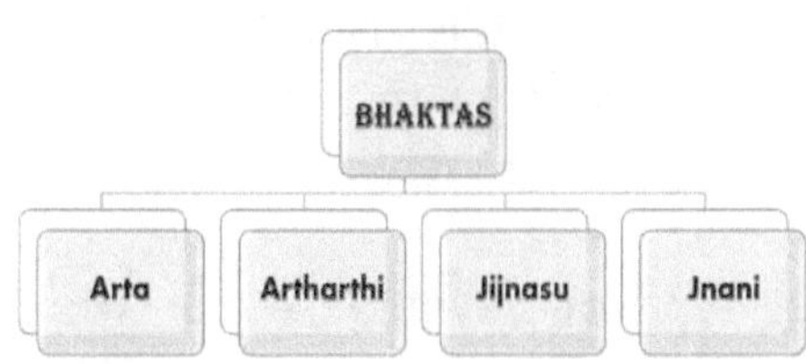


suffering – be it mental or physical. They seek God's help in relieving them of their sorrow and misery. We see many such devotees in the temples doing many types of *Poojas* and '*Vazhipaadu*' (special offering or *Pooja* in a temple) to mitigate their suffering.

The **Artharthi** are the devotees who worship God for material gains like wealth, position, name, fame, good progeny etc. They are also genuine devotees, but their goal is not *Moksha* but material prosperity. They seek God's blessing for attainment of these benefits.

The **Jijnasu** are those inquisitive devotees who seek to know the truth about *Brahman*. They delve into the scriptures, listen to satsangs, debate with scholars and *Gurus* and follow all the precepts in our heritage to seek the truth about the Supreme Consciousness. They seek God's blessings to guide them towards wisdom and enlightenment.

The **Jnani** is the one who has realized the true nature of God – the *Brahman*. He has attained perfection and is devoid of all attachments. He has no desires; he has realized God and realizes his oneness with the *Brahman*. He has attained the ultimate in the goal of Hinduism. He no longer needs idol or  temple worship to realize God.

Another classification is given for the *Bhaktas* in the *Srimad Bhagavatham* in the 11th Canto, 2nd Chapter. They are also ardent devotees.

The first type of devotee is one who sees *Brahman* in everything and every living being in the world. For him, the *Atman* in every living being is the same and he appreciates the unity in diversity. He is called the **Uttama Bhaktan** (<u>superior devotee</u>).

The second type is a staunch devotee of God. He is compassionate towards all beings and other devotees. He partakes in *Satsangs* and worships God with all his heart. He has the qualities of love, compassion, friendship. But he discriminates between the different living beings and man. He does not feel the oneness with all creations. He is called the **Madhyama Bhaktan** (<u>mediocre devotee</u>) .

The third type of devotee is also a sincere bhakta. But he believes that God is in the temple and in the idols which he worships as deities. He does not necessarily feel oneness of all creations, nor does he feel the need to be compassionate towards other devotees. He strongly believes that God will bless him and grant his wishes if he worships the idols. He sticks to ritualistic worship only. He is called the **Praakrita Bhaktan** (<u>inferior devotee</u>).

The details regarding these three groups are exhaustively given in the *Srimad Bhagavatham* and you can read it for yourselves later when you are older. So much regarding the devotees. Now let us look at the diverse types of *Bhakti* (<u>devotion</u>). *Bhakti* itself is also of two types.

**Kamya Bhakti** (*Kama*= <u>desire</u>) which is devotion to God to get something in return like wealth, health, progeny etc. This is devotion with expectations.

**Nishkama Bhakti** (*Nishkama* = <u>without desire</u>) which is absolute surrender and devotion to God without seeking anything from Him. This is devotion without expectations.

**Vijaya wanted to know how children should worship. "What type of worship and japa should children like us do at this stage of life. We cannot do *Poojas* and *Yajnas*, after all. So, how can children like us practice Hinduism?"**

At the very beginning of my series of these discussions, I had told you that Hinduism is a way of life. It is a religion, but it is also a culture. Hence you must study more about the various aspects of Hinduism as you grow older. You must be knowledgeable about the main *Itihasas*, the *Ramayana* and the *Mahabharata*. Both these are available as short, summarized versions in English written by C. Rajagopalachari (Rajaji). You must read them to get an overall idea about these two epics. Later on, you can read larger books on these epics.

Another text that you must compulsorily read is the *Bhagavad Gita*. There are so many versions and commentaries on the book. But for children, there is a simpler book named *"Gita for Children"* written by Swami Chinmayananda. This is available freely and you must get hold of the book and read it.

In your next holidays, we shall discuss the Bhagavad Gita as to how it can help you in your future life. Or we will discuss another aspect of Hinduism which you will easily understand.

The other scriptures like the *Vedas* and *Upanishads* are a bit high-end for beginners like you. If you are interested, I would recommend abridged version of these which are available in English. The process of spiritual education and learning is a gradual but steady one. Swami Chinmayananda aptly called it '*Hastening slowly*'.

Regarding your question as to how children should practice Hinduism, I would suggest that you should inculcate self-discipline in your life. You have heard about the *Karma Yoga* and the practice of Meditation. As children, you can practice the *Hatha Yoga* which is the practice of *Asanas* or the <u>exercise component of the yoga</u>. This will keep your body healthy and fit. Meditation will sharpen your mind and intellect. It will help your memory. As children your *Karma* (<u>duty</u>) is to study. So, devote your energies to study and not get distracted by various evils in society like drugs, bad company, distracting movies, undesirable friends, and videos. Choose your friends carefully. Acquire whatever knowledge you can in your student life. This should include not only your academic knowledge, but also improve your knowledge regarding cultures, science, politics, philosophy, and religion. You should aim at expanding the horizon of your knowledge and skills. You should aspire to keep on acquiring knowledge throughout your life. Remember, '*to rest is to rust*'.

That does not mean you should not play and entertain yourselves. You know that all work and no play makes Jack a dull boy. So go out and play with friends and be happy. Enjoy your childhood. But have a fixed time for play and a time for studies and doing your other duties. Learn to respect your elders and revere your teachers and parents.

The values like honesty, non-violence, cleanliness, non-stealing etc., which are given in the *Ashtanga Yoga* of Patanjali is for everyone. They are the morals and values that everyone should strive to possess. You should mold your character to become a worthy citizen of whichever country you are in.

Regarding worship. Morning is the ideal time for worship. If you are busy with your preparations for school in the mornings, then you may not be able to spend too much time in the *Pooja* room. A ten minute worship would suffice. As youngsters, you should strive to rise early before sunrise, preferably in the *Brahma muhurtam.* Learn simple *slokas* (<u>verses, chants</u>). These are available as books or in a downloadable format. You can also listen to these on YouTube or through recorded CDs or videos. If you play the CD and simultaneously recite the slokas from the books, you will learn them easily and will not mispronounce any words. In the evening by dusk, light the lamp in the *Pooja* room or *Pooja* alcove in your home, sit in front of the deities and chant some of the *slokas* or *bhajans* with your eyes closed to avoid any visual distractions. Wearing the *Tilak* or <u>sacred ash</u> (*Bhasmam/ Vibhuthi*) on your forehead is desirable.

When you go to a temple, do not just go round the temple, and return. Sit for some time in that holy atmosphere, imbibing the divine ambience, chant some slokas in your mind, sit and meditate for some time and feel the presence of God in your hearts. That is how you should worship in a temple. Before leaving the temple, do not forget to prostrate before the deity. When you are in a temple, ask for nothing but blessings from God.

**"Grandpa, why do Hindus wear a Tilak or Bindi on their forehead? What is its significance?" Vijaya, the little one wanted to know why mother always insisted on her wearing a bindi after her bath.**

The *tilak* or the *bindi* is worn on the forehead between the eyebrows. This is the position of the *Ajna Chakra* one of the powerful *Kundalini chakras* and is a powerful energy point on our head. This point symbolizes the third eye of Siva. The *Ajna Chakra* represents the "<u>eye of intuition</u>". Men wear sandal paste on the forehead which we call *tilak* and women wear the *Bindi* or *Kumkumam* (<u>vermilion</u>) as a round dot on the forehead. Married women, in addition wear *Kumkumam* at the hairline on the top of the forehead. Those who worship *Bhagavan Siva* wear the *Bhasmam* or *Vibhuthi* (<u>sacred ash</u>) on the forehead as three horizontal lines. These are worn whenever any rituals or *Pooja* are performed. The *Vaishnavites* (<u>devotees of Maha Vishnu</u>) wear a **U**-shaped Sandal wood paste mark on the forehead, often with a vertical line in the center of the **U** drawn with *Kumkumam*. If you see the idol of *Bhagavan Venkateshwara* of Tirupati, you will appreciate this.

This spot where the *Tilak* or *Bindi* is worn is the site of spiritual power. When we meditate, we focus our mind on this point. Wearing the cooling sandalwood paste on the forehead calms the mind and helps concentration.

It is not mandatory that one should be a Hindu to wear a *Tilak*. A *tilak* on the forehead of a woman, enhances the beauty of the face and is often worn for cosmetic purposes by many women in India.

**"Which is the best time to worship God, and which is the ideal day of the week to worship God?" Jaya wanted to know. "Christians go to church on Sundays, Muslims to the masjid on Fridays. Likewise, do we have a date and time for worship?"**

An apt question. Sri Krishna in his Bhagavad Gita has very clearly said:

अनन्याश्चिन्तयन्तो मां ये जनाः पर्युपासते ।
तेषां नित्याभियुक्तानां योगक्षेमं वहाम्यहम् ।। 9-22 ।।

*Anan'yāścintayantō māṁ yē janāḥ paryupāsatē /*
*Tēṣāṁ nityābhiyuktānāṁ yōgakṣēmaṁ vahāmyahaṁ // 9-22 //*

It means, *"There are those who always think of Me and engage in exclusive devotion to Me. To them, whose minds are always absorbed in Me, I provide what they lack and preserve what they already possess."*

This clearly goes to prove that there is no definite time or day on which you worship God in Hinduism. Your mind should always be centred in His thought. Whatever you do, should be dedicated to God. Your thoughts, words and deeds should be dedicated to God. The word '*Ananya*' is a particularly important word. It means '<u>unique</u>' or '<u>no other</u>'. Meaning, you are no different from God. You are He. Think of him always as not separate from you.

**"Can we see God? If not, why?" Little Vijaya always had amusing queries.**

"Exceptionally good question. You are asking like some atheists do." Grandpa laughed aloud. Can you show God to me, is what the atheists ask. "Have you seen God?" asked Narendra (Swami Vivekananda) to Ramakrishna Paramahamsa when he first met him.

"*Yes, I see Him in you,*" replied Ramakrishna and Narendra, impressed, immediately became his follower.

True, you cannot see God with your anatomical fleshy eyes. *God is not to be seen. He is 'perceived' with your inner Anthakaranam – mind, buddhi and intellect.* You know that honey tastes sweet, isn't it? But can you see the sweetness in honey? No, you can only *perceive* it. Can you explain 'sweetness' to another person? You know that 'gravity' exists in the earth and we all have *experienced* it. But have you <u>seen</u> gravity? You know that electricity runs every appliance in your home right from the microwave oven to your computer. But have you <u>seen</u> 'electricity'? No, but can you deny its presence? You have experienced the *power* of electricity all your life without seeing it. It has no shape, size, smell or taste. Now do you understand that God is also like the taste, gravity or electricity. God is All pervasive but cannot be seen. You have to perceive and feel the presence of God inside you, not *see* Him.

All the idols, images, pictures and ideas we have about God and the various deities are but symbolic representations of that great Truth.

**"What is the concept of '*Moksha*'? Is every soul or *Atman* part of the *Brahman*?" Aditya was perplexed.**

We have gone through this in our previous exchanges. But still, it is worth repeating. The soul of a man or an insect is the same. The soul is very subtle. The word '*Sookshma*' is used in Sanskrit to mean subtle. It is said that the size of the soul is about one in ten thousandth size of the tip of a strand of hair. It is only an  allegorical approximation. The soul which is in a living being keeps on reincarnating and finally merges with the *Brahman*.

For ease of understanding, imagine a blob of metallic mercury which you have seen in your chemistry lab. If it falls to the ground, it breaks into thousands of tiny glistening globules. But each globule is part of the original blob of mercury. When these come together, they merge again into one single large blob of mercury, and you cannot distinguish or separate the tiny original bits. The soul also likewise cannot be distinguished from the *Brahman* and hence will not have further reincarnation once it merges with it.

All rivers end in the ocean. They merge with the ocean. But once they enter the ocean, you can never identify the individual rivers. They are all part of the same ocean. The same holds good for the soul which merges with the *Brahman* and becomes one with it.

This merger of the individual soul with the *Brahman* is what is known as '*Moksha.*'

**"How can a child like me have a *Guru* who teaches me the various concepts of Hinduism?" Jaya had a practical question.**

For every Hindu child, his / her father is the *Guru.* The father and mother teach the basic concepts of Hinduism to their children. Hence the parents are the primary *Gurus* for the children. But later when they are old enough to learn the scriptures, they can seek the private tutelage of a scholar who can become the *Guru* for them. Now a days, many of the scriptures and texts are available in print and as e-books and one can learn them by oneself. But to understand many of the subtle philosophies, one has to resort to the help of a *Guru* or listen to *Satsangs* from scholars and spiritual teachers. I would advise you, children, to listen to as many *satsangs* and speeches of scholars and masters to understand our scriptures better.

**"Do Hindus have a concept called 'Sin'?," Vijaya had a question.**

Sin in Hinduism is called '*Papam*' in Sanskrit. It is also called '*Adharma*' which is the antonym of '*Dharma*' or righteousness. Any deed which is against *Dharma* is a sin. We have seen the *Yamas* and *Niyamas* when we discussed the *Yoga Sutra* of

Patanjali. They are the disciplines and mandates that the Hindu should follow. Going contrary to those ·precepts constitutes *Adharma* or *Papam* (<u>sin</u>). Briefly, if you do anything that is against your conscience, by thought, word or deed, it is a sin.

**"You have discussed *Dharma* previously Grandpa, but can you just summarize it into a few words?" Jaya requested.**

*Dharma* is variously defined. But here I will describe *Dharma* as the *inherent nature and function of a thing or being.* Simple examples will make you understand this better. The *Dharma* of fire is to burn, that of ice is to cool, a tree is to bear flowers and fruit, an electron's *Dharma* is to constantly move around in a fixed orbit around the nucleus composed of protons and neutrons.

I will tell you a short parable. Once a sage was bathing in the river when he saw a scorpion floundering in the water. Gently he removed it with his hand and placed it on dry land. As soon as he picked it up, the scorpion stung him. The scorpion again crawled back and fell into the water. Unmindful of the sting, the sage again lifted the scorpion and put it on the shore. The scorpion again stung him. This continued a few times. One of the bathers nearby asked the sage, why he kept on saving the scorpion if it always stung him. The sage replied, "My *Dharma* urges me to save the scorpion, but the scorpion's *Dharma* is to sting, and it stings me." The *Dharma* of a person is usually unchangeable.

**"Grandpa, what do you think is the role of Astrology in Hinduism? Is it scientific and dependable?" Aditya, the sceptic was up with a logical question.**

Astrology is called '*Jyothisha*' in Hinduism. (*Jyoti* = light; heavenly body). It is called *Vedic Astrology* as it is one of the auxiliary disciplines (*Vedanga*) of the *Vedas*. The word *Jyothisha* encompasses the study of Astronomy, Astrology, and the science of keeping time using the heavenly bodies as markers. Using this the Hindus predict auspicious times for rituals such as marriage, *Upanayanam* and other *Poojas*. They are also used to construct the Hindu calendar.

*Jyothisha* charts are prepared for a person based on the time and date that he was born. This is called the *Kuṇḍali* or *Jathakam* (horoscope). The '*Navagrahams*' (*Nava* = nine; *Graham* = planet) are the nine '*planetary deities*' that control the destiny of man depending on his previous *Sanchita Karmas*. But these *Navagrahams* are under the domination of the Supreme Deity or *Ishvara* (God). The nine *planetary deities* control the life of man on earth. (*Do not confuse them with the planets in the solar system*).

Hindus believe that these '*planetary deities*' are powerful enough to control the destiny of man giving them periods of ascendancy and descent in life. Each *Graham* or 'planetary deity' is under the control of a particular demigod that influences human life. So, humans have good and bad periods in their life. The good periods are when the influences of some of the *Grahams* are favourable and they prosper and have health, wealth and happiness. Whereas the bad periods are those during which they experience pain, sorrow, loss of wealth and other mishaps.

Often people seek the help of an astrologer, who finds the present position of these *Grahams* in the person's horoscope and determines what type of period he is going through. Appropriate *Poojas* or penances may be advised.

In addition to the *Grahams*, in astrology there are twenty-seven *nakshatras* (<u>stars</u>). They are called *Lunar Mansions* or *Lunar ecliptics* and indicate the divisions of the moons orbit as it passes around the earth. They recur cyclically on each day of the month. Every day is thus governed by such a *Nakshatram*. These are given different names as *Aswathi, Bharani, Kartika, Rohini* etc. These twenty-seven *Nakshatras* along with the *Navagrahas*, govern the periods in a person's life. Each person is thus born under a particular *Nakshatram* which governs the day he was born.

Astrology is not an exact science. Some believe in astrology even in this 21st century and swear by it. There are others who seek the services of an astrologer when they want an auspicious time to start a new venture, a new business, buy a new home or land. Many of these predictions of the astrology may not come true. Some positive predictions may affect the individual positively and may be a psychological impetus for his endeavours. But to rely on astrology blindly is not something that anyone would like to do.

Belief in Astrology is something you cannot impose on a person. Have you not heard of the famous Shakespearean quote from the '*Hamlet*' where Hamlet tells his friend Horatio, "*There are more things in Heaven and Earth, Horatio, than are dreamt of in your philosophy.*" That is what I too have to say about Astrology. I leave it to your discretion to believe or not to believe.

**"In this modern age, it is not always possible to worship according to the rituals like *Yagnas* and elaborate *Poojas* prescribed in the scriptures. So, what should a modern Hindu do for worship?" Aditya's questions were pregnant with practical wisdom.**

I will mention the types of worship in various *Yugas*. In the first *Yuga* which is the *Krita yuga* or *Satya Yuga*, the human race was *Sattvic* in nature. *Meditation* was the main method of worship in that age. There were no idols or poojas. The formless *Brahman* was realized by the people through meditation and concentration. *Tapas* (<u>penance</u>) was the order of the day.

In the next *Yuga* which is the *Tretha Yuga* people had a mixture of *Sattvic* and *Rajasic* qualities. In this *Yuga*, sacrifice or *Yajna* was the prescribed mode of worship. The sages and seers worshiped *Agni* (<u>fire</u>) through rituals with the '<u>fire-pit</u>' (*Yajna Kundam*) in which oblations like ghee were poured to the accompaniment of mantras being chanted by one person or a group of devotees. This *Yajna* sacrifice is occasionally done in modern age, by individuals who wear the *Yagnopaveetham* after the *Upanayanam* ceremony.

In the third *Yuga* which is the *Dvapara Yuga*, the people had more of *Rajasic* qualities intermingled with a small proportion of *Tamasic* qualities also. This was the *Yuga* in which Idol worship and *Poojas* became the main mode of worship.

In the present *Yuga*, which is the *Kali yuga*, *Rajasic* and *Tamasic* qualities in people was much more intense and hence, *Namasankeertanam* or *Nama Japam* has been prescribed as the mode or worship as it is the easiest way to realize the *Brahman* and attain *Moksha*.

*Srimad Bhagavatham* says that at the end of the *Dvapara yuga*, Sage *Narada* approached *Bhagavan Brahma* and asked him as to how people should worship in the coming *Kali yuga*. *Bhagavan Brahma* replied that the ideal type of worship is chanting Bhagavan's name through *Namasankeertanam*. Sage *Narada* wanted to know which mantra should be chanted, to which *Brahma* gave the following few mantras, one of which the devotee could choose to chant. There were no special regulations for this chanting as it could be done anytime, anywhere, and by anyone. So, no preparations or any type of arrangements were necessary. The mantras suggested by Brahma were:

हरे राम हरे राम | राम राम हरे हरे
हरे कृष्ण हरे कृष्ण | कृष्ण कृष्ण हरे हरे |
*Hare Rama, Hare Rama, Rama Rama Hare Hare*

*Hare Krishna, Hare Krishna, Krishna Krishna Hare Hare.*

The other mantras suggested by Brahma to Sage Narada were:

The *Gayatri mantra can be repeated mentally. (see previous discussions). Another mantra is:*

ॐ नमो भगवते वासुदेवाय

*Om Namo Bhagavate Vāsudevāya*

Another mantra is :

ॐ नमो नारायणाय

*Om Namo Nārāyanāya,*

Other mantras like **"Om Namah Shivaya"** or any other short mantra can be used for worship in the *Kali Yuga*. In addition, when time permits and, in the mornings, mantras like the *Vishnu Sahasranama Stotram, Lalitha Sahasranama Stotram, Bhaja Govindam, Mahishasura Mardini Stotram, Venkatesa Suprabhatham, Hanuman Chalisa* and any such *Stotram* can be chanted in *Kali Yuga* to achieve liberation.

**"Grandpa, you said that in Kali yuga, individuals have more *Rajasic* and *Tamasic* characteristics. Has this been predicted in our scriptures already? If so, what was said about humans in the *Kali Yuga*?" Jaya was curious about these predictions.**

Yes. *Kali Yuga* and its features have been elaborately described in the *Srimad Bhagavatham* in the 12th Canto, Chapter 2. *Kali yuga* runs for 432,000 years. Of these 5124 years are now over (as of 2023 CE). Another 426,876 years are to go for the end of *Kali yuga*. From the first *Yuga – Satya yuga* to *Kali yuga*, the total number of years decreases incrementally in the ratio 4:3:2:1.

*Kali yuga* is the period when *Dharma* declines and chaos prevails. <u>Truth</u> (*Satyam*), <u>Purity</u> (*Soucham*), <u>Compassion</u> (*Daya*), <u>Patience</u> (*Kshama*), <u>Longevity</u> (*Ayush*) and the human ability to think and act logically decrease to abysmal levels. In *Kali Yuga* <u>wealth</u> and <u>physical strength</u> will become the index of a person's importance and leadership, not *Dharma* or righteousness. People without wealth will be side-lined, however virtuous they may be. The physically strong will rule over the weak. Greed will overcome virtues like generosity and charity.

Marriages will be based on emotions like carnal love and lust. Parents' sentiments and emotions will not be given consideration. Hypocrites will rule the roost. Honesty will be at a premium. The four *Purusharthas* will have no place in *Kali Yuga*. Money will be the main goal for which humans strive. The king (ruler, head of state) will be the most powerful and strong from among the four *Varnas*. Virtue will not be the measure of a leadership. The strong will always try to conquer and subdue the weak. Man's longevity will be markedly reduced in the *Kali Yuga*. Relationships among individuals will decrease. People will become selfish and greedy. The four

*Varnas* will not follow their ascribed duties, and this will lead to chaos in society.

Guests will not be given an honoured place when they visit a household. Drought and famine will occur. The weather will become unpredictable, and extremes of climate will become unbearable. Man will do any cruel or evil deed to gain wealth. New diseases will occur. Man's ego will overcome his humility. Man will become culturally bankrupt. Imagine that all this was predicted over 5200 years ago by our sages ! And all this is happening today!

It is at the end of this *Kali Yuga* that *Bhagavan Maha Vishnu* will incarnate as Kalki to re-establish Dharma in the world.

**"Wow, Grandpa, what you have described seems to be already occurring world over today!" exclaimed Aditya. "I am surprised that our sages predicted all this millennia ago!"**

So, children, I have come to the end of our discussion on Hinduism, and I hope that all three of you were benefitted by the deliberations. I have repeated many of the concepts more than once. Consider that it was done only for emphasis. I, for one, enjoyed imparting this knowledge to you and now your duty is to follow these precepts that I taught you and put them into practice in your daily life. Also, in your spare time and holidays, try to read some of our religious texts and increase your knowledge. Learn how to live the life of a true Hindu. If you have any doubts, you can ask your parents or always contact me. Good luck to you my children and may *Bhagavan Sri Krishna* bless you!

# RESOURCES

1.    Bhagavathamrutham  - CDs of complete 106 episodes by Swami Udit
Chaitanya. Bhagavatham Village Trust.

https://www.youtube.com/watch?v=jZD0363ItH
M&list=PL8ViNJDvLfesOC2K7fVzCOUai41bzdnL
L

2.    MEDITATION  -  YouTube  talk  and meditation exercise.

https://www.youtube.com/watch?v=ihOX_f_Ud
NY&t=392s

3.    HINDUISM ARTICLE AND BLOGS . Hindu American Foundation.

https://www.hinduamerican.org/hinduism-
101?gclid=CjwKCAjw_YShBhAiEiwAMomsENRR
qjn4n2Fg2wC4bseLaIJJaptd-Nri4-
SvElwY6rjYoSRdFAJv_RoCR6kQAvD_BwE&utm
_source=google&utm_medium=cpc

4.  **4** HINDUISM    QUESTION ANSWERS    -
Hindu American Foundation.

https://www.hinduamerican.org/hinduism-short-answers-real-questions

5. HINDUISM  BASIC BELIEFS  - United Religions Initiative

https://www.uri.org/kids/world-religions/hindu-beliefs

6. HINDUISM – WIKIPEDIA

https://en.wikipedia.org/wiki/Hinduism

7.  **12** THINGS TO KNOW ABOUT HINDUISM - Hindu American Foundation.

https://www.hinduamerican.org/blog/12-things-you-need-to-know-about-hinduism/

8. BELIEFS ABOUT GOD IN HINDUISM – Pew Research Center

https://www.pewresearch.org/religion/2021/06/29/beliefs-about-god-in-india/

9. WHAT IS HINDUISM – The Pluralism Project - Harvard University

https://pluralism.org/what-is-hinduism

10. INFORMATION ON HINDUISM – by Mandy Barrow. World Religions.

http://www.primaryhomeworkhelp.co.uk/religion/hinduism.htm

11. HINDU BELIEFS – Facts For Children.  Twinkl

https://www.twinkl.com/teaching-wiki/hindu-beliefs

12. WHAT IS HINDUISM- ART OF LIVING  -  by Sri Sri Ravishankar .

https://www.artofliving.org/us-en/wisdom/theme/what-is-hinduism

13. DIVERSITY IS THE DNA OF HINDUISM – Times of India. 2015 Sri Sri Ravishankar.

https://timesofindia.indiatimes.com/blogs/treasurehunt/diversity-is-in-the-dna-of-hinduism/

14. WHY SO MANY GODS IN HINDUISM – Wisdom from Sri Sri Ravishankar.

http://wisdomfromsrisriravishankar.blogspot.com/2015/10/why-do-we-have-so-many-gods-in-hinduism.html

15. JAGGI  VASUDEV  SADGURU AND HINDUISM   (You Tube Talk)

https://www.google.com/search?q=JAGGI+VASUDEV+SADGURU+AND+HINDUISM&sxsrf=APwXEdcz844AlemnZkwvHD3pUnIH-c58Q%3A1679937950131&ei=ntEhZMSuB5CHwbkP7MCWoAE&ved=0ahUKEwjE9YvGoPz9AhWQQzABHWygBRQQ4dUDCBA&uact=5&oq=JAGGI+VASUDEV+SADGURU+AND+HINDUISM&gs_lcp=Cgxnd3Mtd2l6LXNlcnAQAQAzIFCAAQogQyBQgAEKIEMgUIABCiBDIFCAAQogQ6CwgAEIoFEIYDELADOgYIABAHEB46CgghEKABEMMEEAo6CAghEKABMMESgQIQRgBUIodWItYYLFfaAFwAHgAgAF_iAHpD5IBBBDE2LjaYAQCgAQHIAQTAAQE&sclient=gws-wiz-serp

**301**

16. Idols in the Hindu Way of Life – Why are they worshipped - SADGURU

https://isha.sadhguru.org/us/en/wisdom/article/hindu-idols-gods-worship

17. HINDUISM EXPLAINED by JAGGI VASUDEV SADGURU 2017.

https://thehindugods.org/hinduism-explained-by-sadhguru-jaggi-vasudev/

18. SADGURU – BIOGRAPHY   TEACHINGS QUOTES – Biography Online.

https://www.biographyonline.net/spiritual/sadhguru.html

20 . HINDUISM IS  A WAY OF LIFE   Sri  Ramana Maharishi

https://sriramanamaharishi.com/self-offering/learning/hinduism-is-a-way-of-life/

21.  PURPOSE OF LIFE-  RAMANA MAHARISHI – QUOTES   2021

https://goodqn.com/purpose-of-life-ramana-maharshi/

22.  KARMA AND REINCARNATION – Hinduism Today 2019.

https://www.hinduismtoday.com/hindu-basics/karma-and-reincarnation/

23.  REINCARNATION - WIKIPEDIA

https://en.wikipedia.org/wiki/Reincarnation

24. KARMA AND REINCARNATION -Basics of Hinduism - Kauai's Hindu Monastery

https://www.himalayanacademy.com/readlearn/basics/karma-reincarnation

25. KAIVALYA UPANISHAD-Swami Chinmayananda CLASS 1 1975

https://www.youtube.com/watch?v=ier98k0yXu8

26. KAIVALYA UPANISHAD -Swami Chinmayananda CLASS 2. (You Tube)

https://www.youtube.com/watch?v=ho93BG9q7TE

27. KAIVALYA UPANISHAD -Swami Chinmayananda CLASS 3. (YouTube)

https://www.youtube.com/watch?v=ZJafRKl4wzg&list=PL5B43BA9DB7134F25&index=3

28. KAIVALYA UPAINISHAD Swami Chinmayananda CLASS 4 (You Tube)

https://www.youtube.com/watch?v=oQr4dad5v0M

29. UNTOLD STORY OF IDOL WORSHIP IN BHARAT-Project SHIVOHAM (You Tube)

https://www.youtube.com/watch?v=RMvZyeC8DN4

30. THE SWASTIKA – Project SHIVOHAM (You Tube)

https://www.youtube.com/watch?v=qpeP4Er5PYE

31. SHANKARA Vs SECULARISM     -Project SHIVOHAM  (You Tube)

https://www.youtube.com/watch?v=tlHuhrXhCAc

32. BOTTOM LINE OF BHAGAVAD GITA- Project SHIVOHAM  (You Tube)

https://www.youtube.com/watch?v=hbEA5sQbOUM

33. UNDERSTANDING RAVANASURA  - Project SHIVOHAM  (You Tube)

https://www.youtube.com/watch?v=AflNDhBUfBg

34. RELIGION vs SCIENCE.  Project SHIVOHAM (You Tube)

https://www.youtube.com/watch?v=6ByNA8X3roo

35. STATECRAFT IN THE MAHABHARATA - Project SHIVOHAM (You Tube)

https://www.youtube.com/watch?v=VaTLi4ug5xI

36. HINDU MYTHOLOGY & HISTORY PURANAS ETC - Project SHIVOHAM  (You Tube)

https://hindumediawiki.com/story.php?id=650&title=discussing-mythology-history-itihasa-puranas-in-hinduism

37. THE SECRET OF SRI RUDRAM -Project Shivoham  (You Tube)

https://www.youtube.com/watch?v=GlcEBZuA-Xw

38. HUMAN ANATOMY AS PER SHIVA PURANAM- Project Shivoham  (You Tube)

https://www.youtube.com/watch?v=DIZAMrCD1tc

39. HINDUISM FOR BEGINNERS – Patrick Goodness.  (You Tube)

https://www.youtube.com/watch?v=QovXpBS9isg

40. WHO IS PATANJALI    WHAT IS YOGA   - Project SHIVOHAM  (You Tube)

https://www.youtube.com/watch?v=Bc5UHKO3wWc

41. BRAHMA MUHURTA -  SRI RAVISHANKAR – Art of Living.

https://www.artofliving.org/in-en/lifestyle/well-being/know-about-brahma-muhurta

42.WHAT IS    BRAHMA   MUHURTA    & BRAHMAMUHURTA TIME & BENEFITS.     Dr Pillai  Power time Updates  2021.

https://www.pillaicenter.com/blog/brahma-muhurta/

43.    BRAHMA   MUHURTA    DEFINITION BENEFITS  & TIPS

https://www.yogabasics.com/connect/yoga-blog/brahma-muhurta/

44. WHY DO WE GO TO A TEMPLE ?   Times of India- by Anand Sagar Pathak 2019.

https://timesofindia.indiatimes.com/religion/rituals-puja/why-do-we-go-to-temple-and-how-does-it-help-us/articleshow/68206959.cms

45. 5 REASONS WHY WE SHOULD GO TO A TEMPLE by Chintan Jain.

http://chintanjain.com/journey/why-should-we-go-to-temple.php

46. WHY VISIT A TEMPLE - 10 SCIENTIFIC REASONS. By Anjali Rajendra 2015.

https://www.linkedin.com/pulse/why-visit-temple-10-scientific-reasons-rajendra/

47. 7 REASONS WHY VISITNG TEMPLE IS GOOD FOR YOUR HEALTH by Sandhya Raghavan  2018

https://www.thehealthsite.com/ayurveda/reasons-why-visiting-the-temple-is-good-for-your-health-k0617-499331/

48. HINDUISM   - WIKIPEDIA

https://en.wikipedia.org/wiki/Hinduism

49. RELIGIONS OF THE WORLD  -- HINDUISM – Philosophy of Religions by Donnamarie  Romano 2001.

https://www.qcc.cuny.edu/socialsciences/ppecorino/phil of religion text/chapter 2 religions/hinduism.htm

50. A BRIEF HISTORY OF THE VEDAS - Project SHIVOHAM (You Tube).

https://www.youtube.com/watch?v=S1-17TeZvVo

51. SHANKARA VS SECULARISM      Project SHIVOHAM (You Tube).

https://www.youtube.com/watch?v=tlHuhrXhCAc

52. PHILOSOPHY OF RELIGION.   WHAT IS RELIGION.  By Philip A Pecorino. 2001. https://www.qcc.cuny.edu/socialsciences/ppecorino/phil_of_religion_text/CHAPTER_1_OVERVIEW/What_is_religion.htm

53. HINDUISM -Karma, Samsara, and Moksha  - Britannica.com

https://www.britannica.com/topic/Hinduism/Karma-samsara-and-moksha

54. 25 AMAZING THE SCIENTIFIC REASONS BEHIND INDIAN TRAAITIONS AND CULTURE – Hinduism Facts by Geetanjali   (You Tube).

https://www.youtube.com/watch?v=c-M8l2bdG8g

55. THE DEFINITION AND CONCEPT OF MAYA IN HINDUISM – Hindu website.com.

https://www.hinduwebsite.com/hinduism/essays/maya.asp

56. THE CONCEPT OF MAYA by Vedanta Society of California.

https://vedanta.org/what-is-vedanta/the-concept-of-maya/

57. THE MEANING OF MAYA- THE ILLUSION OF THE WORLD by American Institute of Vedic Studies. 2018.

https://www.vedanet.com/the-meaning-of-maya-the-illusion-of-the-world/2018/

58.	HINDU TEMPLE ARCHITECTURE – Wikipedia.

https://en.wikipedia.org/wiki/Hindu_temple_architecture#:~:text=A%20Hindu%20temple%20is%20a,are%20one%2C%20everything%20is%20connected.

59.	HINDU TEMPLES AND TEMPLE ARCHITECTURE –Hindu Temples - World Religions.

https://factsanddetails.com/world/cat55/sub388/item1351.html

60. SCIENCE – VEDAS - INDIA'S SCIENCE BASE by  MR Suriyan et al. Vedic Heritage – Ministry of Culture, Government of India. 2023.

https://vedicheritage.gov.in/science/#:~:text=The%20Vedas%20and%20its%20concepts,Seekers%20of%20knowledge%20and%20wisdom.

61. SCIENCE IN HINDUISM  by  Rahul  2022.

https://www.hinduismfacts.org/science-in-hinduism/

62. HINDUISM AND THE ARTS – All you need to know about Hinduism.

http://history-of-hinduism.blogspot.com/p/hinduism-and-arts.html

64. SWAMI VIVEKANANDA – by Cultural India.

https://www.culturalindia.net/reformers/vivekananda.html

65.  SWAMI  VIVEKANANDA  -Ramakrishna-Vivekananda center of New York.

https://ramakrishna.org/vivekananda.html

66. The Life of Adi Sankaracharya – Online with Amma 2000.

https://www.amritapuri.org/40614/shankaracharya.aum

67. Sri Adi Sankara  - Kamakoti peetam  2017.

https://www.kamakoti.org/miscl/adi.html

68. Life of Adi Shankaracharya – Stories, Teachings and Stotras. – Isha Foundation

https://isha.sadhguru.org/us/en/wisdom/article/life-of-adi-shankaracharya-stories-teachings-stotras

## BIBLIOGRAPHY

### <u>Books In English</u>


1. Sanatana Dharma – An Elementary Textbook of Hindu Religion & Ethics.  Published by the Board of Trustees Central Hindu College, Benares 1916
2. Chariot of the Gods by Eric von Daniken, Berkley books, New York. 1999.
3. The Holy Geeta by Swami Chinmayananda. Publishers- Central Chinmaya Mission Trust, Bombay.
4. The Complete Works of Swami Vivekananda Published by Swami Bodhasarananda  17th Edition. Advaita Ashrama Publications. 1986. (9 Volumes – in English)

5. Bhagavad Gita by Swami Ranganathananda. (3 Volumes). Advaita Ashrama Publications. 1st Ed. 2000.

6. Brahma Sutras. -According to Sri Sankara  by Swami Vireswarananda. Advaita Ashrama Publications. 12th Reprint 2014.

## <u>Books In Malayalam</u>

1. Srimad Bhagavatham by Pandit P. Gopalan Nair. Guruvayur Devaswom Publications. 2017. (8 volumes – in Malayalam).

2. Ganesh Puranam by  Thottayil N. Krishnan Nair - Vidyarambam Publications. 1st Ed. 2003.

3. Sri Siva Maha Puranam by  Swami Dharmananda Theertha. Kurukshetra Prakasan Publications. 3rd Ed.2001.

4. Mahabharatam  by V Ramakumar. Siso Publications. 12th Ed. 2009.

5. Sampoorna Ramayanam  by  Dr. P.S. Nair. Vidyarambham Publishers. 16th Ed. 2017.

6. Skanda Puranam by  Thottayil N. Krishnan Nair – Vidyarambham Publishers. 3rd Ed. 1998.

7. Garuda Puranam  by  K. Kunhukrishna Pillai. Vidyarambham Publications. 7th Ed. 2004.

8. Srimad Bhagavad Gita Bhashyam – Sri Sankaracharya Virachidam  by K. P. Ramunni Menon. Guruvayur Devaswom Publications. 2nd Ed. 2015.

9. Maha Bhagavatham by Dr. P. S. Nair. Vidyarambham Publications. 13th Ed. 2003.

10. Vishnu Puranam by K. Krishnan Kutty. Published by Devi Book Stall 1st Ed. 2003.

11. Srimad Bhagavad Gita by  Swami Prakasananda. Published by Sri Ramakrishna Math. 1 Ed. 1967.

12. Manu Smriti by Swami Siddhinathananda. Published by Sri Ramakrishna Math. 1st Ed. (third reprint) 2016

# ABOUT THE AUTHOR

Dr K. V. Sahasranam is a distinguished Cardiologist and former Professor of Cardiology at Calicut Medical College, India. With over 45 years of medical practice, he has retired and now resides in the USA. His deep passion lies in educating students and residents, reflected in his book, **"Understanding the Electrocardiogram,"** designed for medical students and physicians, which thoroughly explores the ECG and simplifies its interpretation.

Writing under the pen name *'Sahasranam Kalpathy,'* he has authored 13 more books, spanning both Fiction and Nonfiction including a series on *'Problems of the Elderly'* (2 books), *'Understanding Hinduism'* (3 books), *'Skillsets for Success'* (2 books), three captivating Fiction novels and two books of Short stories for children. All of his books are available on Amazon and Notionpress.com (India).

His latest book named **"Diabetes Demystified"** is the first part of the *'Everyday Health Guide'* series.

9 798223 235002